100 Years of Architecture in Chicago

**Exhibited at the
Museum of Contemporary Art
Chicago**

100 Years of Architecture in Chicago

Continuity of Structure and Form

by Oswald W. Grube, Peter C. Pran and Franz Schulze

Translations and additional text by David Norris

Follett Publishing Company
Chicago

The exhibit was conceived by Oswald W. Grube in collaboration with Peter C. von Seidlein and Wend Fischer. It was produced in Europe in 1973 by Die Neue Sammlung in Munich, Germany.

The American exhibit 1976 at the Museum of Contemporary Art, presented by Stephen Prokopoff, artistic director, Peter C. Pran, consultant.

Designated: Official Illinois–U.S.A. Bicentennial Exhibition 1976

Oswald W. Grube, Peter C. Pran, and Franz Schulze received the Illinois Council, American Institute of Architects, 1976 Annual Award for contribution to the profession for writing this book and organizing the exhibition. Stephen Prokopoff received the same award for organizing the exhibition.

1234567890♦7877

Foreword

This exhibition, a tribute to the extraordinary tradition of innovative building in Chicago, was conceived by Oswald W. Grube in collaboration with Peter C. von Seidlein and Wend Fischer and produced in 1973 by Die Neue Sammlung in Munich. It subsequently toured throughout Europe where it was enthusiastically acclaimed by the art and architectural press. It was only appropriate that this exhibition be seen in the city that inspired it—thus, shortly after the Munich showing, planning for its presentation in Chicago was begun. Although details of the original exhibition have been altered, its basic substance remains the same.

The American version of *100 years of Architecture in Chicago,* presented at the Museum of Contemporary Art in May and June of 1976, has been expanded to include new buildings planned and erected between 1973 and the present. At the same time, more extensive consideration has been given to earlier building. Finally, the show's visual presentation has been proportionately enlarged and cast in a more dramatic format that seeks to remind the viewer of the compelling visual beauty of an architecture whose aesthetic quality is so deeply rooted in structure and technology.

The works of Sullivan, Root, Wright, and Mies represent the high points in the development of the Chicago school. Around these master creators many talented and distinguished architects were ranged who, in their own right, have enlarged the scope of Chicago building and made further innovative contributions to it. Today the broad tradition is still manifest in new projects which demonstrate the continuing vitality of the architectural vision in Chicago and the work that springs from it.

The exhibition is roughly divided into two sections devoted to what have been called the first and second Chicago schools. The first group of architects—Adler and Sullivan, Jenney, Burnham and Root, Holabird and Roche, and Frank Lloyd Wright—were the pioneers of modern architecture who fused a new building technology with clarity of formal expression.

The second Chicago school drew much of its inspiration from the international style brought to the city by Mies van der Rohe and subsequently developed in various ways by a large and talented group of architects. This second wave, incorporating as it does many of the values of the first, has created structures that combine simple elegance with structural rationality. That this kind of architecture meets the requirements of both patron and public can be seen in the wealth of eloquent new buildings in this city and, more recently, in the wide dissemination of the work of Chicago architects around the world.

An exhibition of this scope is only created through the enthusiastic assistance and encouragement of a very large number of people, too many, regretably, to thank publicly here. However, it is most appropriate to note the special efforts of a few individuals and organizations without whose aid this new version of *One Hundred Years of Architecture in Chicago* would have fallen short of its present form. Peter Pran, with Clevon Pran, worked heroically with virtually every phase of both exhibition and this publication; his enthusiasm and devotion to the project have much to do with its success. Franz Schulze was a continuing source of information and encouragement both in editing the book and in helping with details of the exhibition. Carl W. Condit, Peter C. von Seidlein and Linda Legner graciously contributed major articles. David Norris did the translation and editing of the German text assisted by Dr. Marvin C. Dilkey. Additional assistance in translation was provided by Helga Gutschow and Vincent Kling. Linda Docherty gave unstintingly of her time and energy assisting with the rewriting and the editing of the text. And it was J. Philip O'Hara who brought all of the details of text and pictures together to realize this important publication. Dirk Lohan provided assistance of many kinds; and Peter Roesch coordinated discussions with the organizers of the first exhibition. Jack Hedrich provided valuable help in preparing the vast amount of photographic material necessary for the realization of the exhibition and the book. Words cannot express our appreciation of Tom Van Eynde's dependable resourcefulness in coordinating the countless details necessary to the exhibition's physical realization.

The book and exhibition were made possible through financial assistance provided by the Graham Foundation for Advanced Studies in the Fine Arts and its Director, Carter Manny, Jr., and the Illinois Arts Council, its Chairman, Bruce Sagan, and the Program Director of the Bicentennial Architectural Project, Alexia Lalli.

'78–04815

Stephen Prokopoff, Director
Museum of Contemporary Art
Chicago, Illinois U.S.A.

Contents

Introduction to the American Exhibition

by Peter C. Pran
University of Illinois—Chicago Circle
and Franz Schulze
Lake Forest College

"The skeleton of the steel or concrete frame is almost certainly the most recurrent motif in contemporary architecture, and is among the most ubiquitous of what Dr. Giedion would describe as its 'constituent elements. . . .' The frame has been the catalyst of an architecture, but one might notice that it has also become architecture, that contemporary architecture is almost inconceivable in its absence. . . . It would be fair to say that the frame has come to possess a value equivalent to that of the column for classical antiquity and the Renaissance. Like the column, the frame establishes throughout the building a common ratio to which all the parts are related; and like the vaulting bay in the Gothic cathedral it prescribes a system to which all parts are subordinate. It is the universality of the frame and the ease with which it has apparently directed our plastic judgment which has led to the focusing of so much interest upon Chicago commercial architecture. . . . In Chicago seemingly our own interests were so directly anticipated that if the frame structure is the essence of modern architecture, then we can only assume a relationship between ourselves and Chicago comparable to that of the High Renaissance architects to Florence, or of the High Gothic architects to the Ile-de-France, for although no doubt the steel frame did make occasional undisguised appearances elsewhere, it was in Chicago that its formal results were most rapidly elucidated." Colin Rowe, "Chicago Frame," *Architectural Review,* November 1956

The exhibition which Die Neue Sammlung of Munich presented in 1973 under the title *100 Years of Architecture in Chicago: Continuity of Structure and Form* was the most comprehensive survey of its subject ever assembled. The Europeans have an admirable record of receptivity to the accomplishments of architects associated with Chicago. It is enough to recall the milestone 1910 portfolio of Frank Lloyd Wright's work issued in Berlin by Ernst Wasmuth, or the singular effectiveness of Sigfried Giedion's *Space, Time and Architecture* in drawing world attention to the record of Chicago designers.

While the exhibition now at the Museum of Contemporary Art is fundamentally similar in content and principle to the Munich ensemble, it also represents an enlargement of the original version in both respects. More than 130 buildings and projects in the greater Chicago area designed by 100 Chicago architects are now included, and if they trace the strong and continuing line of the Chicago building tradition over the span of a century, they likewise disclose more than a few variations on the theme of that tradition. Moreover, the show is updated to recognize significant work completed since 1973, and this book has been commensurately expanded.

Still, there is the tradition, together with the exceptional mass of work that embodies it: Chicago's most significant contribution to modern architecture has been a rational approach to form and space—as distinct from a more romantic or historically allusive or ideological one—which stresses the derivation of the look of the building from the structural elements that compose it; likewise its interior spaces form an open plan that implies a potential multiplicity of functions. The buildings presented here represent a method of thinking and of approaching problems. Needless to say, the Chicagoans who have followed these principles have varied in their respective talents for giving vivid aesthetic form to their work, as well as in the consistency of their devotion to those principles. But a remarkable continuity of architectural character is discernible in the major efforts of William Le Baron Jenney; H. H. Richardson; Dankmar Adler and Louis Sullivan; Daniel Burnham, John Wellborn Root and Charles Atwood; Frank Lloyd Wright; William Holabird and Martin Roche; Richard Schmidt, Hugh Garden and Edgar Martin; George Fred and William Keck; Ludwig Mies van der Rohe; Myron Goldsmith, Bruce Graham and Fazlur Khan of Skidmore, Owings & Merrill; Jacques Brownson, Gene Summers, Helmut Jahn and Stanislav Gladych of C. F. Murphy Associates; Larry Booth and James Nagle; George Schipporeit and John Heinrich; James Hammond, Peter Roesch and Thomas Beeby; Jerry Horn of Holabird & Root; David Haid; Joseph Fujikawa, Bruno Conterato and Dirk Lohan; Harry Weese; Bertrand Goldberg; Perkins & Will; Gordon & Levin; M. Gelick; Y. C. Wong; Arthur Takeuchi and numerous other gifted men.

The exhibition does not include every good building done in Chicago. But it does feature virtually all the structures which have established the city as the most important single metropolis in the history of modern architecture, moreover, as the one with the most coherent building tradition. The emphasis of the show is on the direction which established that tradition over the last 100 years.

The "first Chicago school," so instrumental in creating a conscious aesthetic based upon clear expression of structure as part of the total architectural work, evolved between roughly 1875 and 1910. Among its masterpieces are Burnham & Root's Monadnock Building, Charles Atwood's Reliance Building and Louis Sullivan's Carson, Pirie, Scott Store. All three of these works are located in the heart of the downtown district of Chicago, whose stupendous growth in the late nineteenth century demanded buildings equal to the needs and aspirations of an industrial society in full momentum. The architects who designed them were daring enough to essay new forms in new materials, but they were also sufficiently cultivated to recognize the aesthetic implications of their assignments.

The skeleton frame was never more lucidly enunciated than in the Reliance Building, nor simplicity of form more persuasively rationalized than in the Monadnock; yet the decoration on the lowest two floors of the Carson Store, like Frank Lloyd Wright's elegant remodeling of the foyer of Burnham & Root's Rookery, dramatizes the attention Chicago's architects also paid to the aesthetic refinements possible with the very industrial materials whose efficiency and economy they were otherwise so committed to.

The structural base of the architecture of the first school was the beam-column type of frame pioneered by Jenney and employed down to the present day, while Wright's open plan and continuous spaces exerted considerable influence on the interpretation of building interiors, especially in the work of Mies van der Rohe. Until his death in 1969, Mies was the central figure of the second Chicago school, which continues to flourish and whose origins may be traced to the earliest buildings that German-born master designed in Chicago after immigrating here in 1938. The second school shares with the first an emphasis on structure and rational design so fundamental as to suggest a qualitative similarity of motive between the two movements.

To be sure, Mies's 860–880 Lake Shore Drive Apartments do not look exactly like Atwood's Reliance Building, and the differences are worth remarking. For one thing, building technology obviously grew more sophisticated during the half century that separated the two projects. Moreover, Mies brought with him a sensibility formed in the Europe of the 1920s, when abstract art movements in the wake of cubism made common cause with a widespread awareness of the aesthetic implications of the machine, resulting in an architecture of clean lines, simple forms and smooth, undecorated surfaces. Moved by these two influences —a respect for the imperatives of technology and a desire to distill architecture to its formal essence—Mies exerted a powerful impact on world architecture as a whole and especially on several generations of younger Chicago designers.

Thus the architects of the second school have tended to eschew almost completely the decorative elements frequently woven into the work of the first school. Recent builders have preferred to let the structural frame speak for itself, animating it only by a fastidious proportioning of its parts, or else they have complemented their designs with monumentally scaled public art work by such figures as Richard Lippold, Pablo Picasso, Marc Chagall and Alexander Calder.

Yet in Chicago both early and late, technology has been the limiting as well as the inspiriting factor. The development of two of the most important urban building types of modern times—the high rise and the clear span hall—would be almost unthinkable without the contribution of Chicago architects, who have arrived at the present forms of these structures by taking maximal advantage of improvements in the quality and capacity of metal, glass and other basic building materials, in elevator design, in heating and air-conditioning equipment, in electrification.

The willingness to utilize these tools has been no less important than the fact of their utilization. For it is a consequence of will, not merely necessity, and it attests once again to a conscious identity in the Chicago tradition. It also helps to explain why Chicago's architects in the years since Mies's death have carried their inventions beyond what he or his predecessors may have envisioned. One has only to think of the great spans and monumental interior spaces of the Civic Center, McCormick Place, Baxter Laboratories Central Facilities Building and the Kemper Arena, or of the spectacular heights of the John Hancock Center and Sears Tower, economically permissible only through the development of the tubular frame.

Economy, indeed, and all it suggests in relation to the more careful use of the environment, have lately become considerations of paramount importance to the practice of architecture. Here too the history of building in Chicago is noteworthy, if for no other reason than that efficient use of structural materials and systems—so long a standard here—must figure heavily in the design of better cities for the future. Energy conservation, minimization of pollution, environmental concerns in general, are clearly affected by the efficiency of the buildings we put up, as well as by the thoughtfulness of the plans we make for our urban establishments. Obviously people have the right to live and work in high-rise or low-rise quarters, and just as clearly, in a metropolis there is a need for both. In the higher density areas of the larger cities, in fact, energy use per capita has been shown to be the lowest in the nation. This fact, together with a revived awareness of the value of urban life to human culture in general, is an argument in favor of cities like Chicago, specifically for the preservation and revitalization of their urban cores through combinations of low-rise and high-rise buildings and multi-functional projects capable of keeping them alive 24 hours a day.

100 Years of Architecture in Chicago; Continuity of Structure and Form addresses itself to these current issues as surely as it documents historical glories. Abuses are cited along with solutions, failures with successes. In the very recording of Chicago's remarkable past, the exhibition has compiled a challenging agenda for the city's future.

On the Exhibition and its Subject
**Excerpted from the foreword to the German edition by Wend Fischer,
Director of Die Neue Sammlung,
the Bavarian State Museum for Applied Art, Munich.**

Why Chicago? Because there is no other city on earth where the origin and growth of contemporary architecture are so clearly discernible. A hundred years ago, following Chicago's destruction by the Great Fire of 1871, a tradition of building was founded that reached its first zenith in the 1880s and 90s with the works of masters of the "Chicago school" of architecture. This peak was followed by several decades of stagnation, after which the tradition so vigorously renewed itself in the 1940s that one can rightly speak of a "second" Chicago school.

Louis H. Sullivan and Ludwig Mies van der Rohe are the central figures of this continuous architectural tradition, unprecedented in its logic and consistency. Their influence has derived not only from their buildings but from their thought and their example.

Sullivan, author of the famous, oft-quoted and almost always too narrowly interpreted maxim, "Form follows Function," wrote in 1896: "It is my belief that it is the very essence of every problem that it contains and suggests its own solution . . . units of structure form the true basis of the artistic development of the exterior."

The same concept was expressed over half a century later by Mies van der Rohe when he said, "In architecture one is confronted with problems for which one must find solutions. The best architecture is the clearest and most direct solution of a problem."

Both statements contain the quintessence of Chicago's architectural tradition. The buildings of both Chicago schools are distinguished by the directness, conciseness and clarity with which function is expressed in architectural form. According to architect John Root in 1890, the strength with which the function was expressed should serve as the criterion for judging the building as a work of art. This aesthetic does not descend from the subjective invention of forms but from the objective manifestation of function. The essence of this principle is echoed in Mies's 1965 statement: "Now, as before, I believe that building has little or nothing to do with the invention of interesting forms or with personal inclinations. True building is always objective."

Since the function determines the character of the form, the principle of functional design has resulted in the terseness which distinguishes the Chicago tradition and so radically differentiates it from the currently fashionable trend toward formal expressionism or the resigned monotony of our mass-produced architecture. . . .

The Architectural Tradition of Chicago
by Carl W. Condit
Northwestern University

Right, panoramic view of Chicago; *far right,* Fair Store in construction, William Le Baron Jenney, 1890

One of the most prominent skyscrapers to be erected in Chicago during the great building boom of the 1960s is the Civic Center, an immense prism of glass and welded steel designed by a group of three architectural offices working under the direction of Jacques Brownson of C. F. Murphy Associates. Anyone familiar with the numerous office and apartment towers that Mies van der Rohe designed in Chicago and many other cities would immediately recognize the influence of the old master throughout the form and the details of the Civic Center, and Brownson was proud to admit his debt to the man who had been his teacher during his student days and his chief mentor throughout his professional career. But the Civic Center is more than a monument to Mies's principles; it is a work that is deeply rooted in the building history of our age and hence in the main stream of high-rise structural technology that has been evolving in its essential elements for more than one hundred years. The English architectural historian Reyner Banham explained its full significance when he wrote in the B.B.C. *Listener* that the Center is the first municipal building to be built in the modern style and the first, at the same time, to spring from the local building tradition. Nearly a century ago Chicago architects began the work of creating a new urban style in the process of developing the first masterpieces of modern architecture, and the very forms as well as the principles of that style are embodied in the leading architectural works of the present day.

The fundamental forms and techniques out of which Chicago made a new architecture did not originate in the city. Chicago had received its municipal charter in 1837, only 34 years before the fire of October 1871 forced it to rebuild its entire working heart. There were no schools of architecture and engineering to provide courses of study, only a handful of architects who could train apprentices and there were no established technical or artistic traditions to draw upon. Yet these very handicaps proved to be advantages: the city was compelled to fall back on its own resources, on the energy, organizing faculty and inventive skills of its predominantly German and Scandinavian population, and on the empirical and pragmatic attitude that everywhere underlay the rapid technological progress of the age. The city was receptive to the inquiring spirit of the new science as well as the innovative spirit of the new technology, and as a consequence

its builders were quick to take advantage of the structural inventions that had been pouring out since the Industrial Revolution of the late eighteenth century, even though the local builders had little to do with creating their original forms. Indeed, the Chicago school may be regarded as the architectural and structural culmination of technical evolution that had begun around 1770, as a flowering into an artistic unification of scientific, technical and aesthetic developments that had reached a stage by 1870 where even the intrenched conservatism of upper-class architects began to be affected.

The Chicago movement grew out of the great body of strictly utilitarian building that was being shaped chiefly by engineers and practical constructors in the nineteenth century, but it was most deeply rooted in the progress of iron-framed construction. A brief summary of the landmarks in that development reveal how extensively the Chicago architects drew upon this kind of work rather than upon the historical revivalism of high design. The creation of the multi-story mill with interior iron framing was primarily the achievement of William Strutt, Charles Bage, James Warr and Matthew Boulton in England in the period of 1792–1810. The experiments of William Fairbairn and Eaton Hodgkinson at Manchester (1826–30) established the necessity of the flanged section for beams and of wrought iron for members subject to deflection and hence tension, while the theoretical researches of Henri Navier at the École Polytechnique in Paris were perhaps most important in transforming structural practice into a rigorous science. The first free-standing iron frames directed attention to the problem of wind bracing, which was first introduced in the form of knee bracing by Charles Fowler for the Hungerford Fish Market in London (1835). The first stage of maturity was reached in Joseph Paxton's celebrated Crystal Palace of 1851. The first fireproof, multi-story, iron-framed, curtain-walled building appeared in the St. Ouen Dock Warehouse in Paris (1865–66), designed by Hippolyte Fontaine. The hinged arch, cantilever trusses and iron-framed domes and vaults came mainly from German engineers, chief among them Heinrich Gerber and J. W. Schwedler, and the theoretical work of Otto Mohr and August Föppl kept pace with the practical inventions of builders. In America Daniel Badger and James Bogardus perfected the cast-iron front, which brought to the crowded urban mi-

lieu an entirely new kind of architecture marked by extremely slender columns of iron enframing bays of glass.

Mechanical inventions were equally important if the promise of the new structural inventions was to be fully realized in a functional urban architecture. If buildings were to rise above the traditional four stories, internal transportation in the form of the power-driven safety elevator was essential. The Chicago fire had demonstrated that the cast-iron columns of fireproof construction buckled and even melted under intense heat, a disaster which could be prevented only by means of a fire-resistant tile covering the exposed metal. If buildings were to be continuously occupied throughout the day, centralized systems of heating, water supply and drainage were necessary to render them habitable to human beings. Office buildings and department stores required maximum open space, natural light and fresh air if they were to provide a milieu for efficient work in comfortable surroundings. By the late 1880s still another factor appeared: illuminating gas began to give way to electricity, restricted at first to artificial light, then in a few years used for telephone communication as well. All these additions to traditional building meant that the architect worked in a new world of problems that pointed to the time when more than half the cost of building would arise from mechanical and electrical utilities, and half the architect's task would be to find ways of incorporating them into the working structure.

The great achievement of the Chicago architects, as I suggested earlier, was their creating a new architectural style, a unified building art, by addressing themselves directly to these practical problems and by deriving the ultimate form from the functional solution. The underlying principles of the Chicago movement were broad enough to give the architect great latitude in the design of individual buildings, but they were also precise enough to give rise to a coherent body of work clearly expressing the philosophy from which it grew. Perhaps the most remarkable feature of this work is that principles easily formulated in abstract terms and the simple underlying geometry of iron framing could lead to great diversity and even a certain richness of formal solutions, a greater diversity, indeed, than one can find in the contemporary equivalents of the Chicago buildings.

The first principle was the most important: a building had to be designed in such a way as to satisfy all the economic, utilitarian and environmental requirements of the completed functioning structure. From this principle the others followed in logical succession. Given the space available, the location, the needs and resources of the owner, the architect's task was to plan the building so as to secure these results to the fullest possible degree and with the utmost economy. The architect and his engineering associate together had to design a supporting structure and an enclosing envelope that would embody most efficiently, safely and durably all the elements of the plan and all the uses to which these elements would be put. For a high building, this structure eventually had to be an iron and later steel or reinforced concrete frame of columns, girders, beams and bracing elements, but it is important to realize that the Chicago architects had created a new architecture before they turned to full skeletal construction. The last step in the process of design was the creation of an external form that was to grow organically out of the functional demands and the structural solution, to express these characteristics in its overall appearance, in the detailed pattern of its vis-ible elevations, and in an ornamental system that enhanced rather than obscured this organic form.

From the beginning around 1880 the Chicago movement developed into two major streams. One was strongly marked by an empirical and pragmatic approach, and tended to be objective and positivistic in spirit, seeking form almost entirely in valid utilitarian solutions that were left to stand largely by themselves. The visible result was usually the strongly articulated or cellular wall of narrow piers and spandrels, frequently marked by a vertical emphasis secured by projecting the pier-like coverings of the columns beyond the main wall plane (which was generally glass). William Le Baron Jenney and the office of Holabird and Roche were the leading designers in this mode, and the foremost examples are the first Leiter Building (1879; now demolished) and the Sears, Roebuck Store, or second Leiter (1889–91), both by Jenney, and the Marquette (1893–94), the Gage group (1898) and the Crown Building (1899–1900) of Holabird and Roche. Yet even in these austerely simple forms the refined and unobtrusive ornamental details are important ("God is in the details," we recall Mies van der Rohe telling us). In the first Leiter Building, for example, the thin flat molding at the top of the spandrel and the little rosettes on the pier face at each floor level are effective devices for heightening or emphasizing the pattern of the chief functional elements in this prism of broad glass openings and narrow brick bands. The knife-edge moldings on the piers and spandrels in the Crown Building play a similar role in stretching out the essential lines, imparting a sense of movement while intensifying the clarity of the articulation.

The other Chicago stream is more difficult to characterize in a few words. It was marked by personal and subjective responses, giving primacy to feeling as much as reason, and it found expression in more plastic and sculptural forms, with an emphasis on mass or fluidity, or on a strongly kinetic quality. Sullivan was easily the foremost figure in this mode of design, and his spirit was reflected not only in the lavish ornament of his buildings, but more in the strong vertical motion of his towers, in the association of arched and rectilinear forms, and in richly colored and textured materials. Yet many would agree that the greatest work in this genre is Root's Monadnock Building (1889–91): an original conception free of historical precedents, a solid block of 16 floors unmistakable in its sober purpose, it is transformed into great architecture by numerous subtle devices—rounded corners and undersurfaces, the slight inward curve of the lower wall and the outward curve of the parapet, the undulations of the projecting bays—which make it a masterpiece of sculptural and plastic form disciplined by structural geometry. In the architecture of steel-skeleton construction the Reliance Building (1894–95), designed by Charles B. Atwood of Burnham's staff, and the Carson Pirie Scott Store (1899–1906) of Sullivan bring together the self-expressive and ornamental spirit with the more scientific attitude underlying Holabird's and Jenney's buildings. In the Reliance Atwood transformed the straightforward rectangular cells of the steel frame into a curtain of glass and terra-cotta of such delicacy and clarity, its visual quality so superbly enhanced and integrated by means of the shallow spandrel ornament and the slender mullions, that most contemporary work seems almost poverty stricken by comparison. The Carson store is Sullivan's triumph and possibly the greatest work of commercial architecture in the United States. Above the richly ornamented glass and iron shell at the base nothing stands in the way of expressing the powerfully articulated wall, with its deep reveals and long horizontal lines, but everything in Sullivan's ornamental vocabulary was used in the most delicate ways to intensify and dramatize the dominant impression.

The Chicago Plan of 1909, the work of Daniel Burnham and Edward Bennett, reveals the same underlying spirit of Chicago architecture in its union of practical solution with aesthetic realization and in its great breadth of vision associated with the most careful attention to detail, although we must admit that the classic forms that Burnham came to love lay wholly at odds with the philosophy of the Chicago school. There is no question that in certain respects the plan marked the last phase of the strictly geometric, Neo-platonic planning of the Renaissance, with balance, axiality and monumental vistas deployed in a hierarchical arrangement, but it is equally true that it represents a transition from the older theories to the three-dimensional, organic and functional planning of the present day. Indeed, the full historic importance of the Burnham plan far transcends its local reference: it was the first metropolitan plan and hence the first to be predicated on an understanding of the unity of the city and its metropolitan context; it represented the next logical stage after Haussmann's plan for Paris, and was thus the first plan conceived on a scale necessary for a city of 2,000,000 inhabitants and a metropolitan area of 3,000,000. It was the first to be concerned with the problem of circulation in the automotive and electric rapid transit age, to provide an adequate answer to the recreational needs of the modern industrial city, and to pay more than passing attention to the conditions of dwelling and daily work. Burnham left Chicago a planning legacy that for 20 years stimulated and guided the most extensive program of municipal public works in America, but 10 years of economic depression followed by 30 years of intermittent war sapped the vitality and the moral idealism of the American city, so that a great civic tradition has been thrown away.

The Chicago architectural tradition fared much better, however recklessly the city has destroyed the works of the past. Mies van der Rohe brought with him in 1938 a new vision of the aesthetic potentiality of steel and concrete framing, while at the same time he brought order and discipline and clarity. He stood close to the old Chicago spirit, most closely perhaps to Louis Sullivan in his concern with the full visual possibilities of the new structural technology. Directly or indirectly he influenced a generation of Chicago architects, by teaching them in the classrooms of I.I.T., by giving them direct experience in office practice and through a multitude of examples. The leading firms and the smaller offices have drawn both on Mies's influence and authority and on a renewed understanding of the Chicago movement as it flourished between 1880 and 1910. The consequence has been, I think, the appearance of a second Chicago school rooted in the spirit of the first, suffering from the loss of the older architects' ornamental skill but commanding at the same time a great diversity of far more powerful structural forms. The new Chicago work, as I have suggested, lies much closer to the evolution of modern structural technology and to the modern urban experience than does the now fashionable work of lumpish windowless masses of brick or concrete, all of which suggest a deplorable return to merely picturesque architecture.

Detail of the Civic Center

The First Chicago School of Architecture
by Peter C. von Seidlein and Franz Schulze

1871

Until the end of the nineteenth century, fire intervened in the fate of cities with a violence comparable only to that of earthquakes and air raids in our own time.

Chicago's historic conflagration broke out on the evening of October 8, 1871, in a small barn behind Patrick O'Leary's frame cottage on DeKoven Street. Ninety percent of the city's neighborhoods were then made of wood: a far-flung tinderbox rendered all the more vulnerable at the time by an uncommonly dry preceding summer. Once started, the fire was swiftly whipped by a southwest wind, first to the east across the river's south branch, then north across the main stem of the stream. It did not subside until almost three days later. By then a third of the city was laid waste and an equal proportion of its population of 300,000 left homeless.

In 1830 Chicago had been a straggling settlement of 50 souls. Twenty years later its population was just under 30,000. During the following two decades that number increased at a staggering rate: by 1870, to 300,000; by 1880, to 500,000; by 1890, to one million; by 1910, to two million.

Otto von Bismarck once said he would like to travel to America, "but only to see Chicago, a city built by free men." The fire did not succeed in halting the growth of that city; indeed, in one brutal stroke it had wiped out a vast portion of the wildly unregulated pioneer settlement, thus creating not only room but the opportunity for new construction more suited to a developing metropolis. The task of rebuilding, of making a larger and handsomer urban establishment, moreover quickly, turned out to be an inspiration rather than a deterrent to the architects and engineers who lived in Chicago or who flocked here in large numbers following the fire.

William Le Baron Jenney
Born: 1832, Fairhaven, Mass.
Died: 1907, Chicago

From 1853 to 1856 Jenney studied engineering in Paris. In 1867, following a tour of duty in the Civil War as an officer of the Union Army, he came to Chicago where he opened his own architectural office.

He was a lively blend of many qualities often associated with the American nineteenth century personality: goal-oriented pragmatism, creative imagination and an indestructible self-confidence, all combined with a hunger for knowledge and an optimistic belief in the unlimited possibilities of an immense, newly opened continent.

His own self-education left him with an abiding distrust of theory and formula, yet it also moved him to write at length, to undertake research, and even to teach in such disparate subjects as architectural history and the nature of building materials. For all that, however, a natural acquisitiveness led him to spend most of his professional time as a combination of architect, engineer and manager. At a time when, relative to today, academies of design played a notably more circumscribed role in an architect's training, the Jenney office was the chief workshop of the first Chicago school. Sullivan, Burnham, Holabird and Roche were all employed there at one time or other.

In the last analysis Jenney was less an inspired form-giver than a canny innovator of building method. In his First Leiter Building of 1879, he took a giant step in the direction of the undisguised revelation of the structural frame, and his Home Insurance Building of 1884–85 was probably the first tall building supported wholly by a metal frame, its exterior masonry functioning as a skin rather than a bearing element.

First Leiter Building 1879
Northwest corner, Monroe and Wells
William Le Baron Jenney

The relatively modest warehouse Jenney erected in 1879 for the merchant Levi Z. Leiter combined traditional building methods with new ones. The

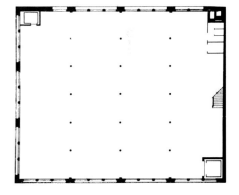

wooden floors, joists and girders rested on cast-iron columns, while the external piers were kept separate from this system and bore only their own weight.

If the First Leiter Building was not a completely framed structure, the exterior nevertheless showed features typical of skeletal construction: the window openings reached from floor to ceiling, and the piers were remarkably slender. There was, to all appearances, no visible wall.

Likewise unusual for the time were the consistent treatment of the upper stories and the sparing use of ornament. Though somewhat pedestrian in design, the First Leiter Building was all in all a bold advance, the first notable structure of the Chicago school.

It was demolished in 1972.

Marshall Field Wholesale Store 1885–87
Adams, Wells, Quincy and Franklin
Henry Hobson Richardson

First Leiter Building

At the time of his arrival in Chicago in the 1880s—during which decade he would eventually erect four buildings here—Richardson was a figure of established renown on the East Coast. Prior to the Field Wholesale Store, his reputation had rested principally on a series of private homes and churches, as powerful in design as they were picturesque, and distinguished often by a use of rusticated stone reminiscent of Romanesque architecture.

In a superficial sense the Field Wholesale Store was faithful to this stylistic approach. In both its structure and the composition of its exterior, it represented no advance whatever beyond Jenney's First Leiter Building. The heavy outer walls were clearly bearing walls, and Richardson's debt to Beaux-Arts principles was still evident in both the varied treatment of window groupings and the decoration of the cornice.

Nevertheless it is worth recalling that the interior, consisting of 61,750 square feet (5737 m^2) distributed over seven stories, was a form of skeletal construction, its floors supported by wrought-iron beams and cast-iron columns. Moreover and most important the Store was an exceptionally lucid and forceful expression of the character of an urban commercial structure. In this respect it was unsurpassed among Chicago buildings of the 1880s. The stupendous mass of the whole and the stern logic with which windows rose from massive units at the base to lighter ones at the top enunciated the building's function with uncommon clarity and consistency. Richardson's eloquent simplicity was his chief contribution to the Chicago school, and it exerted a singular influence on other architects, notably on Adler and Sullivan in their 1889 Auditorium Building.

The building was demolished in 1930.

Louis Sullivan
Born: 1856, Boston
Died: 1924, Chicago

The life work of Louis Sullivan, best known architect of the first Chicago school, consisted not only of a large number of outstanding buildings but of a body of passionately written prose reminiscent of Walt Whitman, in which he argued the case for an architecture integral to industrial society and a democratic way of life.

After a brief term of study at the Massachusetts Institute of Technology and equally fitful stints in architectural offices in Philadelphia and Chicago, the 18-year-old Sullivan made his way to Paris in 1874, where he enrolled at the Ecole des Beaux-Arts. A year later, convinced of the sterility of the curriculum there, he returned to Chicago. By the end of the 1870s he had met Dankmar Adler, a German-born engineer 12 years his senior, with whom he was destined to form a partnership which lasted from 1881 to 1895. The two men produced 26 major projects, several of them among the most significant creations of the Chicago school. Between 1899 and 1904—following his split with Adler in 1895—Sullivan designed the building frequently regarded as his masterpiece: the Schlesinger & Mayer (now Carson, Pirie, Scott) Store.

Thereafter, his fortunes waned. As standards in American architecture changed during the early years of the twentieth century, as the eclecticism he had so strenuously fought began to reassert itself all over the country and no less in Chicago, his major commissions grew fewer. He was obliged to content himself with small buildings, most notably a series of banks in Midwestern towns. Almost pathetically modest in scope and size when compared with the ambitious edifices he had conceived in the 1880s and 1890s, they were nonetheless marked with a vigor of design and ornament that testified to the unflagging genius of the man.

It was not, however, an uncomplicated genius. There were in effect two Louis Sullivans. One was militantly impatient with historicism, with the mindless juggling of decorative styles he had found so superficial an emphasis in the program of the Ecole des Beaux-Arts. Thus Sullivan argued that most of the great structures of his own time came not from architects but from engineers who acknowledged science and technology as the most meaningful basis of building. His own Carson Store, the two lowest floors of which are alive with a very personal form of ornament, is otherwise and primarily an expression of the neutral character of the exposed frame.

Over and against this aspect, however, was the arch-romantic Sullivan who revered Michelangelo and Wagner, and who could never bring himself to believe that the sober discipline of engineering was enough by itself to assure genuinely great architecture. Hence in his exhaustively worked-out prose he sought to reconcile these two basic views in a philosophy that identified ornament as the net by which technology could be captured, domesticated and ultimately transformed into art.

The Auditorium Building 1886–89
430 S. Michigan
Adler and Sullivan

Like so many other phenomena of the Chicago of its day, the Auditorium Building was a titanic undertaking. A combination of deluxe hotel, office

building and a theater seating 4237, it was the most monumental structure of its kind in the United States, if not in the world.

In keeping with customary construction methods of the 1880s, the outer bearing walls were made of brick clad in stone. All other structural elements —interior columns and girders alike— were of iron.

The burdens of an enormously complex set of engineering problems fell mostly to Dankmar Adler. First among these was the construction of the theater, whose 117-foot span was broad enough to call for bridge building techniques. Acoustics represented another challenge, which Adler met by raising an elliptically curved vault with lateral breaks over that span and building a floor with a steep, elliptically curved slope. He also devised a means of stimulating artificial settlement of the foundation of the structure, whose proximity to the lake guaranteed an exceptionally unstable subsoil in which to work.

Adler's methods were often as ambitious as they were unorthodox. The theater, especially the stage, was a marvel of innovative devices capable of a wide variety of changes in size, levels and lighting. He equipped it with an early, but remarkably effective, form of air conditioning. By opening or shutting off sections of the seating he could vary audience size by as much as 1000 people. Even today, virtually the whole spectrum of musical and theatrical performances can be accommodated in this protean space.

Meanwhile, Sullivan played the role of architect as impressively as Adler did that of engineer. The younger man's designs for the interior were spectacular. The generosity of space in the theater, though mostly a result of the great vault overhead, was no less surely conveyed through Sullivan's allocation of parts and his opulent ornamental program. Elsewhere in the building the large hotel bar, the splendid restaurant, the various staircases, suites and rooms, bore consistent witness to their designer's untiring formal imagination. If the composition of the east front of the Auditorium Building is more restless and less unified than that of Richardson's stately Field Wholesale Store, it is nonetheless marked by a taut, robust vigor throughout. The portal frontispiece is one of the most powerful passages in all of Sullivan's architecture.

Uneven settlement of the building, by as much as 18 inches, has caused a slanting of the floor in parts of the interior. The exterior walls are in good condition. The theater, renovated by Harry Weese and Associates in 1967, is a remarkable approximation of the original, though certain rare or expensive decorative elements appear beyond hope of restoration.

For all the grandeur of the Auditorium and its remarkable solutions to a dizzying set of design problems, it is not so important a step forward in the realization of frame structure in the tall building as several projects by Jenney and the firm of Burnham and Root.

Daniel Burnham and John Wellborn Root not only adopted and further developed Jenney's skeletal construction in one of their earliest works, the Rookery, but also devised a new organization of the layout of an office building.

The Rookery, in plan almost a square, in elevation 11 stories high, is built around an inner light court, the lowest two stories of which are covered with a glass roof. The space thus enclosed functions as an expansive and brilliantly lit lobby which underscores the building's commercial character. At the same time the open court provides the upper floors themselves with ample natural light. This latter attribute was of no small consequence, given the fact that artificial lighting was still in its infancy at the time the Rookery went up.

In contrast with the generously decorated street facade, where traces of Richardson and the Beaux-Arts suggest a somewhat conservative expressive approach, the court facade is strikingly innovative in character. Its rows of windows are consistent throughout the nine visible floors, and the narrow terra-cotta bands that frame those rows suggest an early version of the ribbon window.

In turn, the vault of the lobby is an outstanding example of the iron-and-glass roof construction pioneered in Europe during the second half of the nineteenth century. The lobby was re-

Monadnock Building 1889–91, 1893
53 W. Jackson
Burnham and Root (northern part)
Holabird and Roche (southern part)

It is not without irony that the definitive early embodiment of the skyscraper aesthetic was a wall-bearing structure. To be sure, the 16-story Monadnock features interior cast-iron columns and wrought-iron beams. But by 1891 these were standard elements in buildings of its kind, and in any case, the most distinguishing characteristic was the somber brick walls. Whatever their other virtues, they represented an altogether conventional construction system.

Nonetheless, the Monadnock was a triumphant expression of the principles of Chicago construction. Its ground plan, a long, narrow rectangle which provided natural illumination in all interior office spaces, was a prototype of the slab-shaped high-rise buildings that followed it in the twentieth century.

The chief importance of the Monadnock, however, lay in the aesthetic implications of its uncompromising simplicity of form. In outlining the program of the building, the developer, Owen Aldis, early instructed designer John Root to keep the exterior decoration to a minimum. Aldis' motives were utilitarian, and Root, who had loaded the Rookery with a profusion of external ornament, was at first unenthusiastic about the directive handed him. Later, however, he reversed his attitude and not only willingly but eagerly eliminated all references to historical styles, arriving at a majestically simplified volume whose sparing deviations from a perfectly prismatic form seemed only to animate rather than detract from the overall simplicity of the design. Those deviations include a fastidious outward curve at the very top of the structure, a gentle and echoing curve at the base

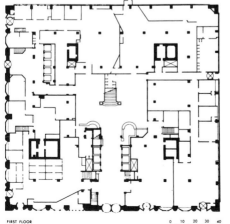

FIRST FLOOR   0 10 20 30 40

modeled by Frank Lloyd Wright in 1905, and the elevator foyer further changed by William E. Drummond in the early 30s.

The building is in excellent condition and essentially unchanged.

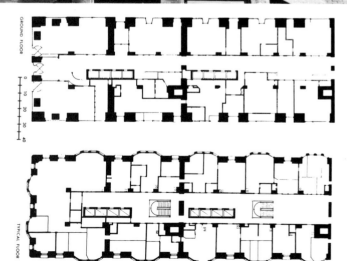

of the second story, ranks of oriels on the north and east elevations and a chamfered corner edge that tapers with almost tantalizing understatement to a sharp edge at the base. The resultant sum of forms and material is meticulously shaped, proportioned and executed throughout.

Here, then, is the Chicago aesthetic manifest: decoration is meant to be either subdued or banished altogether, in favor of the direct expression of structure and function, which in turn may take on its own elegance solely through the designer's attention to proportion of line, plane and volume, and to the frank expression of materials and natural colors.

Two years after the completion of the Monadnock, an annex to the south was added by Holabird and Roche, who mirrored the original rectangular plan and the basic form of the earlier structure, but utilized a steel frame rather than bearing wall construction. Thus the windows are noticeably larger in the southern building, though the finished product lacks some of John Root's precision and sensitivity.

The building is in generally good condition; the ground floor interior has been largely and indifferently altered.

Daniel H. Burnham
Born: 1846, Henderson, N.Y.
Died: 1912, Chicago

John Wellborn Root
Born: 1850, Lumpkin, Ga.
Died: 1891, Chicago

Compared with the sure sense of purpose that marked the development of other architects in the Chicago School —and even more in view of the great success of his own later years—Burnham's youth was a slough of failure.

He was a dreadful student, failing the entrance exams at both Harvard and Yale and thinking little enough of himself to approach any other schools. Instead, he repaired to Chicago, where he took a job as a clerk in a retail store. He rather hastily quit this assignment to enter Jenney's firm, with a view to becoming an architect. That post he likewise abandoned, in favor of what turned out to be a disastrous gold mining expedition in the West. He tried politics, even running for office, with similarly discouraging results. He had just opened an architectural office of his own in Chicago when the city burned down and his partner left him.

At this point Burnham's father intervened, and secured his 26-year-old son a post in another architectural firm as a draftsman—the one capacity for which he had earlier shown a flair in school. In 1873 he met John Root, with whom he formed a new partnership. It was the turning point in the lives of both men.

Root, on the other hand, had an early life almost totally opposite to that of Burnham. He was precocious and adroit in all the arts, especially music and drawing. After schooling in England during his teen years, he returned to New York, where, at New York University, he continued to turn all he touched into creative gold. He eventually took a degree in civil engineering, a discipline which dovetailed nicely with his aesthetic bent. For a time he worked in the office of James Renwick, architect of St. Patrick's Cathedral, then moved to the Chicago firm of Carter, Drake and Wight—in the same year (1871), when poor Burnham's first partnership was coming apart at the seams.

The union of Burnham and Root was a study in complementarity. The former was the organizer, the idea man; the latter, the visionary and philosopher

(in this respect Root was comparable to Louis Sullivan in the quality of the thought he gave to creating a vital architecture out of the tools of modern industrial technology). The partnership quickly flourished. Structures such as the Montauk Building, the Rookery and the Monadnock were already recognized as masterpieces when erected, and they were instrumental in the appointment of Daniel Burnham as chief consulting architect for the Columbian Exposition of 1893.

Root never fulfilled his own role in this commission. He died, at 41, in 1891. Burnham pursued his plans for the vast fair, and in the meantime collaborated with Dwight Perkins, himself destined for a brilliant role later in Chicago architecture. Perkins, however, was unable to dissuade Burnham from endorsing the opinion of those Eastern architects who proposed that the Exposition be carried out in the neo-Renaissance mode then highly fashionable along the Atlantic Coast.

However, Burnham's own later buildings, like the Reliance, the Fisher and the Railway Exchange, testify to his continuing devotion to the principles of the Chicago structural tradition. Nevertheless he persisted in his yearning after the classical style as well, and both Sullivan and Frank Lloyd Wright criticized him severely for his conformity to East Coast architecture and to what they regarded as a generally debased public taste.

During the final decades of his life, Burnham's interests turned increasingly to city planning projects. His Chicago Plan, completed in 1909, remains one of the great early achievements in the field of total urban design.

William Holabird
Born: 1854, American Union, N.Y.
Died: 1923, Chicago

Martin Roche
Born: 1855, Cleveland
Died: 1927, Chicago

Born and raised in the East, William Holabird spent two years at West Point before coming to Chicago in 1875. Shortly after his arrival, he decided to become an architect, having apparently given the profession little previous thought. He entered Jenney's office as a draftsman, and left five years later to form an independent partnership with Ossian C. Simonds.

Martin Roche moved to Chicago with his family at the age of two. He was educated in the public school system here. Upon graduation in 1872 he also went to work in Jenney's firm.

In 1881, Roche joined Simonds and Holabird as a co-designer specializing in interior work, and the partnership was expanded to include his name. The following year the firm became Holabird and Roche. Unlike the other great duos of the first Chicago school, this union was not based on a clear division of labor between engineer and architect or between administrator and designer. Although Roche was apparently responsible for most of the designs and Holabird is credited with the engineering assignments, indications are that it was a close collaboration and that the work was often divided, especially on major design programs.

Almost from the beginning, the first Chicago school took on something of a dual character as individual architects were often forced to make a choice between considerations of beauty and utility. Sullivan and Root tended to give priority to the demands of aesthetics, approaching their work first in an emotional and romantic way and only subsequently addressing themselves to points of practicality. Holabird and Roche, on the other hand, aimed for maximum utility and sought to make their buildings aesthetically satisfying within this framework.

All four of these men passed through Jenney's office, but Holabird and Roche were his true spiritual heirs. Like their teacher, they approached commissions from an objective, practical and businesslike point of view. The cellular wall, which had emerged from Jenney's efforts to create the most economical and functional form for the tall office building, appeared with many variations in the work of his students; but it was Holabird and Roche who gave the steel frame its purest expression until Sullivan struck that perfect and delicate balance between beauty and utility in the Carson, Pirie, Scott Store.

A good deal of criticism has been levied against Holabird and Roche on the grounds that, once they had perfected their formula for the skyscraper in the Marquette Building, they continued to use it to the point of monotony. The criticism is justified to some extent, but it fails to acknowledge that the Holabird and Roche "formula" worked, largely because of its straightforward rationality. In the course of 45 years of existence (1882–1927), the partnership produced no fewer than 72 buildings in the central commercial area of Chicago.

Tacoma Building 1889
Northeast corner, LaSalle and Madison
Holabird and Roche

If the Tacoma Building was a somewhat inelegant work, it was also an original one, a strikingly resourceful response to the opportunities and problems implicit in the metal frame. It was the first large Chicago office building with a clearly open facade, expressive of the fact that the outer wall was little

more, indeed theoretically no more, than a skin. As such, the exterior could

penetrate the interior to an unprecedented degree. Moreover, by breaking up the facade with bay windows, the architects coaxed light to enter from three directions, not merely from one. Air was drawn in by the same principle and means: the oriel maximized ventilation as well as illumination. It even provided a wider view of the street.

Added to this were several other distinctions. The Tacoma was the first building to be erected with rivets rather than bolts, a method which assured faster and more secure construction. Its foundations, floating rafts of concrete reinforced with I-beams, were likewise revolutionary. It was, all in all, a building typical of the pragmatic design manner of Holabird and Roche.

The building was demolished in 1929.

Marquette Building 1894
140 S. Dearborn
Holabird and Roche

By 1894, five years after completing the Tacoma Building, Holabird and Roche had added a considerably refined aesthetic consciousness to their already evident gift for technical innovation. The Marquette Building is the most impressive single testimony to this. It has all the major characteristics of Chicago skyscrapers of the mid-90s: boldness of expression, regularity of form, clear revelation of the structural steel frame. But it is also far more assured in its proportions than the Tacoma.

It employs a wide-ranging program of classical ornament. The end bays are of chamfered stone, and Roman motifs animate the second-story cornice. Four panels in high relief, each depicting a scene from the lives of the seventeenth century French explorers of Illinois, Pere Marquette and Louis Jolliet, are ranged over the Dearborn Street portals. They are echoed in a

24

Steel Construction in Tall Buildings

Advances in the commercial manufacture of steel in the middle of the nineteenth century, notably the invention of the Bessemer and Siemens-Martin processes, together with the further development of methods of producing rolled sections, made it possible to substitute rolled sections for cast iron in the erection of the supporting steel frame.

Whereas European designers had confined their use of iron mostly to structures like bridges, train stations and exhibition halls—which could not

series of sparkling mosaics that decorate the foyer immediately within. Still, all these Beaux-Arts reminiscences are kept restrained; they enhance rather than detract from the candor of the overall design. The frame remains triumphant; the spaces between piers and girders are fully opened up, and on the lowest two stories the "Chicago window"—two sashes flanking an expanse of plate glass—appears in mature form, possibly for the first time.

The building is in good condition and well preserved; the original cornice was removed after World War II, to the detriment of the design.

be erected by then-conventional building means—cast-iron parts for residential and multi-story business buildings were already being produced in the U.S. as early as the mid-1800s. With the appearance of rolled steel sections, Chicago designers began to employ steel as the primary constructive material of their multi-storied buildings.

The major disadvantage of both iron and steel is their vulnerability to great heat. Cast-iron buildings had fared no better in the 1871 Chicago fire than wooden ones. Thereafter it became quickly evident that both iron and steel, despite their great building potential, had to be sheathed in fire resistant material. Several early metal frame structures like Jenney's Home Insurance Building did indeed make use of such cladding. But Jenney seemed moved more to endow that work with the appearance of traditional masonry than to take maximal advantage of the possibilities of great spans which steel suggested. It remained for other designers to exploit that advantage.

Reliance Building 1894
32 N. State
D. H. Burnham & Co.
(chief architect: Charles B. Atwood)

Burnham and Root carried on under the former's name following John Root's death. Indeed the firm developed into one of the great "architectural factories" of the turn of the century, at which time its work could be found all over the country. The exceptional level of quality of which Burnham & Co. was capable is manifest in the Reliance Building.

The typical commercial facade of the early 1890s, whether built on bearing walls or a metal frame, tended to give expressive priority to the strength, and often the massiveness, of the materials

it was made of. In the Reliance, as in the Tacoma before it, the opposite character of lightness and transparency is affirmed. The Reliance, however, suffered from none of Tacoma's ungainliness. A soaring 15-story shaft whose components are unfailingly graceful and precise in their proportions, it demonstrated more convincingly than any building of its day the buoyancy which steel and glass together can produce in a tall building.

Nine years earlier, in the court facade of the Rookery, Burnham and Root had evoked the impression of a continuous band of windows, by stressing all horizontal elements and underplaying the vertical. In the Reliance this principle of modular continuity was brought as close to perfection as the means of the time permitted. But it was expressed less as a direction—be that horizontal or vertical—than as a total transparency of structure. Reflected light became the major expressive device, gaining variety and complexity from the shifting rhythms of the bay windows.

The building is in rundown condition; the ground floor was subjected

level. This caisson technique, though borrowed from bridge construction, was without precedent in tall commercial buildings.

Sullivan's facade in turn was a strong but curiously mixed composition. To some extent it was consistent with the majority of his buildings from the late 1880s and early 1890s, which by and large revealed his debt to Richardson. In the Field Wholesale Store Richardson had grouped the windows of the middle three stories into rows of vertical units topped by arches. Sullivan repeated this device in the base of the Chicago Stock Exchange, with the result that the verticality of the building was strongly asserted at that point. At the same time this clustering suppressed the sense of the modular skeletal frame which in the upper floors was far more frankly expressed.

The detailing and the ornamentation of the Stock Exchange were among its most winning architectural features. The gigantic portal arch, the grillwork on the elevators and the embellishments of the Trading Room—all, happily, preserved today at the Art Institute of Chicago—testified to Sullivan's originality and fertility of formal invention. In these respects he was matched by no other architect of the first Chicago school.

In 1908 the Chicago Stock Exchange moved to quarters in the Rookery Building; its former spaces were remodeled over the years for a variety of tenants. Despite widespread public protest the building was declared "economically unviable" and was razed in 1972 to make room for a taller structure. Richard Nickel, a gifted architectural photographer noted for his efforts in behalf of landmark preservation, was accidentally killed in the course of documenting the demolition. Ironically, the mediocre new building on the site

to a shabby "modernization" after World War II, and the handsome original cornice was removed, leaving the facade flat and unarticulated at the attic level.

Old Stock Exchange 1894
Southwest corner, Washington and
** LaSalle**
Adler & Sullivan

Whereas Adler and Sullivan's Auditorium Building was constructed on the principle of the bearing wall, their Old Stock Exchange was supported by a

skeletal steel frame. Adler's engineering talents were again much in evidence here. In view of the building's relatively low profile, he elected to forego all wind bracing. It was a rather daring decision, given the 13-story height. Nevertheless the building never suffered notably from wind stress. Moreover, Adler constructed a new type of foundation along the west wall. Instead of following the standard practice of resting the structure on wood pilings, he built it on large watertight drums filled with cement and sunk to hardpan, some 50 feet below ground

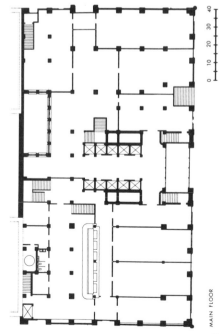

MAIN FLOOR

has proved to be even less "viable." Shunned by renters, it has gone into receivership.

Top, facade of the Old Stock Exchange; *bottom,* Second Leiter Building

Second Leiter Building 1889–91
403 S. State
William Le Baron Jenney

With the Second Leiter Building, a department store of dimensions impressive even today, Jenney reached the climax of his career as a designer. The eight floors encompass an area of roughly 55,000 square feet and, as in the case of the First Leiter Building, the constructional elements—metal columns and beams—furnish the basis for the expression of the exterior. The large spans and unusually high stories result in a generously proportioned facade.

The structure is in generally respectable condition, though the interiors are greatly altered. The building is now the main downtown store of Sears, Roebuck & Co.

Fisher Building 1895–96
343 S. Dearborn
D. H. Burnham and Co.

A major element of Burnham's success was his ability to adapt to rapidly changing public taste. Influenced by the World's Columbian Exposition, which had taken place in Chicago in 1893, this taste turned more and more to a preference for ornament borrowed from historical styles.

Burnham's Fisher Building, finished two years after the Reliance, reflected that change and the attempt of the architect to follow it. Although the facade is structurally almost identical with that of the Reliance, its 18 stories make it taller and more slender. It is one of the most elegant buildings of the first Chicago school. Only the Gothic ornament inappropriately applied to spandrels and upper stories detracts from its clarity. Nevertheless, it would be far better to retain this ornament than to subject the building to the "renovation" that deprived Sullivan's Gage and Carson Buildings of their cornices.

The building has been cleaned recently and is in excellent condition.

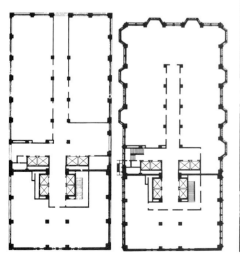

Gage Group 1898–99
30, 24, and 18 S. Michigan
Holabird and Roche
(Louis Sullivan designed the
facade of the northernmost
of the three buildings)

The Gage Group demonstrates how closely the views of the early Chicago school architects had come to paralleling each other by the end of the century. Sullivan's facade can be distinguished from the other two in its use of ornament, its more subtly complex fenestration—a consequence of the functional demands of the client—and the more elegant profile of its piers. The two buildings by Holabird and Roche are nevertheless more powerful and straightforward. Yet these distinctions are minor; nothing could suggest the emergence of a unified school of thought in Chicago commercial architecture more than the fact that its concurrences far outweighed its differences.

For Sullivan, who had already dissolved his partnership with Adler, his contribution to the Gage Group carried him a step closer to the Schlesinger & Mayer Store. Holabird and Roche evidently moved abreast of him; all three architects were clearly heading toward a maximally frank exterior expression of the interior frame.

The building bearing Sullivan's facade was originally eight stories high. Four floors were added in 1902. The ground floor facades have been modernized—and impoverished—in all three structures. Similarly unfortunate has been the replacement of all three original cornices by flat parapets. A seventh floor was added by Altman-Saichek Associates to the southernmost building in 1971. The effect of this last alteration was considerably more respectful of the original design.

McClurg Building 1899–1900
218 S. Wabash
Holabird and Roche

The McClurg Building possesses one of the most consistent facades of any building of the first Chicago school. Without resorting to eclectic styles or retreating behind ornament, the architects have here created a building of superior proportions with a sensitive articulation of structural elements. Bearing and non-bearing members are clearly differentiated; through the interruption of the subordinated elements the progression of column, beam and mullion is made clear.

Two decades after Jenney made his attempt in the First Leiter Building to express the load-carrying function of iron construction, the McClurg reached an admirable clarity in its expression of the steel skeleton.

The building is in good condition and still in use.

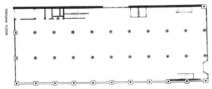
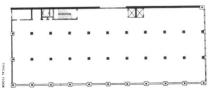
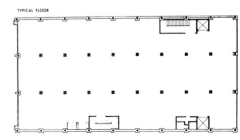

Above, Gage Group; *left*, floor plans of the Gage Group; *right*, floor plan of the McClurg Building

Carson, Pirie, Scott Store 1889, 1903–04, 1906
1 S. State
Louis Sullivan

"The . . . office unit . . . naturally predetermines the standard structural unit. . . . In turn, these purely arbitrary units of structure form . . . the true basis of the artistic development of the exterior."

Three years after Sullivan wrote this in an essay titled "The Large Office Building Artistically Observed," he received the commission for his last major work, destined also to be his most significant: the Schlesinger & Mayer (now Carson, Pirie, Scott Store).

The structure of the building was simple enough, and by 1899, rather standard: a modular frame, consisting of columns and beams, their respective spans and heights determined by functional requirements alone. If Sullivan had meant what he said, this and nothing more would be the basis for the composition of his facade.

He was true to his word. The skeleton was never more clearly expressed than here. The brilliant white terracotta sheathing accents it and the boldly recessed windows dramatize it even more. Seen at close range or from a distance, the State Street face of the Carson Building is one of the strongest and most uncompromisingly direct statements in all of modern architecture.

Sullivan thus strode firmly into the twentieth century. Yet one cannot leave his accomplishment at that. We have earlier affirmed that he was committed as surely to romanticism as to technology, and for all the muscularity of his engineering here, Carson's is distinguished by some of the most lavish and ingratiating ornament he ever conceived. As if to make up for the ascetic

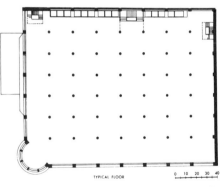

TYPICAL FLOOR

0 10 20 30 40

simplicity of the upper stories, he covered the lowest two floors with a magnificent mesh of filigree, restless, rich and fantastic, a valedictory to the decorative tradition of the Beaux-Arts, but a declaration personal enough to be free of the mechanical sterility into which the Beaux-Arts by then had fallen.

Until this time Sullivan's buildings marked him as one of the reigning architects of the Chicago school, yet one for whom the building art seemed to represent more what the nineteenth century, and especially Richardson, had understood, than what the new methods of construction implied. In the latter respect, that is, in their embrace of the principle of the frame, Jenney, Burnham and Root were probably ahead of him. His romantic utterances together with his unswerving devotion to ornament had established him as something of an outsider among his contemporaries. But this special position was not the least of the factors that gave him the very sovereignty and independence to summarize in the Carson Building the essential elements of the first Chicago school's development, and thus to bring them to culmination.

The exterior is in excellent condition; the interior is much altered. The earliest part of the structure, built for the Schlesinger & Mayer Department Store, is a three-bayed, nine-story section on E. Madison St. It dates from 1899. The main mass, 12 stories high, three bays wide and seven long, was erected in 1903–04. Schlesinger & Mayer sold the building in 1904 to its present occupant, the Carson, Pirie, Scott Store. In 1906 D. H. Burnham & Co. added five more bays to the south, closely following Sullivan's plans. The original cornice was replaced by a parapet in 1948. In 1960–61 Holabird and Root added three more bays to the south. The ornament, sketched by Sullivan, was worked out by his assistant, George Grant Elmslie.

Montgomery Ward Warehouse 1906–08
Along the north branch of the Chicago River, directly south of Chicago Ave.
Schmidt, Garden & Martin

After the turn of the century Holabird and Roche continued to build in the idiom of the Chicago school. But younger architects as well joined in the creative use of construction methods and forms developed during the last two decades of the nineteenth century. Indeed this next generation carried its predecessors' ideas forward, devising new methods and giving them vital shape as late as the years immediately following World War I.

Notable among the younger group was the trio of Richard Schmidt, Hugh Garden and Edgar Martin, who formed a partnership in 1906 which lasted into the 1920s and whose heirs continue today under the name of Schmidt, Garden and Erikson.

Schmidt, who was born in Germany in 1865 and spent a period of study at Massachusetts Institute of Technology, was a master of concrete construction. His most impressive achievement in that medium is the Montgomery Ward Warehouse, an immense edifice which follows the contours of the north bank of the Chicago River. It is supported by a reinforced concrete frame on wood pilings. Rising to a height of nine stories and containing about 144,000 sq. ft. (16000 m²) of area, it was for a long time the largest reinforced concrete building in the city.

Save for the brick cladding of the spandrels, the facade is composed of the outer edges of the undisguised frame itself. The accent is unmistakably horizontal, a fact which not only follows from the building's great length, but celebrates it.

The building is in generally good condition.

The Chicago Plan (known popularly as The Burnham Plan) 1909
Daniel H. Burnham, with Edward H. Bennett

By 1909, when Burnham submitted his ambitious scheme for a new Chicago, he had already gained a substantial reputation as a city planner. His experience as chief consulting architect for the Columbian Exposition had launched him in that direction, and in the years following the Fair, he advanced plans for San Francisco, Cleveland, Washington and Manila.

In 1906 he received a commission from the Merchant's Club (later the Commercial Club), with instructions to evaluate the overall physical condition of Chicago and "to record some conclusions in the shape of drawings and texts which shall become the guide for the future development of the city." Together with Edward H. Bennett, he worked intensively for three years on the assignment. The city formally adopted "The Chicago Plan" in 1910, and it served as a framework of official policy over the next 50 years. For a variety of reasons many of its details were never realized, but those that did come to fruition have left a deep imprint on the face of the city. Among them are:

The broad formal layout of Grant Park, extending east from Michigan Avenue to the lake. Burnham also proposed a long strip of open parkland along the lakefront to the north and south of Grant Park. It was to be interspersed with lagoons and grand, symmetrically disposed jetties. A sizeable amount of it was achieved, but at the cost of some of the grandeur of the concept and much of its symmetry.

A program of parks throughout the city, which are interconnected by many, though not all, of the broad, treelined parkways which Burnham hàd in mind.

The two-level embankment of Wacker Drive, along the Chicago River.

The east-west axis of Congress Street, which is, however, an expressway rather than the boulevard Burnham meant it to be.

The Forest Preserves, located along the inland edges of the city, a partial green belt between city and suburbs.

What Burnham foresaw but could not accurately measure—and thus could not adequately plan for—was the eventual stupendous pressure of the city's automobile traffic, which began to increase markedly between the wars. The parkland along the lakefront has lost much of its once untrammeled freedom to the teeming Outer Drive which cuts through it, dividing green land from shore. Cars in ever-increasing quantities have also robbed the interior boulevards of their intended identity as verdant, ingratiating connectors between parks. Moreover, while the expressways built during the last two decades follow paths laid out in the Plan, they are hardly what Burnham had in mind, either in function or in aspect.

Neither could Burnham envision the shifts that were imminent in the city's social structure. The southern blacks who began to move here in large numbers during World War I were quickly segregated into vast and sordid ghettos on the south and later the west sides. These infected areas fester to the present day. In addition, the morale of the city suffered immensely from the effects of the Prohibition-provoked corruption and gangsterism of the 1920s, and thereafter from the disastrous De-

pression of the 1930s. What was once an enthusiastic and widely-remarked identification on the part of Chicago's larger public with the destiny of the city as a whole (the popular acceptance of the Burnham Plan itself was a reflection of this) had largely vanished by the onset of World War II, and the social changes which followed that conflict did nothing to restore it.

In the wake of such developments the Burnham Plan, conceived for gradual realization but never equipped with any sure means for achieving it, was bound to founder. Even Burnham's vision of business, residence and government districts composed of buildings of the same height—the classical expression of a prosperous and orderly society—fell victim to the altered social and economic priorities of the second half of the century.

Despite these broken dreams, however, the Burnham Plan was the first total plan for an American metropolis. Much of what is attractive about the city's present countenance is traceable to those of its details that did eventually see the light of day. Moreover, the Plan stimulated a keen interest in city planning here which, for all its many frustrations, continues unabated today.

"Make no little plans..." said Burnham as he submitted his plan, "...for they have no power to stir men's blood."

Glessner House 1886–87
1800 S. Prairie
Henry Hobson Richardson

The Glessner House, designated a landmark in 1971, is the one remaining Richardson structure in Chicago. Erected on one of Chicago's foremost residential streets of the 1880s, its laconic facade of roughhewn granite

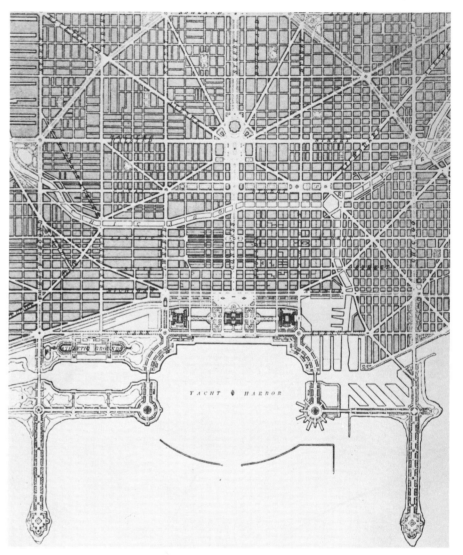

suggested a medieval fortress to many of its contemporaries who criticized it —especially its street facade—on grounds that it was a rebuff to the viewer.

On the other hand, the more open south and west sides, which face an interior court and are thus not visible from the street, offered the house's residents a more relaxed type of urban

living than the customary free-standing villas of the time were capable of providing.

The building was acquired in 1966 by the Chicago School of Architecture Foundation. Under the direction of Brenner, Danforth & Rockwell, it has been gradually restored to good condition, though work continues. In 1976, it was designated a National Historic

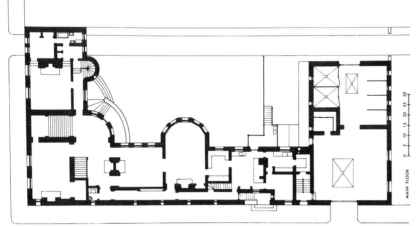

MAIN FLOOR

Landmark by the National Park Service of the Department of the Interior. Plans for further renovation and incorporation within the Prairie Avenue Historical District are proceeding under the guidance of Wilbert Hasbrouck.

Frank Lloyd Wright
Born: 1869, Richland Center, Wis.
Died: 1959, Phoenix

Wright's relationship to Chicago building at the turn of the century was not unlike that of Richardson's in the 1880s: both men exerted considerable influence on the Chicago school of architecture without ever being full-fledged members of the movement.

At 13, after passing much of his childhood in Boston, Wright made the first of many returns to his native Wisconsin. He later studied engineering at the state university, but did not graduate; before he was out of his teens, he was working as a draftsman in the Chicago firm of Lyman Silsbee.

That too was a brief engagement, lasting only two years. But what followed—a six-year term in the office of Adler & Sullivan—had an incalculable influence on his thinking and the direction of his life's work.

Nevertheless, Wright remained at all times his own man. At 25 he opened his own practice, significantly enough in suburban Oak Park, well away from the city. He was in fact never much committed to the urban ideal: his chief contribution to architecture lay in the splendid corpus of residences he produced over an extraordinary creative span of seven decades.

In 1909 Wright once again returned to Wisconsin, and once again left it, in 1915. The following two decades were restlessly spent in a variety of farflung locales, including California and the Far East. The last 25 years of his life found him alternating between the "Taliesin" complexes—residence-studio-school facilities—that he had built for himself near Spring Green, Wisconsin and Scottsdale, Arizona. All the while he ceaselessly recorded his views of architecture and society, pub-

lishing several books on those subjects, as if in emulation of the example his mentor Sullivan had earlier set for him.

Twenty-eight years of Wright's early career were spent in or near Chicago. During that time he developed his concept of an "organic" architecture, embodying it in the Prairie Style house, whose ground-hugging profile, interpenetrating volumes and flow of interior spaces influenced a whole school of younger architects.

Ward W. Willitts House 1902
1445 Sheridan Rd., Highland Park, Ill.
Frank Lloyd Wright

A coherent relation between interior plan and an exterior form expressive of it was achieved by Wright shortly after the turn of the century. The Willitts House is one of the most revealing examples of this synthesis, and it ranks among his early masterpieces. The great chimney in the center of the house acts as a stable core from which all parts move dynamically outward. The wide eaves of the low-hipped roof and the rhythmic rows of casement windows establish the horizontal emphasis characteristic of the Prairie Style, while echoing externally the complex flow of interior spaces. The off-white stucco of the facades, enlivened by strips of dark-stained wood, suggests an influence from Japanese traditional domestic architecture.

Still used as a single family residence, the house is in excellent condition.

Unity Church and Parish House 1906
Southeast corner, Lake and
Kenilworth, Oak Park, Ill.
Frank Lloyd Wright

The Unity Church was one of the relatively few public buildings Wright

Above, Willitts House; *top right,* Unity Church; *middle right,* interior of Unity Church; *bottom right,* detail of Unity Church; *bottom left,* floor plan of Unity Church

erected during the years when he was early associated with Chicago. It was his first structure in concrete, a material he was later to use repeatedly, with striking virtuosity.

The two volumes of the building, one square in plan, the other more nearly a rectangle, are handsomely related to each other in scale and detail. A low foyer links the two. It is a typical revelation of Wright's architectural psychology, so to speak: after entering, the visitor is led to the main auditorium by a circuitous route which effectively prepares him for the spectacular larger space beyond.

The auditorium, illuminated by a splendid coffered ceiling, is a remarkable study in the counterpoint of rectilinear volume and void which comes about as close to cubism in architecture as any designer ever did. Nor is it idle to recall that the Unity Church antedates Picasso's earliest studies in the interpenetration of geometric form and space by some two years.

The building is in good condition: it has been periodically refurbished.

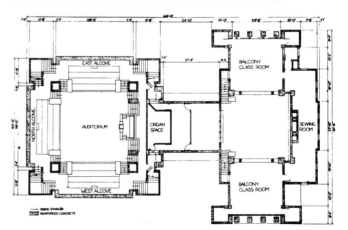

Avery Coonley House 1908
300 Scottswood Rd., Riverside, Ill.
Frank Lloyd Wright

One of the most sumptuous of Wright's Prairie Houses, the Coonley residence was in fact built as a full-fledged estate, complete with a garden and gardener's cottage, a stable, a wooded park and a variety of comparably luxurious accoutrements. The program of ornament—colorful wall tiles, richly decorated leaded windows and skylights—was the architectural counterpart of a lush natural setting to which it was consciously related. The elevation is low and generous, with interlocking volumes. Just as characteristically, the interiors are alive with movement and a constant play of spatial surprises which result from the flow of passages one into another. "This broken rambling horizontal extension," writes Norris Kelly Smith, "seemed to Wright to connote as fitly the meaning of personal freedom in the individual's 'social space' as had the loftiness of the cathedral the meaning of order and authority."

The house has been divided into condominium apartments, but is relatively intact.

Robie House 1909
5757 S. Woodlawn
Frank Lloyd Wright

The Robie House, a single-family residence at the edge of the quadrangles of the University of Chicago, is probably Wright's single most accomplished work from the pre-World War I years. It is also a typical example of Prairie Style architecture: the silhouette is long and low, in deference to the flat land beneath it. The eaves are wide and generous. The rooms seem to grow outward from the hearth, in an open, interconnected arrangement that contrasts markedly with the closed-off, box-like spaces characteristic of traditional American house design in the eighteenth and nineteenth centuries. The exterior forms derive directly— "organically"—from the dynamic but well-defined spaces within them. And over all, Wright's feeling for proportion, detail and materials prevails.

The building is in good condition. It was restored by Wesley Peters in 1964 and by Skidmore, Owings & Merrill in 1967. Owned by the University of Chicago, it now houses the Adlai Stevenson Institute of International Affairs.

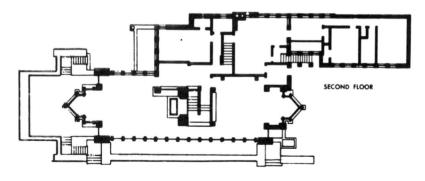

SECOND FLOOR

Left, Coonley House

Preservation
by Linda Legner

Chicago, the city that framed its first skyscrapers in steel and thereby gained an undisputed reputation as a leader in the building arts, has lately been caving in to the pressures of redevelopment. Today it is locked in a preservation battle fiercer, perhaps, than that raging anywhere else.

Immediately at stake is the cohesive collection of masterpieces produced in the late nineteenth and early twentieth centuries, though, by implication, newer buildings are likely to be threatened eventually by the same danger.

One by one these old landmarks, most of them modest in scale by today's standards, are being squeezed off their sites by leviathan successors that promise to bring in more dollars more "efficiently." In the process, Chicago is destroying something substantially more precious than bricks and mortar. With every great building that falls, a little more of the city's sense of history and civic respect dies with it.

Unfortunately, the case for preservation is too often confused with stagnation and a resistance to change. In fact, what the most enlightened of the preservationists advocate is selective retention: *everything* needn't stay; on the other hand, the best doesn't have to go.

Yet in a lunge for more money, distinguished if aging buildings do not seem to have a chance. Structures too small on lots too narrow are not considered "fiscally responsible." So away with them.

Already gone are the First Leiter and Home Insurance Buildings of Jenney, Adler and Sullivan's Garrick Building, Holabird and Roche's Cable, Tacoma, and Republic buildings, all but two of Burnham and Root's masterworks, and the last major casualty (to date), the Old Stock Exchange of Adler and Sullivan. From the lessons of these losses, preservationists have discovered that, while they may have God on their side, moral rectitude will not safeguard landmarks. Only cash can do that.

As long as communication channels to the power elite stay closed, preservationists will occasionally assume guerrilla tactics. But on the whole, the preservationist community in Chicago has settled down to serious, long-range planning. As might be expected, their interests and efforts have grown sophisticated.

Deferring at last to architectural treasures west of the Hudson, the National Trust for Historic Preservation has opened a Midwest field office in Chicago. Under the capable direction of a dedicated staff, the Trust has supplied a good deal of concerned but rational advice, sponsored special projects and supported as well as organized a host of conferences and seminars.

The U.S. Department of the Interior has released the Chicago Theme Study, urging a national cultural park in the Chicago metropolitan region, to be focused on, though not limited to, remaining Chicago and Prairie School buildings.

Historic districts, which gave rise to the idea of the national cultural park, have proven to be surprisingly workable means of saving valuable neighborhoods. It has been easier to mobilize support for them than for individual buildings, if for no other reason than that designation of a district tends to have an upgrading effect on all real estate within and around it. This broadstroke approach has been effective on streets like Prairie Avenue and Alta Vista Terrace as well as in whole communities: Riverside, Pullman and Oak Park.

Responding to citizen concern, local landmark commissions have formed in several suburbs, most recently in Evanston and Oak Park (where the village not long ago bought the Frank Lloyd Wright Home and Studio, and created a special foundation to assure its wellbeing).

A number of communities and groups like the Chicago School of Architecture Foundation pursue effective and popular educational campaigns featuring tours, talks and training classes.

The Landmarks Preservation Council is probably the most catholic of local preservation groups since it is not preoccupied with ownership or restoration of landmark properties. LPC has, therefore, assumed responsibilities for drafting legislation that, it is hoped, will put muscle into the movement.

The press is somewhat more attuned to preservation issues than in the past, as are some government administrators and many segments of the lay and professional public.

Progress, primarily in the private sector, has been realized. But enormous difficulties still exist.

The federal government, for instance, fairly radiates enthusiasm but has virtually no budget to make its sympathies effective. The State of Illinois, meanwhile, seems decidely more interested in the natural than in the built environment. Fish, game and land conservancy takes up most of its attentions. What's more, implementation of any state preservation package is flawed by Illinois' home rule powers, which leave landmarks at the mercy of political machinations.

But the overwhelming obstacles to preservation lie squarely in established economic and political systems where change comes slowly and the stakes are high. Official city actions seem almost calculated to frustrate solutions.

Within the municipality, for example, two voluntary committees deal with preservation. The Mayor's Commission for the Preservation of Chicago's Historic Architecture was convened in 1972, in the aftermath of the Stock Exchange fight, and charged explicitly with unraveling economic entanglements. Composed of high-ranking civic leaders and major figures of the real estate and finance worlds, this special commission looked far more impressive at its inception than it has proved to be. The full committee has never met on its own, or produced a study, or even issued a public statement. It seems little more than an exercise in blue ribbon tokenism, a discredit to the good faith of many Chicagoans who saw it initially as a genuine attempt to solve problems.

The other group is the Commission on Chicago Historical and Architectural Landmarks. First formed in 1957 and reorganized in 1968, it consists of eight mayoral appointees (non-salaried and not exactly representative of the business community) plus the city Commissioner of Development and Planning.

Under the governing landmark law, the Commission is vested "with the responsibility of recommending to the City Council the adoption of ordinances designating . . . 'Chicago Landmarks' . . . and thereby necessitating their preservation, protection . . . and perpetuation."

All this legal jargon boils down to the uncomfortable fact that the Commission can only *recommend* designation, not dispense it. That latter power rests solely with the City Council of Chicago, a legislative body.

The Commission's public hearings have become increasingly inequitable. Despite rules of procedure to the contrary, preservation proponents are standardly not allowed to question the commissioners, to cross-examine the owner of a building in question—or any of his witnesses—or to offer arguments in rebuttal. Evidence in favor of designation is frequently presented and the hearing summarily continued to a later date, thus affording any owner who objects to landmark designation the opportunity to review his opposition's case *before* introducing his own. He is, however, not required to submit a brief in advance.

The city hasn't hesitated to deny landmark designation when it interfered with what has been regarded as "important" redevelopment. The ordinance, in effect, permits the designation process to be interrupted on behalf of a politically well-connected owner. The Commissioner of Development and Planning can delay a recommendation. A City Council committee can bury it. It is hardly surprising, then, that proceedings limp along feebly or that few recommendations have become landmark reality.

Over the years, the city administration has done nothing to address the economic dilemma. Landmark owners, with rare exceptions, will not forego private gain for community benefit. By standards of traditional property law, designation circumscribes the owners' freedom to dispose of their property as they wish. So they will opt to demolish rather than preserve unless afforded the benefits of reasonable remuneration. But what city is in a financial position to remunerate an owner directly?

Or even indirectly? The way the landmark ordinance is now written, the owner of a *designated* structure may tear it down as long as he goes through the motions of negotiating with the city for the prescribed duration of the examination procedure . . . unless, that is, the city is willing and able to buy his building at fair market value—which means at the price of redevelopable land, not just the worth of the building.

Tax structure, inflationary land values and particularly zoning laws, militate against designation. Landmarks, in contemporary thinking, are "underscaled" to begin with. According to attorney John Costonis, they are also "typically located on small parcels. This factor would hardly bear notice were it not for the so-called zoning bonus system. A zoning bonus permits a developer to erect a larger building in return for providing an open space amenity, such as a plaza or arcade, at his own expense. Owners of small parcels, however, cannot effectively utilize bonuses because they are left with insufficient land on which to build an economic structure.

"The introduction of zoning bonuses has brought development of small lots to a standstill and hastened the amalgamation of smaller holdings into land assemblies of sufficient size—usually a quarter block or more—to exploit the bonuses. It is an unfortunate paradox that bonuses, which were intended to enhance one type of urban amenity, have had such a destructive impact on another."

Urban landmarks, you might say, are in the right place at the wrong time. It is a complicated but not unresolvable quandary. In *Space Adrift: Landmark Preservation and the Marketplace,* Costonis developed a proposal, dubbed the Chicago Plan, which just could answer the needs of all concerned.

As a relief for insistent redevelopment tension (which is, after all, why landmarks fall), he suggests a reinterpretation of the conventional property definition. To wit:

Instead of controlling a plot of ground, an owner would be asked to recognize that he actually controls a cubic development package, part of which can be sold as readily and perhaps as profitably as his land alone.

Through a development rights transfer mechanism, an owner could subtract the volume of his landmark from the total development envelope of his site. What remains would be available for sale or transfer to another owner who might wish to build higher than zoning on his parcel allowed.

All transfers would be carried out within a specified area, much like current zoning districts. Thus the city could keep tabs on basic bulk and density build-up. In return for the prerogative to sell his rights, an owner would convey to the city a preservation restriction which would prohibit redevelopment and require present and future owners to maintain the building.

Because he would have "decreased" the value of his property, the landmark owner would receive a tax deduction. Likewise, the development rights' buyer would pay proportionately more since he would have significantly increased his site's inherent worth. The city would not lose a tax penny.

But what if an owner were to reject the transfer option? Costonis suggests the creation of a developments rights bank owned and operated by the city. Into it would go rights over municipally owned landmarks (like the Water Tower or, soon, the Rookery), condemned rights and those donated by sympathetic owners. The city, naturally, would be enabled to sell the pooled rights to private developers and build up a cash reserve. Then, if an owner declared his intent to demolish, the city would have the money for purchase, and not a cent of it would have to be extracted from general revenue funds.

The strength of the Plan as Costonis reads it is that "development rights transfer largely shifts preservation costs from the city and the landmark owner to the downtown development process itself." As long as the city officially refrains from granting variances and unofficially making deals, transfers remain marketable, and the Plan's thesis is upheld.

"The posture of the property system vis-a-vis development rights transfer at the present time," Costonis reminds us, "is much the same as it was when the concepts underlying condominium ownership and air rights sales were being fashioned. In each sense, a prolonged period of trial and error was necessary during which legislatures, courts, the real estate community, and the marketplace all made their contribution." It seems little enough to ask that similar cooperation be accorded the concept of development rights transfer.

Chicago 21, a shiny new plan for the city's central communities, recognizes development rights transfer as a possible tool and calls for three legally designated preservation districts—one of them in the heart of the Loop. Indirectly, it lays the framework for a transfer district by encouraging new construction in development corridors located primarily on the perimeter of the Loop, not inside it.

In the Chicago Theme Study, the Department of Interior not only affixed its imprimatur to the Chicago Plan but made federal assistance in a national cultural park contingent upon it. In return for seed money toward a development rights bank, the Department asked the city to express equivalent commitment by legislating the transfer system.

Some observers have suggested that by endorsing the envelope benefits of the planned unit development ordinance—which was designed for superblock sites and isn't effective for smaller plots—the city has, in a round-about way, welshed on its part in any future involvement with the Chicago Plan.

In any case, neither Chicago's business contingent nor the city fathers have taken direct or affirmative action on Costonis' proposal. Official indifference? Maybe. Or perhaps a political aversion to climbing out on a limb. Admittedly, no one can be sure the Plan will work. It hasn't been tried. But one conclusion *is* distressingly certain: few landmarks can survive the present civic delay.

Curiously enough, the energy panic and an economic recession may prove to be preservation's trump cards. A glutted office market, financial insecurity and scarcity of building materials have virtually halted new downtown construction and encouraged (if only by default) recycling and adaptive reuse of older buildings. But such conditions will not persist indefinitely. Once the market revives, demolition is likely to intensify.

In the final analysis, the only guarantee of preservation may be the outright ownership of landmarks by sympathetic private title holders or preservation organizations. Thus, several groups have begun exploration of revolving purchase funds similar to those in Savannah. In Chicago, however, that would require tremendous working capital.

Clearly, preservation failures go deeper than the inability of good guys to prevail over bad. What preservationists are really combating is, in the short run, an economic deadlock, in the long run a deficiency of attitude.

Who *will* pay?

Chicago Architecture Between the Two World Wars
by Franz Schulze

One of the more dogged myths of modern architectural lore is that the 1893 Columbian Exposition destroyed the first Chicago school. Those who have held this belief argue that the Fair gave renewed national legitimacy to the Beaux-Arts manners in which it had chosen to present itself, and therewith drew attention away from the bold clarity of the great Chicago office buildings of the 1880s and 1890s.

More facts contradict this notion than support it, but it is a provocative point of departure for any discussion of Chicago buildings between the first school—which did, after all, come to a close—and the so-called second one, a development of the post-World War II period.

To begin with, a significant number of good commercial buildings, done in accordance with the principles of the first school, were erected in the first decade of the twentieth century, rather well after the Exposition. In fact, Holabird and Roche, that most characteristic of Chicago offices, produced most of its best work after 1900, including the Republic Building (1905–09), the Champlain Building (1903), and the Mandel Brothers Annex (1900, 1905). Moreover, we have already observed earlier here the rise of a lively second generation of commercial architects—albeit none of them geniuses—whose work was clearly indebted to that of the pioneers. Buildings utilizing the typical Chicago frame were designed, and designed well, as late as the second decade and, in some isolated instances, as late as the 1920s. Further, and finally, Frank Lloyd Wright's work, and with it that of the entire Prairie School, did not mature until after the turn of the century.

World War I, then, and not the Fair, seems to have been the chronological barrier which the first school, as an identifiable and vital movement, was unable to leap. By the middle of the second decade most of the great early figures were gone: Root died in 1891, Adler in 1900, Jenney in 1907, Burnham in 1912. Sullivan lived on until 1924, but during the last two decades of his life he was awarded no major commissions in the city. In 1914, tragedy befell Frank Lloyd Wright when several members of his household were murdered at Taliesin in Wisconsin. Two years later he departed for Japan.

By the time American commercial building resumed on a major scale following a quiescence imposed upon it by World War I, a new national temper prevailed, and with it an altered set of architectural values. At this point one may rightly acknowledge that the Columbian Exposition had an *eventually* deleterious effect upon the growth of the American modernist idiom which had been born in late nineteenth century Chicago. The Fair had undoubtedly stood for eclecticism, that is, for architecture based on an assortment of historical styles, and this was the chief expressive impulse behind the costumed skyscrapers that sprang up in American cities, most notably New York, after 1900.

The Chicago Tribune Competition

Following World War I, East Coast designers set the pace for the rest of America, while in the Midwest no significant new talents emerged. Instead, Chicago architects fell in line with the mood of conservatism. The clearest evidence of this, indeed one of the most highly publicized events in American architecture of the 1920s, was the *Chicago Tribune* competition of 1922. In that year the *Tribune,* the city's most powerful newspaper, announced plans for a new office building, and offered $100,000 in prizes as an incentive to architects submitting proposals for it. The winning design, executed by Raymond Hood and John Mead Howells of New York, was a glittering, vertically continuous tower clad in Gothic masonry and capped by an ornately buttressed Gothic chapter house. Like most technologically sophisticated skyscrapers of its day, the building was supported by a steel frame which was, however, almost totally concealed behind shafts of stone and decorative excrescences. The Tribune Tower undoubtedly gratified its sponsors; it stood for "beauty" in architecture, a value associated in the early 1920s with stylistically identifiable embellishments from the past. All the other entries from American architects to the competition were variations on the eclectic theme: Egyptian, Greek, Renaissance and Baroque styles, or fanciful permutations of them, dominated the contest. The contrary idea that a tall building might gain in architectural authority through the candid acknowledgment of its structural base and even through the formal celebration of it— an idea postulated by the 1880s–1890s generation in Chicago—was by now nearly forgotten among architects working in the United States.

The proposals which arrived from Europe were a different matter. Though some of them were among the most grotesque of the entire competition, several others bore little or no resemblance to the reigning American eclectic manners. Instead they were marked by a striking modernity. Walter Gropius, then director of the Bauhaus in Weimar, collaborated with Adolf Meyer in a project whose severe geometry and indifference to decorative elements reflected the machine aesthetic then gathering momentum in Europe. The frame of the Gropius-Meyer project was clearly expressed and its fenestration noticeably reminiscent of the "Chicago window"—a pair of attributes which suggest that the two Germans were more respectful of early Chicago architecture than were Chicago's own builders of the 1920s. Designs submitted by Knut Lönberg-Holm of Sweden, by Max Taut of Germany and by the Werkstatt für Massenform of Vienna further underscored the fact that a modernist revolution in Europe was already well under way. The progressive younger architects there, inspired in part by avant-garde movements in European painting, in part by earlier Euro-

pean designers such as Perret, Behrens and Berlage, and to some extent even by Frank Lloyd Wright and the first Chicago school, were forging a new functionalist philosophy of building at the same time American architecture was content to express itself in a wide, if not to say wild, variety of generally more traditional forms.

America survived the Tribune Tower competition: in fact the design which took second prize in the event—by Eliel Saarinen of Finland—had considerable influence on the development of skyscrapers during the later 1920s and early 1930s. Saarinen's concept, which elicited praise even from crusty old Louis Sullivan, was a lofty, gently tapering, stepped edifice marked by numerous outcroppings and an overall sculptural look. It eventually served as an inspiration to the New York design-

ers of the later 1920s who were seeking attractive ways to create set-back massings in their buildings as an architectural response to the limitations imposed by the city's 1916 zoning laws.

Thus, as of 1930, the standard American skyscraper was an aggregate of numerous influences. It derived its form more from a traditional concentration on outer mass than from any expression of inner structure, and it was still rather lavishly decorated, though the decoration had become streamlined, in keeping with simplicities lately learned from European modern movements, including what is now known as Art Deco. In short, it was something of a pastiche, symptomatic of the fact that U.S. designers had not yet decided whether they belonged in spirit to the old or the new architectural worlds.

It is imperative to point out here that good design could be consonant with this ambiguous expressive attitude, but ambiguous it remained. The story of Chicago architecture during the 1920s and 1930s—insofar as it was distinguished, and much of it was not—is one of isolated architects and individual buildings. And that effectively is the story of American building during the same decades. The next major development in this country came as a result of the importation of European modernism, a phenomenon hastened by World War II and the events leading up to it. By 1940 some of the best architectural talents of Europe had emigrated to America. These were the men who resolved the ambivalence of the 1920s and 1930s, and made modernism the nearly universal language of American architecture.

The greatest of these European emigrés, Ludwig Mies van der Rohe, settled in Chicago, bringing with him a devotion to lucidity of expression in design and a reverence for structure in architecture which he had learned more from his own experiences in Europe than from any special knowledge of Chicago building. Though he had been influenced early in his career by the house plans of Frank Lloyd Wright, the expressive kinship between him and the Chicago pioneers was for the most part fortuitous. Nonetheless, it was his presence and productivity as much as any other factor that revived an interest in the history of the first Chicago school at the very time the second was developing under his immediate impress. Some of his followers, indeed, having learned lessons about structure from him, went on to

Eliel Saarinen

Walter Gropius

Max Taut

"Werkstatt für
Massenform," Vienna

Completed
Tribune Tower

learn others from the masters of the first school. For all the differences between the romanticism which Louis Sullivan assimilated from Walt Whitman and the respect for classical rectitude which Mies gained from his own nineteenth century idol, Karl Friedrich Schinkel, the two modern architects are historic comrades in the same Chicago tradition. There is no neater summation of the rationale of that tradition than these remarks of Ludwig Hilberseimer, who, though he was referring specifically to Mies, might just as well

have been talking about Sullivan and the first Chicago school:

"His work is based on the conviction that no contradiction should exist between architecture and structure; that the two should be in harmony; that structure, while not in itself architecture, can be a means of architecture, if the builder understands the organic principle of order which relates every part of the building to the whole, according to its importance and its value."

The Century of Progress Exposition

If the Tribune Tower competition was the most pronounced evidence of a retreat from the spirit of adventure on the large scale in Chicago, it would be a misconception to suggest that nothing of architectural merit or originality was produced in this city between the two World Wars. Such a view has indeed been all too commonly held over the last several decades, probably because the dramatic post-World War II achievement of Mies van der Rohe and his followers has made it seem that they were not only the chief but the sole revivers of the early Chicago tradition.

In an historic sense they were; surely no overt development of the 1920s and 1930s resuscitated the structural aesthetic in Chicago so forcefully, above all so sustainedly, as Mies's advent did. Nonetheless, talent and vision were not lacking in the Chicago architectural world, even during the dark Depression years. Otherwise why, as early as 1935, did a group of local architects representing Armour Institute of Technology approach Mies—who was nothing if not a pillar of the international avant-garde—with a request that he head Armour's architecture school and reorient its curriculum from a Beaux-Arts emphasis to a modernist one? (Mies finally accepted the offer in 1938.) For that matter, how should one account for the collection of respectable Chicago skyscrapers executed in the Art Deco manner: works like the Palmolive Building (Holabird and Root, 1929, now known as the Playboy Building), the Civic Opera House (Graham, Anderson, Probst and White, 1929), the Field Building (Graham, Anderson, Probst and White, 1934)? Moreover: even acknowledging that these buildings were not intimately related to the

structural tradition in Chicago architecture which this text takes as its principal subject, there was in fact some work done in Chicago between the wars that is worth comment with that very tradition in mind. One of the more noteworthy sources of it, though seldom acknowledged in standard architectural histories of Chicago, was the Century of Progress Exposition of 1933. It was built at a time when scarcity of money forced experimentation of ideas.

At first glance, this second Chicago World's Fair would seem to recall its predecessor, the 1893 Columbian Exposition, in its apparent indifference to the local architectural heritage. Its organizers looked east for planning talent; notably to the fashionable Raymond Hood, of New York, co-designer of the Tribune Tower, and the conservative Paul Cret of Philadelphia.

Yet the Exposition also marked the rise to national prominence of Louis Skidmore and Nathaniel Owings. Both served as planners on the Fair's architectural commission. There can be little doubt that they tirelessly promoted the modernist idiom, bringing more than a little architectural daring to the programs they supervised. Moreover, it was a trio of Chicagoans with distinguished Chicago names—Edward H. Bennett, Jr., John Holabird, and Hubert Burnham, all sons of earlier architectural pioneers—who designed one of the more structurally experimental works of the Exposition. The Travel and Transportation Building has been called the first suspended structure in the United States, bridges excepted. First or not, it was surely atypical for its time and far-reaching in its potential implications. Its domed roof was supported by twelve steel cables strung from towers arranged in circular plan. The aesthetic result was

Skyride

House of Tomorrow

Travel and Transportation Building

clumsy: structure partially and awkwardly concealed behind a sleek Art Deco costume. Yet one cannot help remarking in it an ancient Chicago congeniality between the need—in this case Depression-inspired—for economy and efficiency on the one hand, and resourceful structural solution on the other.

Several other works at the Fair are likewise worth recalling, such as the enormous Skyride, a creation of the bridge engineers David B. Steinman and Holton D. Robinson. This was in effect a suspension bridge, between whose 628-foot (191.4 m) towers, separated by a 1850-foot (565.9 m) span, observation cars moved back and forth on cables at a height of 218 feet (66.5 m). It was the most spectacular entertainment feature of the Fair, the counterpart of the Columbian Exposition's huge Ferris wheel. George Fred Keck's

House of Tomorrow was yet another audacious endeavor, which contained an all-electric kitchen and a central air-conditioning system, both elements highly unusual for the time.

Shown also at the Century of Progress Exposition was the remarkable three-wheel Dymaxion Car of R. Buckminster Fuller, who had spent an early portion of his revolutionary career in Chicago. There he had designed the Dymaxion 4D House in 1927. It demonstrated great technical advantages in the creation of a controlled environment. Structurally the house was supported by a radial system of cables branching out from a central mast. Within the mast was located the whole mechanical system. The name *dymaxion* means "maximum gain for minimal energy input."

In the final analysis, American architecture was not significantly affected

by the Century of Progress Exposition. World War II broke out just as recovery from the Depression was getting under way, and following that cataclysm, the rush to embrace the ideas of the European modernists—Mies, Gropius, Le Corbusier—ushered in a new era. But the Fair remains one of the more sparkling moments in the history of Chicago architecture during the often murky and confused second quarter of the century.

Dymaxion House

The Second Chicago School of Architecture
by Oswald W. Grube , Peter C. Pran and Franz Schulze

(Note: Since the buildings of the first Chicago school have been rather fully discussed in the past, the authors have elected to devote more space in this book to an examination of the work of the second Chicago school.)

The Resurgence of the Chicago Tradition of Architecture

Engine Factory 1938
La Grange, Ill.
Albert Kahn, Inc.
Cosmetics Manufacturing Plant 1938
Albert Kahn, Inc.

In the decade prior to World War II, advances in the mass production of machinery, vehicles and consumer goods led to the development of a new type of factory, with large interior areas capable of housing long assembly lines. The form of these factories was straightforward and simple, usually dictated by economy and function alone.

The Detroit firm of Albert Kahn, Inc. was the first to exploit the possibilities of new materials and new structural methods in these factories. Often employing wide spans, Kahn created compact, yet functionally flexible buildings. They were realizations in the American vernacular of some of the same concepts which members of the European vanguard—most notably Mies—were advancing at a more formal level. As such they are among the early links between native and foreign elements in the evolution of the modernist idiom in this country.

Lake County Tuberculosis Sanatorium 1939
Belvedere Road, Waukegan, Ill.
Ganster and Pereira

The design and construction of this facility were preceded by a careful analysis of its intended function, and use was made of large south-oriented glass areas overlooking the pleasant rural site. The "International Style" was chosen as the architectural form granting the most freedom for expressing that function. The building is noteworthy for the success with which the grammar of that style was employed.

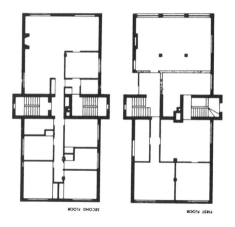

University Building 1937
5551 S. University
George F. and William Keck

In the 1930s, prior to the arrival of Mies, the European contemporary architecture which had come to be known as the "International Style" was only hesitatingly accepted in Chicago. Among the best of its early local manifestations is this small apartment building near the University of Chicago campus, a work notable for its simple surface articulation and carefully balanced proportions.

Ludwig Mies van der Rohe
Born: 1886—Aachen, Germany
Died: 1969—Chicago

Mies van der Rohe, whose work and thought are central to the resurgence of the Chicago architectural tradition, remained in his native Germany through the rise of Hitler. After the Nazi government made it virtually impossible for him to continue practicing architecture, he accepted the offer of Chicago's Armour Institute of Technology to become director of that school's department of architecture and immigrated in 1938.

Mies's teaching was as important a factor in the development of the second Chicago school as was his architecture. Like many of the architects of the first Chicago school, he had received no formal architectural training, yet his concept of what such an education should accomplish was as sure and logical as the character of his structures. In his 1938 inaugural address at Armour Institute he said: "We must make clear, step by step, what things are possible, necessary and significant . . . Education . . . must lead us from chance and arbitrariness to rational clarity and intellectual order . . . Therefore let us guide our students over the road of discipline from materials, through function, to creative work. Let us lead them into the healthy world of primitive building methods, where there was meaning in every stroke of an axe, expression in every bite of a chisel."

Illinois Institute of Technology 1940–72
3300 S. Federal
Mies van der Rohe

In 1940, Armour Institute merged with Lewis Institute to form the Illinois Institute of Technology. Under its president,

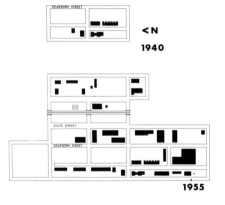
1940

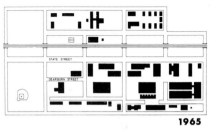
1955

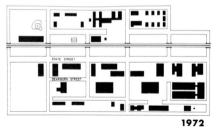
1965

1972

Henry T. Heald, the new, privately-funded educational facility began a period of growth that has since turned it into the third largest teaching and research institute in the U.S.A.

Following the 1940 merger, I.I.T. decided to remain on the old Armour campus on Chicago's near south side —this, despite the disintegration of the surrounding neighborhood. Shortly after Mies's arrival, he was awarded the commission to plan the redevelopment and extension of that campus. The objective was not only to accommodate the institution's rapid growth, but also

Mies finally developed was based on a 24-foot (7.3 m) module, which was intended to govern the bay size of the new buildings as well as the distances between them. The structures he designed for I.I.T. over the following years are dependent for their quality on a harmonious relationship of material, structure and proportion. Their carefully considered placement and subtle landscaping (by Alfred Caldwell) create a series of handsome outdoor passages and courts. The various and intriguing relationships between buildings and open spaces produce an abiding sense of visual balance and harmony. Freedom and order are here united by a comprehensive discipline.

Mies was responsible for all the new buildings added to the I.I.T. campus until he retired from teaching in 1958. By then Dr. Heald had left the school, and the succeeding administration replaced him as campus architect. Although the later buildings erected by SOM were scaled to and integrated with Mies's original scheme, the visual unity of his plan was compromised. The campus might have been changed from a cohesive urban unit to a mere collection of buildings were it not for the fundamental soundness of Mies's concept.

A 1972 issue of *Architectural Forum* called the I.I.T. campus "certainly the most meaningful contribution" of Mies to urban planning, and "of special international significance as an exemplary prototype of university architecture and planning."

Minerals and Metals Research Building, I.I.T. 1942
Heating Plant, I.I.T. 1949
Mies van der Rohe

Among the earliest of the individual structures at I.I.T., the Minerals and Metals Research Building and the Heating Plant—standing side by side at the southwest corner of the campus—embody the limits of Mies's approach to the expression of form. The east facade of the former is one great horizontal expanse of glass, a study in the architecture of transparency. The Heating Plant on the other hand is a cubic block, more vertical in feeling and solid, nearly opaque, save for four narrow bands of windows which divide the brick wall on the east. Yet the frame in both cases enunciates the ordering

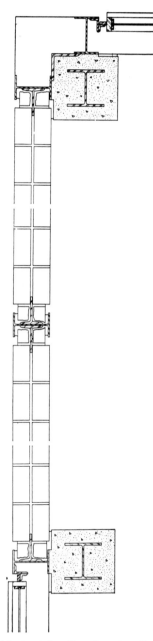

Typical horizontal sections through wall

to serve as inspiration and impetus for urban renewal in the adjacent slums. The long-range master plan which

principle common to all the buildings at I.I.T. Indeed, Mies's American buildings nearly without exception are variations of the two themes laid down here.

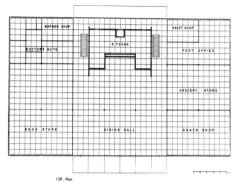

139. Plan

**Institute Buildings at I.I.T. 1945
Mies van der Rohe**

"Clarity of structure presupposes not only understanding of structure but the development of its characteristic order. There is freedom to choose a structure; but once chosen, there is freedom only within its limitations. To discover these limitations and to develop the structure accordingly is the requisite of any architectural work."
Ludwig Hilberseimer, 1956

The I.I.T. campus was the first of Mies's projects in which he chose to employ skeleton construction throughout. In all multi-story buildings the load-bearing structural members—steel fireproofed with concrete—lie be-

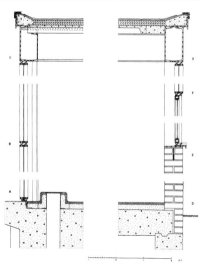

hind the facade but are expressed on it by black-painted steel spandrel fascias and mullions. The bays are filled with either buff-colored brick or glass, and ivy on the walls of the buildings integrates them nicely with the overall landscaping of the site.

**I.I.T. Campus: Commons Building 1953
3200 S. Wabash
Mies van der Rohe**

Since the Commons was classed by the fire code as a single-story struc-

ture, concrete cladding of the steel skeleton was not required. This unusually economical structure, distinguished by its carefully studied proportions, has proved its adaptability to changing interior functions.

49

I.I.T. Campus: Crown Hall 1952–55
3360 S. State
Mies van der Rohe

Set apart by its scale and transparency from the other buildings on the campus, Crown Hall was Mies's first and most convincing realization of his concept of a "universal space." His intention to create a space capable of many functions and changes of function over an extended period of time has resulted in what architect Werner Blaser describes as a "unity of spatial, aesthetic and technological organization." The main floor of the 120 x 220 ft. (36 x 66 m) structure is a single column-free room 18 ft. (5.5 m) in height. It houses both the architecture and planning departments in a single spacious atelier which functions alternately or simultaneously as drafting room, lecture hall and exhibition area.

The roof plate of this room is suspended from four plate girders spanning the full width of the building and continuously welded to wide-flange columns. The lower divisions of the all-glass facade are translucent, while those above contain clear plate glass backed by venetian blinds.

In the high basement are the classrooms and workshops of the Institute of Design, an outgrowth of Laszlo Moholy-Nagy's "New Bauhaus," transplanted from Germany to Chicago in 1937.

Of Crown Hall Mies himself said, "I think this is the clearest structure we have done, the best to express our philosophy."

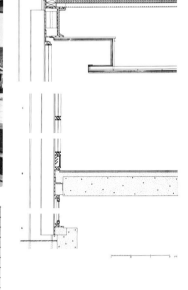

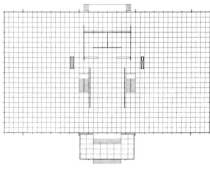

I.I.T. Campus: Arthur Keating Hall 1968
31st and Wabash
Skidmore, Owings & Merrill
(Myron Goldsmith, design partner,
Michael Pado, project designer)

Built on a crowded site at the northern edge of the campus, Keating Hall contains I.I.T.'s indoor athletic facilities. Plate girders span the 115 x 228 ft. (35 x 68 m) column-free gymnasium which occupies the entire main floor. There courts are provided for individual athletic events, but the area can also be used for large social gatherings and assemblies. A swimming pool, handball courts and locker rooms are located on the floor below.

Keating Hall continues the tradition of Mies's buildings at I.I.T. in its precision and clarity. On the other hand, in contrast with Crown Hall, its structural elements are placed within the glazed enclosure. In the longitudinal direction, the floor and roof slabs are cantilevered the equivalent of one window module beyond the girders, thus setting the transverse facades away from the interior columns. The factory sash curtain wall is glazed with an impact-resistant laminate of gray-tinted sun control glass on the exterior and clear tempered glass on the interior bonded together with sheets of matte plastic. Awning windows on the long facades provide natural ventilation.

Viewed from the exterior, the translucent volume of the gymnasium is defined by the clear glazing in the ground level windows of the lower floor. When lit from within at night, the otherwise hidden structural system is revealed in striking silhouette.

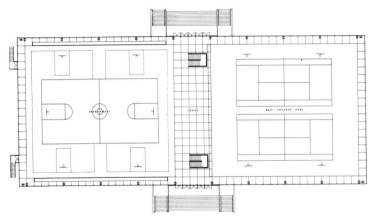

Farnsworth House 1945–50
Plano, Ill.
Mies van der Rohe

"Nothing can express the aim and meaning of our work better than the profound words of St. Augustine: 'Beauty is the splendor of truth.' " Mies van der Rohe, 1938

This weekend house on a wooded bank of the Fox River expresses Mies's concept of structural truth with an economy of means and purity of proportion that remain unsurpassed. The structural elements of the house are reduced to the barest essentials: eight exterior columns on 22 ft. (6.7 m) centers support both the floor slab and roof plate. The column-free interior, with its clear height of 9 ft. 6 in. (2.85 m) is divided only by the asymmetrically-placed wardrobe and the kitchen/bath/utility core. The exterior walls are entirely of glass, all exposed steel is painted white, and travertine marble is used on the floor, terrace and stair treads.

Whereas Frank Lloyd Wright sought to make his houses part of nature while emphasizing their role as shelters from the forces of nature, the Farnsworth house is, metaphorically speaking, an homage to nature. Floating lightly above the ground so as to escape the flooding that seasonally occurs, it serenely observes its natural surroundings; the landscape rather than the walls of the house seems to define the limits of its spatial sovereignty.

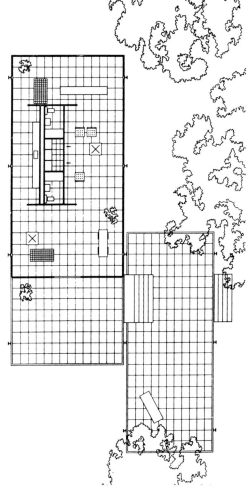

Promontory Apartments 1949
5530 South Shore Drive
Mies van der Rohe
(with Pace Assoc. and Holsman,
Klekamp & Taylor)

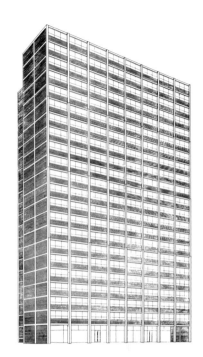

By 1929, the year Le Corbusier proposed his "skyscrapers in a park" for Buenos Aires, a group of tall, free-standing apartment towers could already be seen on a spacious lakeshore site in Hyde Park. The open arrangement of these structures, which later impressed Corbu during a visit to the U.S.A., was in fact partly accidental: the Depression had halted the construction of additional buildings which would have made the neighborhood identical with other densely built-up high-rise areas of the city.

Twenty years later another great European-born architect addressed himself to a Hyde Park site, this time as designer rather than spectator. Mies's Promontory Apartments was his first Chicago project outside the I.I.T. campus, and the first tall building in the city to effectively revive the structural tradition of the first Chicago school of architecture. The only reinforced concrete skeleton among the fourteen apartment buildings Mies was eventually to erect along the lakefront, Promontory is designed with his usual concern for exactitude and austere simplicity. Horizontal joints articulate the frame into stories. The stepping back of the columns every five floors expresses the relationship between decreasing dead load and building height —a visual concept later repeated in steel in the Chicago Civic Center. The U-shaped plan contains in actuality two independent but united towers, each with its own stairs and elevators. The skeleton frame insures the variability of interior divisions.

Mies's alternate proposal for the fa-

cade of Promontory is the first true example of his use of the curtain wall, a feature destined to appear frequently in his later projects. It is worth noting that this type of facade does not articulate the load-bearing frame behind it, since its equal modular divisions remain uninterrupted by the skeleton.

Thus it is not the same form of direct structural expression customary to such older Chicago buildings as the Carson, Pirie, Scott Store or to newer ones like the Civic Center. Nevertheless, its modular clarity and simplicity share a common architectural grammar, since both are dictated by the

frame. In fact in Mies's best efforts (if not in those of his less inspired imitators), the curtain wall produces a structural transparency altogether consistent with Chicago principles of transforming technological devices straightforwardly into aesthetic form. On the other hand, it has little relationship with the American skyscrapers of the 1910s and early 1920s whose cladding—sheathing might be more apt— is characteristically dependent on allusions to historical styles that are often expressively irrelevant of the frames they conceal.

860–880 Lake Shore Drive Apartments
1948–51
Mies van der Rohe
(with Pace Assoc. and Holsman, Klekamp & Taylor)

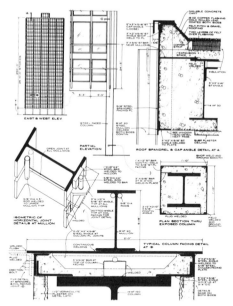

None of Mies van der Rohe's buildings had as immediate or as powerful an impact on his American contemporaries as his two 26-story apartment towers at 860–880 Lake Shore Drive. In the consistency and simplicity of their expression Mies proved that his vision in the 1920s—of an architecture based on a distillate of structure—was not a Utopian impossibility but a bold prediction of the future. Thus the significance of these buildings lies not so much in the sophistication of their technology and structure as in the compelling formal—one might say abstract—*expression* of structure and technology.

Walther Peterhans, who taught with Mies at I.I.T., said, "These towers testify to a new and until now unknown spirit. They are built out of the familiar materials, steel and glass, and yet it is as though they introduce the era of steel and glass, as if steel and glass are seen for the first time."

The steel structural elements of the towers are sheathed with concrete fireproofing. Load-bearing irretrievable formwork of galvanized steel clads the concrete, and helps reduce the sway factor present in tall structures. Thus the black-painted steel skin, welded without horizontal joints, is a direct expression of concealed structural function. Prefabricated in sections one column bay wide and two stories high, the facade elements were hoisted up at the site, and welded to the skeleton, making possible the absorption throughout its entire mass of interior and exterior temperature differentials. Finally, aluminum framed windows were fitted to

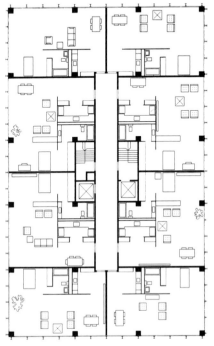

the steel mullions. Off-white, light-reflecting curtains intensify the contrast between skeleton and glazing.

The wide column spacing permits

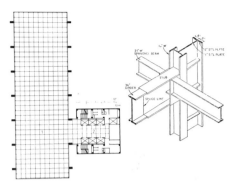

this direction first revealed in the alternate proposal for the Promontory Apartments, the lesson of 860–880 in continuing the structural expression found in the great buildings of the first Chicago school was grasped and carried forth by a succeeding generation —most notably by Mies's pupil Jacques Brownson.

Inland Steel Building 1957
30 W. Monroe
Skidmore, Owings & Merrill
(Bruce Graham, designer in charge)

The curtain wall as a uniform and unarticulated envelope for skeleton structures has found less acceptance in Chicago than in other large American and European cities. While such facades may be a logical consequence of economical prefabrication techniques, architectural developments in Chicago in the last decade have proved that the clear architectonic expression of structure often results in facades which are also structurally superior. In the Inland Steel Building, the first architecturally significant high rise in the Loop since the days of the first Chicago school, the building's form and architectonic expression reflect not only its structure but a completely new solution to internal function. The 10,000 sq. ft. (930 m^2) area of the 17 floors is completely column-free, and can be subdivided with prefabricated moveable partitions. All load-bearing supports are positioned outside the facade, and all mechanical and service rooms, stairs and elevators are concentrated in an asymmetrically-placed 25-story service tower. Over a third of the site remains open at the ground floor as an extension of the pedestrian area.

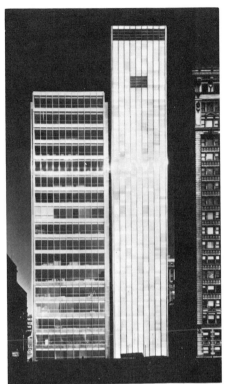

Inland Steel

flexible and open apartment plans in these buildings; all utilities and mechanical spaces are concentrated within the interior bays. Large windows, extending from floor to ceiling, bring the resident into direct visual contact with his environment, the most dramatic element of which is the great sweep of Lake Michigan.

Almost without exception in his later tall buildings, Mies abandoned the type of facade of which 860–880 was the prototype in favor of equally-spaced aluminum curtain walls which conceal the dimensions and placement of the structural frame. Although he chose

Chase Manhattan, New York

The depth of the 36 in. (90 cm) transverse girders, which carry openings for ducts, can be clearly read on the facade. The suspended ceiling is set back from the glass line and visually a clear distinction exists. The green-tinted sun control glass, contrary to the usual practice elsewhere, reaches from floor to ceiling—a characteristic of the Chicago school.

The separation of served and servant spaces, later elevated to a dogma by Louis Kahn, is in tall structures more tour de force than functional requirement, since it is more feasible economically to place vertical elements within the useable floor areas. Here they also serve as a portion of the wind bracing, and their position shortens the horizontal distances traversed by ducts and utilities.

For these reasons the floor plan organization of the Inland Steel Building remains an exception; the rule is, in Chicago, as elsewhere, to strive for high-rise buildings with the greatest allowable depth, and cores positioned as wind bracing in the middle zones.

The great spans and clear expression remain significant, and the shining stainless steel cladding and cantilevered end bays give the building a lightness which is in strong contrast to the weathering steel and bronze glazing of later buildings of the Chicago school.

Equitable Building 1965
401 N. Michigan
Skidmore, Owings & Merrill
(Bruce J. Graham, design partner)

This elegant and yet strongly articulated 35-story building is notable for its excellent siting as well as its innovative, carefully-detailed curtain wall. Its location is on the north bank of the Chicago River, near the site of Fort Dearborn and the first settlement in Chicago. Equitable defines the eastern limit of the immense open plaza formed by the river as it bends from Dearborn Street to Michigan Avenue, an urban space unsurpassed in magnitude, scale and variety.

Central District Filtration Plant of
Chicago 1966
1000 E. Ohio
C. F. Murphy Assoc.
(Stanislav Gladych)

The Filtration Plant, located on the lake north of Navy Pier, is surrounded by landscaped grounds and several illuminated fountains. It is the largest facility of its kind in the U.S. The superb siting of the complex and the handsome sweep of its horizontal lines make this project comparable in quality to the better high-rise buildings that have gone up in downtown Chicago.

Continental Center 1961–62
Wabash at Jackson
C. F. Murphy (Jacques Brownson)

The 23-story Continental Center was built as an annex to a large insurance company office building on Michigan Avenue. The large rectangular plan of the new edifice, which is directly connected with the older one, is divided into twelve bays. Cores preempt the two interior bays, while the remaining peripheral bays are column free and can be divided on a module of 5 ft. (1.52 m). On the ground floor the glass has been set back to create a covered walkway, thus greatly increasing the area given to pedestrian traffic.

The wide spans of the Continental Center required girders built up of the heaviest sections ever used in high-rise construction up to the time. The additional cost of these spans was compensated by the flexibility of the floor plan and the reduction in number of the expensive column footings, which had to reach 100 ft. (30 m) down to bedrock. The unusual depth of the floor girders resulted in two additional advantages; the welded connection between girder and column was sufficient to provide all the bracing the structure required, and in the zero stress zone of the girders it was possible to provide openings for mechanical and duct installation.

The Continental Center, in contrast to the light-reflecting stainless steel sheathing of the Inland Steel Building, has a welded, unclad skin of carbon steel originally painted black, now red. The current trend toward curtain "envelopes" finds its antithesis here, in a form derived from Mies's 860–880 Lake Shore Drive.

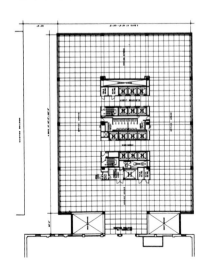

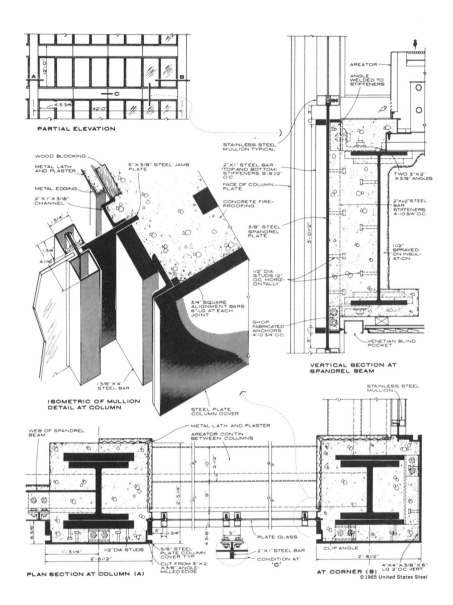

PARTIAL ELEVATION

ISOMETRIC OF MULLION
DETAIL AT COLUMN

VERTICAL SECTION AT
SPANDREL BEAM

PLAN SECTION AT COLUMN (A)

AT CORNER (B)

© 1965 United States Steel

Chicago Civic Center 1963–66
Randolph, Dearborn, Washington and Wells
C. F. Murphy Assoc., supervision architects
(Jacques Brownson, chief architect)
Skidmore, Owings & Merrill, associate architects
(Bruce Graham)
Loebl, Schlossman, Bennett & Dart, associate architects

The Civic Center and the Continental Center are some of the clearest and most persuasive structural and architectonic manifestations of the second Chicago school of architecture.

The program for the Civic Center required that provision be made for a variety of rooms and groups of rooms distributed throughout the building. Seven different types of courtrooms, some two stories high, as well as jury and conference rooms, were placed in the interior of the structure. There lighting and air conditioning could be most economically installed. In contrast, the private chambers of the judges are located on the east and west facades, from whence they connect with the courtrooms via internal corridors. Under the granite-paved plaza are walkways, city administration offices, restaurants and stores.

The functional justification for the extremely large spans of the Civic Center is the need for maximum flexibility. Large, column-free areas were guaranteed, which could be subdivided as required; and in addition this flexibility was evident in the third dimension, so to speak: in some areas the intermediate floor slabs were omitted to gain courtrooms two stories high. Even here alterations can be made later and new rooms or intermediate floors installed.

The columns of the Civic Center are constructed of high-strength steel and rest on caissons. Their cruciform sections were welded together at the steel mill into two story sections. All connections made during assembly on the site were also welded. As in the case of Mies's Promontory Apartments, the columns are reduced in section in several stages, to reflect diminishing dead load. The steel cladding of the concrete fireproofing covering the columns is bonded to the concrete as a composite construction, thus playing an essential role in the total stability of the structure.

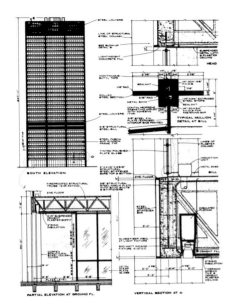

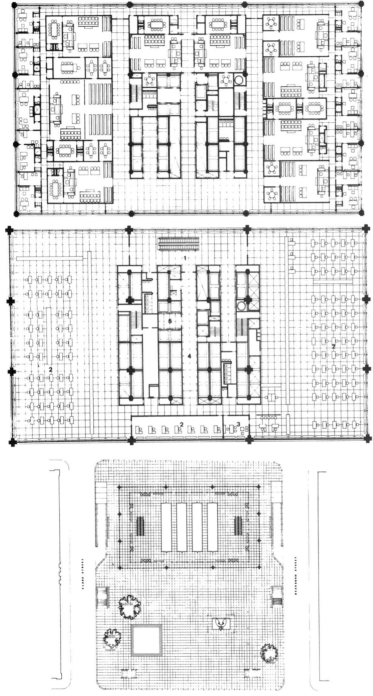

The length of the bays, 87 ft. (26.5 m) was unprecedented in high-rise construction at the time the Civic Center was built. Warren trusses 5 ft. 4 in. (1.62 m) deep were required, with openings in the webs for mechanical installations. These are covered with composite construction steel and concrete ceilings.

The Cor-Ten steel employed in the Civic Center was first developed in 1933 for railroad hopper cars exposed to extreme weather conditions. Its first use in a building was by Eero Saarinen in his 1962–64 John Deere complex near Moline, Illinois. The Cor-Ten surface oxydizes over the years to a deep reddish brown, and requires a minimum of maintenance.

The Civic Center is further proof that contemporary technology can respond to extremely complex problems with solutions that are not only rational but also simple and consistent in their expression.

The English writer Reyner Banham saw the Civic Center as: ". . . a unique,

Federal Center 1959–73
Dearborn, Adams, Clark and Jackson
Ludwig Mies van der Rohe, C. F.
Murphy Assoc., A. Epstein & Sons,
Inc., Schmidt, Garden & Erikson

The site planning for the new Federal Center began in 1959, and its first component, a 30-story high-rise building on Dearborn Street (now called the Dirksen Building), was completed by 1964. The second tall structure, of 45 stories (now called Kluczynski Building), plus a one-story post office which completes the ensemble, were finished in 1973.

This trio surrounds a plaza on three sides, with the fourth open to a view of the facades along Adams Street. All the buildings in the immediate vicinity, some of which are visible on Clark Street above the low silhouette of the post office, are massive prisms marked by a noticeable uniformity of cornice lines. By situating the 45-story office building of the Federal Center to the south, Mies enabled his own powerful group to address its neighborhood forcefully, while simultaneously sustaining and even adding to the unity of the neighborhood. Directly across from the 45-story building is the splendid old Marquette Building of Holabird and Roche. The plaza thus provides the setting for a dialogue, as it were, between masterpieces of the first and second Chicago schools.

and uniquely Chicagoan, achievement . . . Technically this sober prism of civic pride is remarkable enough, but what is really remarkable is this simple fact: this is the first public building in the world which is both modern and conceived in the local building tradition. Chicago has no tradition but modern; almost as long as it has been a city, its natural style has been the most severe metal skeleton construction.''

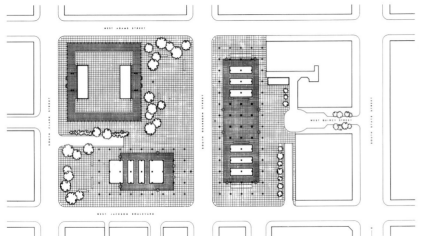

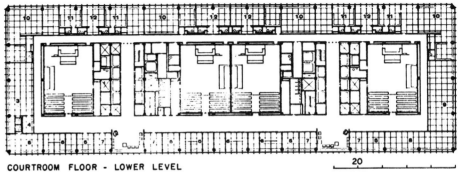

COURTROOM FLOOR - LOWER LEVEL

20

61

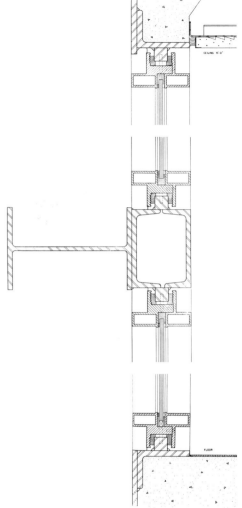

The two tall buildings of the Federal Center are steel-framed, with rigid connections and transverse reinforced concrete stiffening walls in the elevator cores. The foundation work was especially difficult: 104 reinforced concrete caissons were required, driven to a stratum of limestone.

Here Mies employed the principle of the non-isolated curtain wall, for the last time in Chicago. The IBM and the

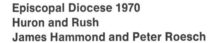

**Episcopal Diocese 1970
Huron and Rush
James Hammond and Peter Roesch**

The delicate, bronze-colored frame of this near north Side building creates a

pleasant contrast with the heavy load-bearing limestone walls of its neighbor, the St. James Episcopal Cathedral. An underground connection with the Cathedral avoids a link at the plaza level that might have disturbed the clarity of

Illinois Center projects received isolated aluminum curtain walls.

In the clear span structure of the post office Mies strove again for a "universal space." The square floor plan is only slightly smaller than that of the National Gallery in Berlin. The first proposals featured two plate girders above the roof, after the manner of Crown Hall, but eventually cruciform columns were adopted which divide the building into bays. Because of the large amount of fixed equipment, no visual disadvantage results.

One and Two Illinois Center 1969–72
111 E. Wacker
Office of Mies van der Rohe
(Joseph Fujikawa, partner in charge)

This pair of office buildings, the first elements of the new Illinois Center development, are closely related to the scale and height of nearby structures along Michigan Avenue. The buildings form the visual boundary to the southeast of the great space surrounding the junction of Michigan Avenue and the Chicago River. Both Illinois Center structures are positioned in the close arrangement characteristic of Mies's other projects, and both indeed have taken up only half of the site available to them. The rest is given over to plaza areas. With this grouping at the extreme northwest corner of the IC site, Mies indicated his intention of creating a balanced and yet dynamic interrelationship of building volumes, continuous vistas and plazas. A pedestrian level of shops and restaurants beneath plaza level is connected to the two building lobbies by escalators. Seven hundred parking places are distributed throughout three basement levels. Economic feasibility studies suggested reinforced concrete rather than steel skeleton construction, with concrete stiffening walls in the core and coffered concrete floor slabs. The structure is concealed behind a curtain wall

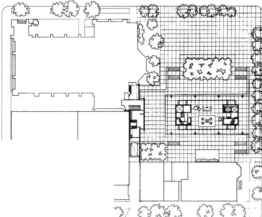

the two building shapes. A landscaped plaza and sculpture court are terraced upward, forming a base for the new building, and this open space is implicitly continued into the glass-enclosed lobby. The 45-ft. (13.5 m) clear span structure, with column-free interiors and cantilevers on two sides, is reminiscent of the structural system of the Inland Steel Building.

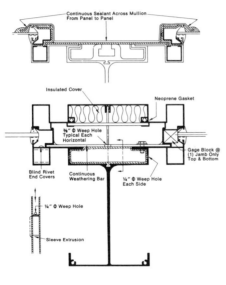

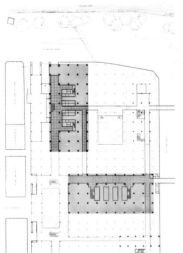

**IBM Building 1972
One IBM Plaza
Office of Mies van der Rohe
(Bruno Conterato, partner in charge)
C. F. Murphy Associates**

The IBM Building, one of the last tall buildings Mies erected in Chicago, is surely one of his finest, a fitting valedictory to the exemplary body of work he contributed to the city. Situated on the north bank of the Chicago River at State Street, it is close enough to the great Michigan Avenue Bridge area to the east to be part of that splendid space, and large enough to have added significantly to the volumetric composition of the entire river district. At 52 stories, it is the tallest building by Mies

in Chicago; in fact, only the 56-story Dominion Center in Toronto surpasses it in height among his other works.

In short, IBM is a huge structure and a monumental one, yet so carefully proportioned and exquisitely detailed that it seems a model of buoyancy. Its fully-glazed lobby, walled on the interior with travertine and set back from supporting columns on all four sides of the building, reveals a comparable balance of grace and large scale.

To the west are the twin towers of Bertrand Goldberg's Marina City. Though its designer worked with Mies at the Berlin Bauhaus, Marina represents a strikingly different concept of the tall building. Side by side, the two

projects by master and pupil are a measure of the wide spectrum of structural possibilities which Chicago architecture has exploited.

IBM was placed as far to the north of its site as possible, so it would not obstruct the view from Marina City, while gaining for itself a wider panorama of river and lake. Its curtain wall, in contrast with those used in the Federal and Dominion centers, is a completely isolated skin. It features insulating glass, thermal insulation and a pressure equalization system. Studies have shown that it is one of the most economically designed buildings in Chicago from the standpoint of overall energy consumption.

of bronze-anodized aluminum sections with tinted glazing. The relatively large bay size, 30 x 30 ft. (9 x 9 m) allows sufficient flexibility of floor planning, and the four by nine bay plan lends itself to large undivided offices where required.

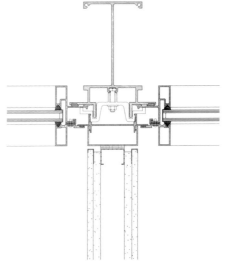

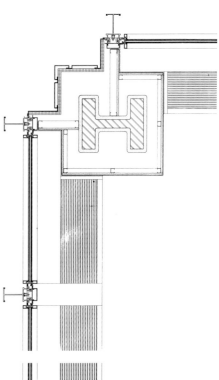

Left, IBM Building; above, curtain wall detail; below, detail of Seagram Building for comparison

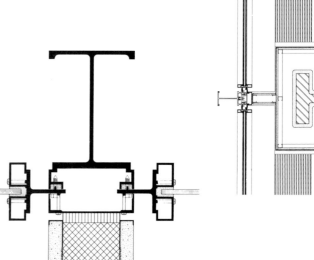

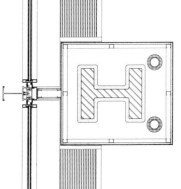

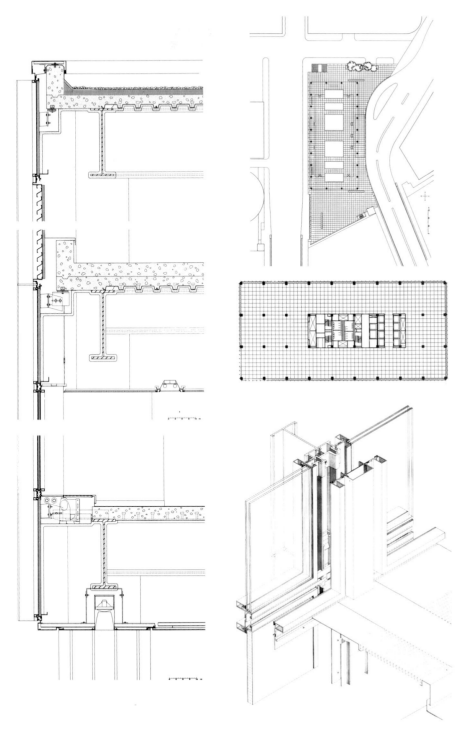

Two First National Bank 1968–73
40 S. Clark
C. F. Murphy Assoc., and The Perkins & Will Partnership

Located on a difficult site across Clark Street from the new 55-story First National Bank, this 30-story annex possesses a clarity of structural expression and refinement of detailing that make it not only the more significant of the two, but one of the best new skeleton constructions in the city. The site, hemmed in on both sides by existing buildings, was crossed by a public pedestrian thoroughfare which could not be closed. This requirement, in addition to a necessary access ramp to the underground garage, determined not only the column spacing, but also the placement of the two elevator cores, each with its own glass-walled lobby, on either side of the pedestrian passage. On the upper floors these cores are surrounded by column-free floor areas, which can be further divided as required.

The steel facade evolved here is a logical development of those employed on the Continental Center and Civic Center. U-formed sheathing elements of ⅜ in. (ca. 1 cm.) steel plate, each one bay wide and one story high, are separated at column and sill line by reveals. Vertically these joints create not only a visual orientation to the spacing of the columns behind them, but also provide a track for the window-washing platforms. The use of double-glazed sun-control glass results in a continuous thermal separation of the facade, and the weight of the mullions between the individual panes, while sufficient for their function as stiffeners and as determinants for the placement of moveable partitions, is not so great that they become dominating visual elements.

IBM Self Park 1974
George Schipporeit

Located just north of the Chicago River on State Street, this garage defers handsomely to its lofty neighbor, the IBM Tower. An intricate ramp system formed in concrete is hidden on the exterior by a delicate screen of self-weathering Cor-Ten, while the narrowly spaced, vertical metal fin profiles likewise conceal the parked cars within. The gentle curve of the southeast exterior wall toward Wabash Avenue lends the building a simple but effective sculptural quality. Scissor ramps minimize driving distance. Eight hundred cars can be accommodated within this twelve-story-high garage.

In the austerity of a spandrel and column sheathing which is free of any willful attempt at arbitrary vertical emphasis through the addition of non-functional mullion elements, proof is

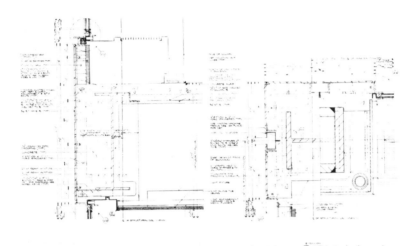

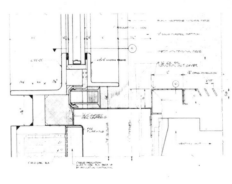

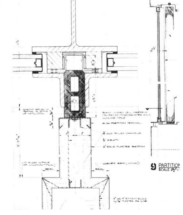

once more offered that a simple and economical facade can be developed which not only expresses but actually emphasizes the underlying structure.

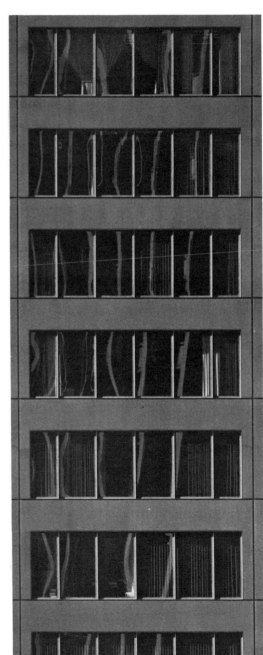

Time & Life Building 1970
Ohio and Fairbanks
Harry Weese & Associates

A number of the features in Harry Weese's Time-Life Building—principally the elevator system and the solar reflecting glass—have been cited as innovations in the design of the tall building. Yet no less impressive an aspect of this work is the obedience—call it even the conservatism—with which it follows the historic canon of Chicago construction. Weese is not customarily associated with the second Chicago school, having long established himself as an independent figure, fluent in a variety of expressive modes and forms. The arhythmic and minimal fenestration of his 1975 Cook County Jail suggests how far from the Time & Life Building his own concepts of the skyscraper have roamed.

In the latter structure, however, Weese affirmed the rectilinear character of the frame as candidly and vigorously as any other Chicago designer of his time. The frame, of reinforced concrete faced with Cor-Ten steel, rises to a height of 28 stories from a site divided among three-by-seven 30 x 30 ft. (9.14 x 9.14 m) bays.

Eventually all the office space in the building will be taken over by Time-Life. That client early insisted that all its employees arrive at and depart from their offices at the same times daily. The traffic problem thus posed was solved by the expedient of double-deck elevators, each capable of stopping at two floors simultaneously. The loading and unloading of passengers was facilitated by creating a lobby of two levels, either of which passengers may use depending on whether they are coming from or going to odd- or even-numbered floors above. This device avoided an unwieldy number of eleva-

tors and freed a good deal of space in the lobby. Moreover, the two lobby levels (actually a third and less conspicuous level connects with an extension of the building to the rear) encouraged the architects to enliven the foyer space with considerable volumetric variety. The sculptural massing of the all-granite levels and staircases, balustrades and seating areas has resulted in one of the bolder interiors of its kind in Chicago. The double-deck system, used for the first time here, has been repeated elsewhere in the meantime.

The mirrored glass of the facade is another feature of the building whose compelling visual effect is a result of a distinctly functional motive. About 90 percent of the sun's ultra-violet rays are reflected back, thus achieving a sufficient saving in air conditioning costs to permit the humidification of the entire structure. This gain is achieved with only a slight diminution in the intensity of natural illumination. Besides, the design of the office spaces is open, with few floor-to-ceiling partitions, thus employees are provided a nearly unimpeded view of the outside.

Harris Bank (Addition) 1975
LaSalle and Monroe
Skidmore, Owings & Merrill
(Bruce J. Graham, design partner,
Robert Diamant, project partner)

The new addition to the Harris Bank, which completes a row of three buildings serving that institution on West Monroe Street, is a palpable measure of the refinements that have gradually appeared in the work of the second Chicago school over the course of two decades.

The easternmost of the Harris trio was built by SOM in 1960 as an addition to an earlier Beaux-Arts edifice which dates from 1925. Like the 1975 unit, the 1960 structure is a steel frame, rather clearly indebted to Mies in principle, though more akin in its glistening aspect to SOM's Inland Steel Building, which stands a block to the east. (SOM's Hal Iyengar was in charge of the structural engineering.)

Yet the 1975 building is a more assured and authoritative work than its 1960 predecessor. Bolder in concept, it is less fussy in detail. The massive columns which mark off its 45-foot (14 m) bays are vigorously expressed, as if in greater deference to C. F. Murphy's Civic Center than to any specific piece by Mies. These bays suggest a largeness of scale on the exterior that is substantiated in the spacious three-story banking lobby, while the stainless steel cladding lends an elegance to the building which is also reflected in the easy, open grace of the interior.

Executive offices are located on the fourth floor, an auditorium seating 400 on the seventh through ninth floors, and a guest dining room on the 37th floor. A fountain sculpture occupies the eastern edge of a simply landscaped granite plaza.

The Dearborn Street Plazas
Civic Center Plaza
First National Bank Plaza
Federal Center Plaza
U.S. Courthouse Annex Plaza

The exceptional clarity and regularity of Chicago commercial architecture are as much a factor of the space in which the city's buildings have gone up as those buildings are, individually and intrinsically. An ambient rectilinearity reigns: even the river runs at a right angle from the lake into the land, then neatly encloses the main business district with a 90 degree turn to the south. Meanwhile, the facades that have risen in the heart of that district, the Loop, constitute a massive repetition in elevation of the rigorous grid of the street plan.

One of the more remarkable post-war developments in the history of this formal/spatial consistency is the row of plazas that took form along Dearborn Street in the 1960s. Each of them is a spatial extension of some major project of those boom years: the Civic Center (C. F. Murphy Associates, SOM), the First National Bank (C. F. Murphy Associates and Perkins & Will) and the Federal Center (Mies van der Rohe). The three buildings and their attendant spaces run in a perfect north-south axis exactly through the center of the Loop. Each is separated from the next by one block, which is also the distance that divides the Civic Center from the north boundary of the Loop, Lake Street, and the Federal Center from the south boundary, Van Buren Street. The First National Bank is located in the precise

born—thus securing axial unity with the Civic Center to the north. The architects of the First National Bank, last of the three works to be built, quite intentionally maintained and underscored this axis.

At the same time, the components of these individual plazas are in handsome accord with their immediate surroundings. The Cor-Ten steel frame of the Civic Center carries on a lively dialog with the concrete screen wall of

the Brunswick Building, while to the west Holabird & Roche's 1911 City Hall strikes a note from the past which is more than sentimental—since its powerful columns echo the great piers of the Civic Center—but which is surely symbolic, since City Hall and the Center are paired municipal buildings.

The Federal Center, meanwhile, is magisterially sited and the First National Bank Building is harmoniously attended by Two First National to the

geographic center of the Loop.

Such symmetry tempts one to infer a *genius loci* of sorts. The fact is, it was essentially the result of an accident of fate, since all three sites, as well as the intention to place plazas on them, were determined independently of each other. Nevertheless, once the designers recognized this, they worked consciously to maximize interrelation-

ships. Mies, for instance, originally envisioned one very tall tower for the Federal Center, to be flanked by twin plazas, one on the east side of Dearborn Street, the other on the east side of Clark Street. He later decided to put up a complex of three buildings instead of one, and to combine the proposed pair of flanking spaces into one major compact unit on the west side of Dear-

west, and Inland Steel Building to the east. The space below is unique among the three plazas for its variety of levels and assorted consequent volumetric surprises—not to mention the splendidly shifting configurations of its great fountain—all of which contribute to a highly sociable atmosphere. The other two plazas are, relative to First National, formal, dignified, uninflected. They are meant more for pedestrians than sitters. But the vastness of all three is tempered and humanized by the trio of monumental art works that

embellish them: Pablo Picasso's looming 50-foot head of a woman, executed in the same Cor-Ten steel of the Civic Center behind it; the colorful, 70-foot-long mosaic wall on the theme of the four seasons by Marc Chagall at the First National Bank; and the 54-foot abstraction in vermilion-painted steel, "Flamingo," by Alexander Calder at the Federal Center.

The most recent building to be added to the Dearborn Street corridor is the Monroe Center by C. F. Murphy Associates (with Helmut Jahn as chief de-

signer) scheduled for completion in 1978. The curved facade will turn the southeast corner of the Monroe Street intersection and form part of the southern limit of the First National Bank Plaza; the landscaping will continue the tree pattern of the plaza. To conserve energy and yet bring as much natural

light as possible to the interior, only the north facade will be glazed floor to ceiling. Thus the building differs in both concept and form from the existing rectangular structures on the street and constitutes a refreshing new approach to the speculative office building.

New Structural Systems for Very Tall Buildings

"The future of (the) high rise in America, and in fact in the world, depends, of course, on the future of urbanization and social attitudes. But if the population density in all parts of the world continues to increase, combined with a higher level of industrialization and more need for urban space for living, working and recreation, it will be hard to avoid buildings that will be taller than those we are building today. Our civilization may never develop in that direction; but if it does, and we have to erect those buildings, we might as well be prepared to construct them in ways that are socially functional, economically efficient, that can create interesting, pleasant and exciting new environments in which to live, work and play." Fazlur Khan, 1972

Chicago during the 1960s was the crucible in which a number of radical new theories in the statics of very tall steel and reinforced concrete structures was developed, tested and applied. Therewith contemporary highrise construction took on a new dimension, both literally and figuratively. It is not unreasonable to suggest that the tradition of the city's structure-oriented architecture may have entered a major new phase for the third time in the past 100 years.

By current expectations, the number of white collar jobs in America will shortly outnumber blue collar jobs by two to one, and in the meantime the cost of land in the large cities will have increased at a comparably staggering rate. Mechanical systems will be more advanced; elevators requiring no more than a 20-second wait will be able to evacuate the tallest building in five minutes.

Yet on cramped sites, the optimum height of a structure depends largely on its economic feasibility, as determined by the amount of usable floor space not preempted by mechanical cores and elevator shafts. The feasibility of all modern structural systems is determined by the analysis of certain known factors—ratio of height to depth and the resulting resistance to wind loads. In tall buildings with curtain wall facades, the limiting factor is usually the allowable horizontal deflection of the entire structure, since too great a movement will not only cause damage to interior partitions and ceilings but also physical discomfort to the building's occupants. For calculation of this deflection the term "sway factor" is employed; it is defined as the maximum horizontal deflection at the top of the building in relation to the total height of the building. Based on recent experience this ratio should not exceed 1:600. If skeleton structures without wind bracing are calculated in terms of sway factor, they can be considered economically feasible only up to a height of ten floors. The reason is that an analysis of the horizontal forces causing sway indicates that 90 percent of the deflection is caused by shifting or "wracking" of the building frame (also called "shear sway"). The remaining 10 percent is due to the tendency of the entire building to tip over. In conventional construction (without wind bracing) this shear sway must be absorbed by increasing the cross sections of the columns and beams. Calculations for the dead and live loads—that is, the vertical loads—would result in selection of smaller sections than indicated by calculations based on wind load. Thus wind load is the decisive factor. With steel structures, feasibility calculations have shown that the traditional frame system carried higher than 20 floors is uneconomical due to the

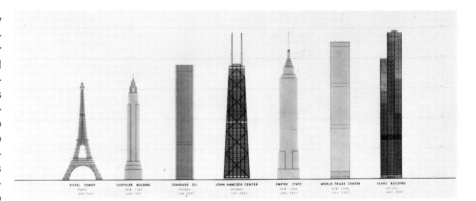

"over-dimensioning" (excessive size and scale) required in structural elements if they are to resist wind load.

Fazlur Khan and Myron Goldsmith are partners of SOM and also professors of architecture at I.I.T. In cooperative efforts between that school and the SOM office, numerous studies have been carried out with the objective of developing economically feasible solutions for the construction of very tall buildings and, specifically, of evolving structural systems which efficiently resist horizontal forces or wind load.

Goldsmith is a structural engineer as well as an architect. Much of the work he has done since a period (1946–53) spent in Mies van der Rohe's office, has been directed toward these very objectives, which he has approached with a singular concern for the blending of function and architectonic conviction. It is significant that his master's thesis was titled: "The tall building—The Effects of Scale." Clearly, each structural system determines the specific scale in which it can be realized; its dimensions cannot be altered by whim. Goldsmith's aim, then, has been to find adequate solutions for each progression of size and span, as reflected in choice of materials, dimensioning and resultant economics.

An even more specialized interest of

Goldsmith is the further development of reinforced concrete construction, a discipline which he studied with Pier Luigi Nervi in Italy in 1953. He had previously had practical experience in the subject while working with Mies on the Promontory Apartments. At that time it was generally accepted that 25 stories was the height limit of structures in which reinforced concrete is used as a load-bearing structural material. Later, however, Goldsmith proposed a 50-story structure, and, for his master's thesis, one of 86 stories, both of reinforced concrete. Both forms had been considered unrealizable—at best, projections of the future. By 1948 Goldsmith had already introduced diagonal bracing on the facades of his tall building projects, but their first appearance in an actual structure was in 1967 on the John Hancock Building.

Up until the time Myron Goldsmith joined SOM in the early 1960s, steel had been the preferred material for skeleton frames of moderate height; later, and largely through Goldsmith's example, reinforced concrete was "rediscovered" and used both in framed structures and sports arenas. In 1963, Dr. Khan, collaborated with SOM partner Bruce Graham, designed the first "tubular cantilever" buildings in reinforced concrete.

This development comprises a num-

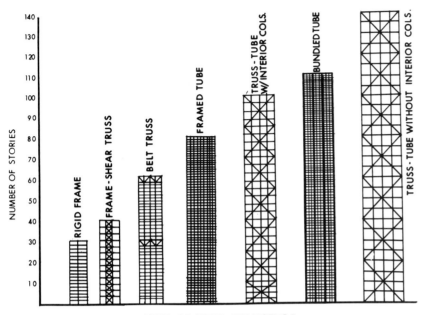

TYPE OF STEEL STRUCTURE

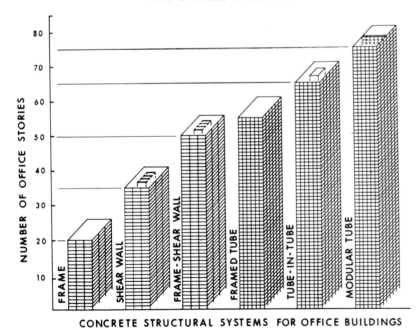

CONCRETE STRUCTURAL SYSTEMS FOR OFFICE BUILDINGS

need for expensive interior bracing and curtain wall. Tubular systems, which generally eliminate the premium on height while reducing the expense of dealing with wind forces, have opened up new economic possibilities in high-rise design.

Even before tubular structures were developed, Khan found a way to make buildings 50 percent stiffer by the use of the rigid frame shear truss interaction. Such a device is utilized in the Chicago Civic Center. There the frame is designed to withstand gravity load and the shear truss is intended to take the rest of the wind effect plus gravity. The frame resists the wind load at the top; the shear truss resists it at the bottom. This is also a very efficient system for concrete structures, since they act as rigid frames, and it was therefore used—with closely spaced exterior columns—in the 35-story Brunswick Building (1962). To open up the entrance area on Brunswick, a large transfer girder was erected above the ground floor.

The first tubular structure in Chicago was the 43-story concrete Chestnut-De Witt Apartment Building (1963). Here a framed tube structure was used, which created the rigid tube effect by placing exterior columns very close to each other: in this building, 5 ft. 6 in. (1.7 m) from center to center. The closely spaced column system eliminated the need for a curtain wall.

Another version of the tubular structures, the belt-truss system, was later employed in the BHP Building in Melbourne and in the First Center in Milwaukee, Wisconsin, both designed by SOM. This variant is most economical in buildings of 35 to 60 stories, and is capable of increasing stiffness by 30 percent. The exterior trusses at the top and the middle of a given building are connected inward to the

interior truss between the elevators. On the facades, the belt trusses can be made a clear part of the architectural expression.

A system capable of reaching greater heights is the tube-in-tube, which is applicable to concrete commercial structures, and most efficient in buildings from 50 to 80 stories. Because office buildings have large elevator and utility cores, these can be formed as a tube within the perimeter tube. The inner tube can accommodate the dead load, and the outer tube, the wind forces. This system was first used in the 52-story One Shell Plaza in Houston—again by the same designers and engineers at SOM.

The John Hancock Center (1968) is the single existent example of the column diagonal truss tube system. Because diagonal structural members were used, the steel weight in the 100-story John Hancock was brought down to only 29.7 pounds per sq. ft. (as compared to 44 pounds per sq. ft. for the Empire State Building, built in 1930) and a saving of $15 million was realized.

Finally, there is the bundled tube concept, used in the Sears Tower (1975). Here a collection of nine framed tube modules, each 75 ft. (23 m) square, was employed. They were held together by external belt trusses and internal diaphragms. Computer analysis produced the optimum 15 ft. (4.6 m) column spacing, which worked out well with the structural efficiency of the 75 ft. (23 m) square tube dimension. This structural system translated the framed tube into floor layouts of very large areas, while at the same time reducing shear lag. In the 110-story, 1,450 ft. (442 m) high Sears building, the bundled tube system brought down the steel weight to 33 pounds per sq. ft. and resulted in a $10 million saving.

ber of structural engineering systems, collectively called tubular structures, implying the treatment of a building as if it were a rigid tube. The rigid tube of the structural perimeter is meant to provide the wind bracing for the entire building and to carry its own gravity load, thus reducing or eliminating the

In the bundled tube system, tubes can be individually terminated at any level. "It is a new vocabulary of form. A building can be massed eccentrically, like a pipe organ," says Khan.

Clearly, each tubular system is best suited to a specific range of height, material and function. The revolutionary implications of these tubular systems, as well as the striking number of outstanding buildings that have grown from it, are to be credited not to the first Chicago school of architecture nor to Mies, but rather primarily to Bruce Graham and Fazlur Khan of Skidmore, Owings & Merrill in Chicago. This is another testimony to the continuing role of Chicago architects as world pioneers in structural and rational architecture.

No less important than structural advances is the concept of the multifunctional high-rise building, like the John Hancock Center, where apartments, offices, restaurants, health clubs, parking and commercial areas are placed in one building. This development has resulted in 24-hour-a-day buildings that have helped to revitalize the city center.

Mounting socio-economic pressures demand a more attractive urban environment. According to the New York Regional Plan Association, big cities consume about half the energy per resident as the rest of the country. "Higher population density means lower energy consumption," says the Association's report. "Urban sprawl wastes not only land and time, but also energy." This is an argument in favor of high-density and high-rise construction.

Studies have shown that no more energy is used per resident for downtown high-rise living—with elevator systems and short walking/driving distances to work and shopping—than for

low-density low-rise suburban living—with long and extensive networks of roads and rails for transportation and service systems. The elevator in a high-rise building provides a gentler, more efficient and less polluting means of transportation than auto-clogged highways sprawling over vast surface acreages.

City centers require high-density living, and high rises offer a good solution to this problem; instead of stretched-out, compact city centers full of five-story buildings, often with less light and fresh air reaching the ground, high rises with the same or higher density can open up for restaurants, shopping plazas, parks and recreational areas.

Clearly it is necessary to plan these taller structures with all such amenities provided for. Moreover, the high rise should maintain a continuity with its surrounding cityscape. For the centers of most very large American cities, a judicious mixture of high-rise and low-rise structures seems, for the foreseeable future, to be the most logical way of securing a vital, efficient and livable urban environment.

Hartford Insurance Building 1959–61
100 S. Wacker
Skidmore, Owings & Merrill
(Bruce J. Graham, design partner
Robert Diamant, senior designer)

This 20-story office structure west of the Loop at Monroe Street and the south branch of the Chicago River was, at the time of its construction, one of the tallest reinforced concrete buildings in the U.S.A. The columns, on a spacing of 21 x 21 ft. (6.50 x 6.50 m) take only vertical loads; they are proportionately reduced in section from bottom to top as the loads decrease. The haunches between columns and

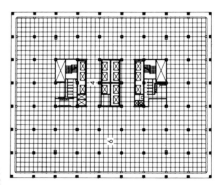

floor slabs visually indicate load transference. All wind loads are absorbed by the elevator/utility core.

The Hartford reflected the ultimate in reinforced concrete construction techniques at the time it was erected. Such techniques could no longer be economically employed if buildings were to grow either taller or of more slender proportions. Only the advent of the tubular cantilever concept made such further growth possible.

Chestnut-De Witt Apartments 1963
860 N. De Witt
Skidmore, Owings & Merrill
(Bruce J. Graham, design partner
Myron Goldsmith, senior designer
Fazlur Khan, structural engineer)

For tall buildings with narrow floor plans—a condition required in residential buildings if natural illumination is to be guaranteed—the skeleton frame is economically impractical, since the dimensions required of both load bearing elements and the rigid connections between them would be excessive. For the 43-story Chestnut-De Witt apartments, whose dimensions are 125 x 82 ft. (38 x 25 m), Khan for the first time employed a load-bearing screen structural system, calculated as a tubular cantilever anchored in the ground. The exterior walls are monolithically connected with each other at the corners, and all horizontal forces (such as wind load) are distributed almost equally over the statically highly-indeterminate screen of all four sides of the structure. The ideal form for such a load-distribution system would be, of course, a cylinder—a form not employed here since circular apartment layouts were dismissed as too inflexible. (See Bertrand Goldberg's Marina City apartments for a contrary view of the cylinder.) Instead, flexibility in

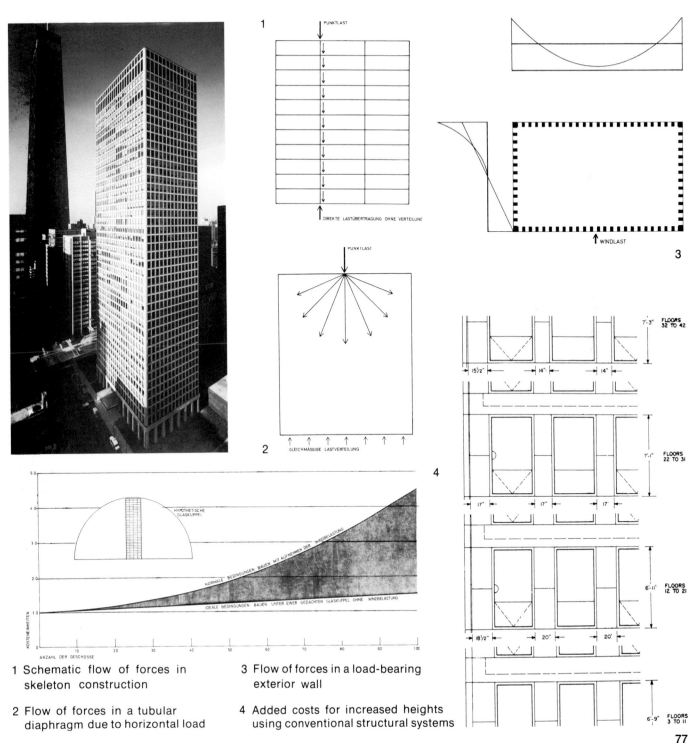

1 Schematic flow of forces in skeleton construction

2 Flow of forces in a tubular diaphragm due to horizontal load

3 Flow of forces in a load-bearing exterior wall

4 Added costs for increased heights using conventional structural systems

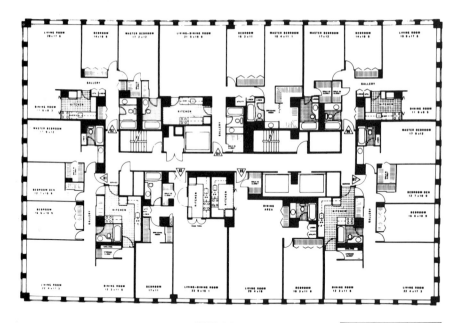

UPPER FLOOR PLAN

0 5 10   20   30

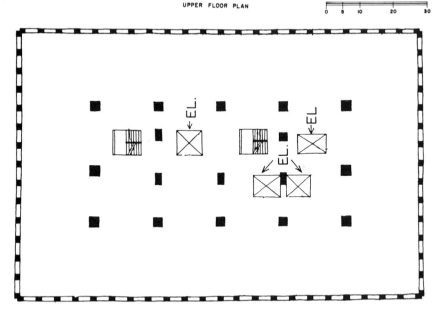

Brunswick Building 1966
Dearborn and Washington
Skidmore, Owings & Merrill
(Bruce J. Graham, design partner
Myron Goldsmith, senior designer
Fazlur Khan, project structural
engineer)

The economically feasible limit of a single reinforced concrete tubular cantilever is about 40 stories. The step necessary to go beyond this limit was taken with the development of the interior core as a second tube, acting in concert with the facade: the so-called "tube-in-tube." Such a structural system makes it possible to free the zone between the tubes of all columns and transverse shear walls, with a resulting flexibility in the placement of interior divisions. Since the presence of an interior core in office structures is a given factor, the double tube system would be a logical device in such office buildings. In fact it was so used for the first time in the 35-story Brunswick Building in Chicago, and in the 38-story CBS Building designed by Eero Saarinen in New York.

In the Brunswick as in the Chestnut-De Witt project, the windows—regarded as openings in the tube diaphragm—increase in size with the building's height, reflecting a decrease in tension on the diaphragm as the height increases. This increase is not, for reasons of realistic construction techniques, continuous, but occurs rather in several stages. Nevertheless, a contribution is still made toward a direct structural expression of the construction principle. To open up the entrance on the ground floor, and to take account of the difficult soil conditions in Chicago, the Brunswick Building is provided with a massive transfer beam above the ground floor. All loads from the exterior tube are thus trans-

plans of the 407 apartments was augmented by the relatively large spacing of the interior columns. This device was made possible because the exterior screen was able to absorb all wind loads. The dimensions of the windows, determined by computer calculations of various alternatives, are 5 in. (1.65 m). They reach from floor to ceiling.

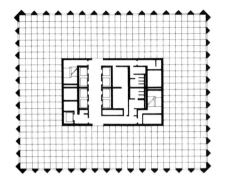

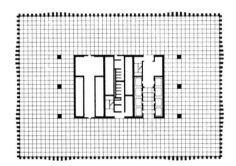

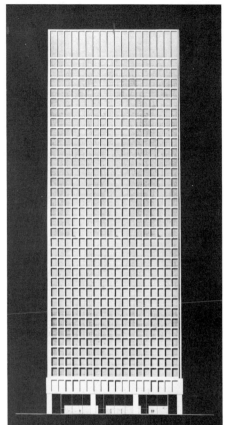

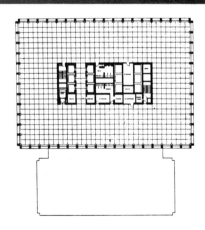

mitted to only 10 exterior footings. The placement of this beam, which is in itself two stories deep, causes a visual interruption which compromises the image of the Brunswick as a horizontal cantilever. But the scale and transpar-

ency of the entrance are well adapted to the progression of structures and plazas lining Dearborn Street.

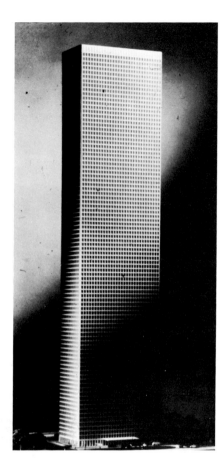

**92-Story Apartment Tower 1965
(project)
K. Menon
Advisors: Prof. Myron Goldsmith and
Prof. Fazlur Khan
Dept. of Arch., I.I.T.**

The continued development of the new structural systems proceeded with the design at I.I.T. of a 92-floor reinforced concrete apartment house. It was part of a thesis undertaken by K. Menon under the tutelage of Professor Goldsmith. To secure the stiffening of the exterior walls of the tube, without resorting to a second tube, two transverse bulkheads were provided which

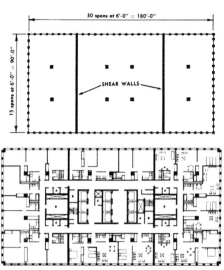

connected the long sides of the building but still offered a justifiable variability in the floor plans. The result consists actually of three tubes which work in combination—a precursor of the form of the Sears building. As mentioned above, in buildings of 100 floors and more, steel was considered the sole practical structural material until the middle of the 1960s. It was the work of R. L. Hodgkison in 1970, however, that added significantly to the economic feasibility of reinforced concrete in heights of that range.

Between 1965 and 1970 SOM designed two steel-framed skyscrapers in Chicago of 100 and 109 floors respectively. Both structures could have been realized only through the employment of the tubular structural system, although they differ in type of system as well as in the consistency of its implementation.

**John Hancock Center 1969
Michigan, Chestnut, Seneca and
Delaware
Skidmore, Owings & Merrill
(Bruce J. Graham, design partner,
Fazlur Khan, senior project engineer,
Robert Diamant, senior designer,
Richard Lenke, project manager)**

This daring multi-functional building has dramatically revitalized the upper Michigan Avenue area. It represents a new trend in the design of urban projects: away from the "office building city," so often dead after 5 P.M., toward a downtown that is vigorous both day and night. A section through the building illustrates how the functions are divided. From the ground floor to the 5th floor, entrances, shops and commercial areas are located; the next seven floors (from 6th to 12th) contain parking stalls (for 1200 cars), reached by a spiral ramp from the ground floor; the following 28 stories (from 13th to 41st) are given over to column-free office space. The "sky plaza" serving the apartments takes up the 44th and 45th floors. It includes a lobby, shops, a restaurant, a swimming pool and a health club. The next 48 floors (46th to 93rd) contain the apartments. The observatory is situated on the 94th floor, with restaurants and bars on the 95th and 96th. Finally, on the 97th level, communication equipment serving Chicago TV stations is installed. The building shape grew from the functional and structural requirements. Shops, car parking and offices require large, undivided floor areas. The apartment floors need less floor space, as well as smaller cores and shorter distances to exterior walls. The apartments were thus placed at the top of the building, well above street noise, moreover in sight of splendid city panoramas, while offices

were located below. Hence the tapered shape.

Architectural Forum said of the Hancock Center: "Its form descends from a structural concept that can be grasped intuitively, as can the Eiffel Tower." The same magazine added: "The Hancock Center alters the essence of Chicago . . . it symbolizes the belief of the city in its technological accomplishments and the possibilities of its economic development. It looks like an isolated monument accidentally positioned, but as the symbol of Chicago this tower is exceptionally expressive."

The 100-story, 1127 ft. (343 m) high edifice is the tallest multi-functional building in the world. The exterior is a clear structural statement, and the column-diagonal truss tube system used for the building represents the most advanced structural thinking for this kind of project. It has permitted a great reduction in both the cost and the weight of the structural steel.

The original plan for this site called for two structures set side by side on the same plot. One was to be a combination of garage and office building, the other a taller apartment house. Bruce Graham decided finally to merge the two structures in one.

The Hancock houses nearly 4,000 office workers, and 1,700 residents in 603 dwelling units. A daily total of nearly 4,000 visitors come and go at different time periods. The observation platform on the 94th floor and the restaurants on the 95th and 96th floors are reached through their own express elevators, and attract many visitors during the evening. Thus rush hour traffic is avoided and a nearly constant round-the-clock use attained. Many residents work in the building, and many workers live within walking distance.

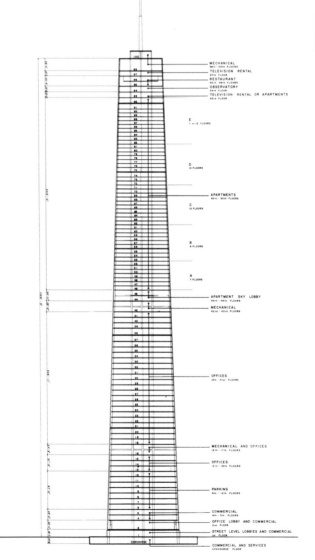

THREE BEDROOM APARTMENT
FLOORS 82 THROUGH 71
APARTMENTS 02/05/08/11
JOHN HANCOCK CENTER
875 NORTH MICHIGAN AVENUE
CHICAGO, ILLINOIS 60611

MECHANICAL
98th -100th FLOORS
TELEVISION RENTAL
97th FLOOR
RESTAURANT
95th -96th FLOORS
OBSERVATORY
94th FLOOR
TELEVISION RENTAL OR APARTMENTS
93rd FLOOR

E
71 to 92 FLOORS

D
10 FLOORS

APARTMENTS
44th - 92nd FLOORS
C
10 FLOORS

B
9 FLOORS

A
7 FLOORS

APARTMENT SKY LOBBY
44th -45th FLOORS
MECHANICAL
42nd -43rd FLOORS

OFFICES
18th -41st FLOORS

MECHANICAL AND OFFICES
16th -17th FLOORS
OFFICES
13th -16th FLOORS

PARKING
6th -12th FLOORS

COMMERCIAL
4th - 5th FLOOR
OFFICE LOBBY AND COMMERCIAL
2nd FLOOR
STREET LEVEL LOBBIES AND COMMERCIAL
1st FLOOR
COMMERCIAL AND SERVICES
CONCOURSE FLOOR

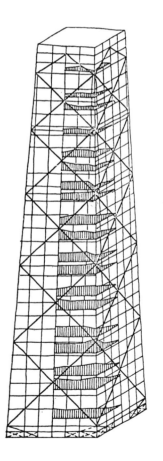

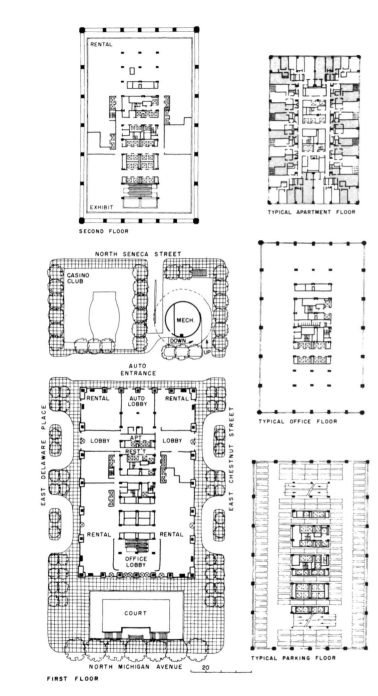

RENTAL

EXHIBIT

SECOND FLOOR

NORTH SENECA STREET

CASINO CLUB

MECH.

DOWN

UP

AUTO ENTRANCE

EAST DELAWARE PLACE

RENTAL | AUTO LOBBY | RENTAL

LOBBY | APT | LOBBY

REST'T

RENTAL | RENTAL

OFFICE LOBBY

COURT

EAST CHESTNUT STREET

NORTH MICHIGAN AVENUE   20

FIRST FLOOR

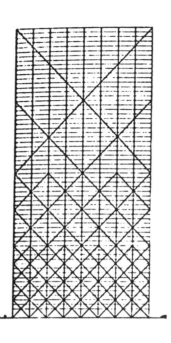

TYPICAL APARTMENT FLOOR

TYPICAL OFFICE FLOOR

TYPICAL PARKING FLOOR

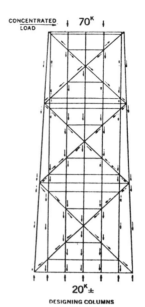

CONCENTRATED LOAD   70ᴷ

20ᴷ±

DESIGNING COLUMNS

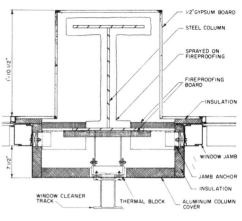

1/2" GYPSUM BOARD

STEEL COLUMN

SPRAYED ON FIREPROOFING

FIREPROOFING BOARD

INSULATION

WINDOW JAMB

JAMB ANCHOR

INSULATION

WINDOW CLEANER TRACK

THERMAL BLOCK

ALUMINUM COLUMN COVER

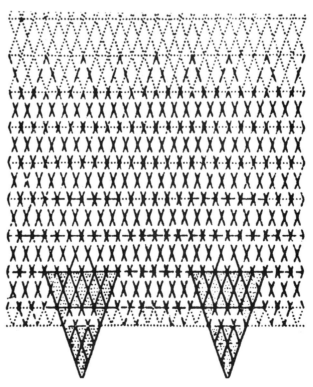

**Downtown High-rise Building 1961
  (project)
Mikeo Sasaki
Advisors: Prof. Myron Goldsmith and
  Prof. Fazlur Khan
Dept. of Arch., I.I.T.**

The "optimum column-diagonal truss tube" system of exterior X-bracing in 80 to 100 story buildings—whose purpose was to avoid paying premium for increased lateral load due to extreme height—was first used in a 6 x 6 bay tower, designed by Mikeo Sasaki. The structural concept of the John Hancock Center is traceable to this thesis design.

**Sears Tower 1974
Wacker, Adams, Franklin and Jackson
Skidmore, Owings & Merrill
  (Bruce J. Graham, design partner,
  Fazlur Khan, structural engineer
    partner,
  Richard Kruetz, project manager,
  William Drake, senior designer,
  Hal Iyengar, project engineer,
  Ferd Scheeler, job captain)**

In contrast to the John Hancock Center, the 110-story, 1,450 ft. (442 m) tall Sears Tower is exclusively an office building. It consists of a bundle of nine structural tubes, 75 ft. (23 m) square. Sears's bundled tubes are a synthesis of the other SOM tubular precedents. The client did not want diagonal bracing—it would have supplied optimum rigidity—and in this case it was not needed. Sears's tandem diaphragms, trisecting the structure, supply that rigidity here, working in concert with the columns. The built-up, wide-flange columns are on 15 ft. (4.5 m) centers, inside and out, connected by 40 in. (1 m) deep steel beams. In addition, two-story high diagonal member trusses belt each tube at mechanical levels on the 29th to 31st, and 66th and 89th floors. Two corner tubes drop off at the 50th floor, where there is no truss, inasmuch as there is proportionally less stress relative to the structure. Two more drop off at the 66th floor, and three at the 90th, leaving only two rising to the building's full height.

The client-owner, Sears (formerly Sears, Roebuck & Co.), largest mail-order house in the world, formerly had its offices spread over numerous locations in the city and suburbs. On the downtown site, Sears built the largest private office building in the world; with its 4,000,000 sq. ft. (400,000 m²) total floor area it is surpassed only by the Pentagon in Washington, with its

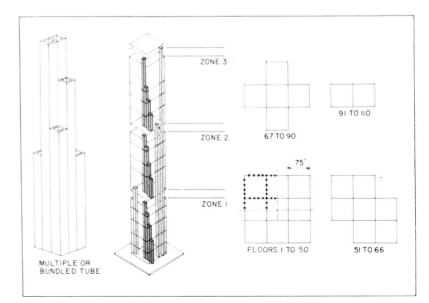

ZONE 3

ZONE 2

ZONE 1

MULTIPLE OR
BUNDLED TUBE

91 TO 110

67 TO 90

75'

FLOORS I TO 50

51 TO 66

Project of Adler and Sullivan, 1891

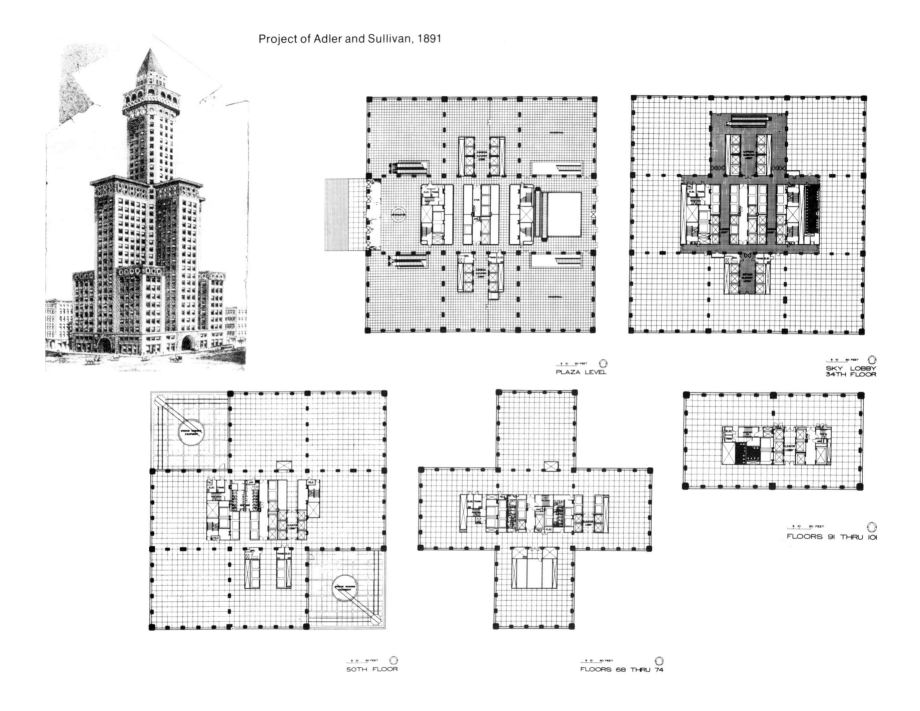

PLAZA LEVEL

SKY LOBBY
34TH FLOOR

50TH FLOOR

FLOORS 68 THRU 74

FLOORS 91 THRU 101

6,000,000 sq. ft. (600,000 m²). It is also the tallest building in the world.

By locating the building along Wacker Drive, close to the railroad stations, and the Eisenhower and Kennedy Expressways, traffic congestion has been avoided.

The nine clustered tubes, considered as vertical cantilevers, have the advantage of relatively continuous floor areas, since each tube floor area is column free and fully flexible in its interior divisions. The larger columns are shown on the exterior, and help to emphasize the system of the nine bundled tubes.

It is a superb building both architecturally and structurally. In her article "Chicago: A city of Architectural Excellence" in the New York Times (May 1975) Ada Louise Huxtable wrote:

"Chicago is probably the best city in the country for building quality . . . The Sears Tower is there, all right, presiding over the city with an almost nonchalant understatement, if that can be said of a 110-story skyscraper . . . Beyond its exceptional height and unusual shape—it is made up of a cluster of square tubes rising to different heights —it makes no aggressive call for attention. Personally, I think that is fine . . .

"The structural formula, an ingenious and precedent-setting one in engineering terms, by Fazlur Khan of SOM, is notable for its economy and strength. Considering that quite enough, the architect, Bruce Graham, partner-in-charge for SOM, has sheathed the structure in the simplest, cleanest, flatest glass and metal skin. This is the sleek curtain wall so elegantly defined by Gordon Bunschaft, of the New York office of SOM, at 140 Broadway in lower Manhattan. The skill and finesse of the well-done, shear skin wall are today vastly underrated.

"Mr. Graham has an architectural

philosophy which holds that there is no point in overreaching (except in height), overcomplicating, striving for dubious originality or going gratuitously beyond what amounts to an unbeatable basic solution. He thinks that good is good enough. There is no straining for effect. This is a principle that should be pasted in a lot of so-called 'creative' hats. And if that makes for the paradox of an unpretentious tall building, so be it . . .

"The interior lobbies at ground and mezzanine level also eschew theatrics for simple, undramatized solutions: plain, beautifully fitted metal and glass rails, smoothly curved travertine wall corners (they will not chip), flat white surfaces and incandescent lights. The 75-foot square proportions of the nine bundled tubes are handsome . . .

". . . And for such a behemoth, the public spaces seem to function surprisingly well, with a human, casual and cheerful air, immensely enhanced by one of the liveliest, wittiest and most colorful Calder compositions around. Sculptural movement works with people movement in a natural orchestration of activity."

86-Story High Rise 1948 (project)
Myron Goldsmith
Advisor: Mies van der Rohe
Dept. of Arch., I.I.T.

For this thesis project Goldsmith proposed a reinforced concrete skeleton of eight haunched columns connected every 15 floors by transverse floor slabs which progressively decrease in depth. Within the "primary" structure, which would be erected first, is placed the "secondary" structure containing the individual floors. It was proposed to rest seven intermediate floors upon each transverse slab element, and to suspend another seven floors from the

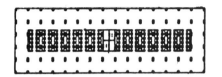

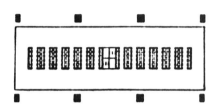

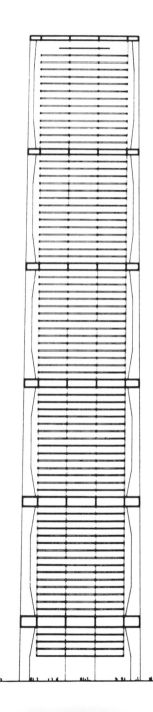

element above. The remaining floor between two such seven-floor sections would thus be column-free.

The massive primary structure requires fewer foundations than a conventional skeleton frame, and the calculation of each seven-story increment of floors as if it were a separate building results in a light secondary structure, the identical elements of which permit the use of prefabricated facade and finish elements.

Goldsmith pointed out in his thesis that the ultimate height of such structures would be limited not by strength of materials but by the fact that the increased number of elevators required would preempt the usable space of the lower floors. In this project, for example, 48 percent of the lower floor area was taken up by vertical transportation shafts. More recently the introduction of the "sky lobby"—intermediate floors where passengers transfer from express to local elevators—has removed this earlier height restriction by reducing the number of elevator shafts required.

Round Apartment Tower at Wolf Point
1963 (project)
Pace Associates
(Charles Genther, design partner)

Planned for a site west of the Merchandise Mart overlooking the fork of the north and south branches of the Chicago River, this 50-story hollow cylindrical apartment tower would have been a realization of the division of load-bearing elements into primary and secondary structures as proposed by Myron Goldsmith in his 1948 thesis. The inner and outer steel frames, built and left exposed in the manner of bridge construction, would have carried four stacks of 16 floors each, for a total of 1,300 apartments 770 ft. (235 m) in height, with an outside diameter of 260 ft. (80 m). The apartment building would have been entered from a 125-ft. (35 m) diameter interior court whose peripheral glass-roofed galleries would have created the atmosphere of a garden conservatory.

It is unfortunate that this project, which had been carried almost to the point where construction could have begun, was not realized.

Transverse-truss Tube Megastructure
1971 (project)
Dr. Fazlur Khan

In tubular cantilever structures various means have been employed to resist the gravity loads of the individual floors. In a "bundled-tube" system—Sears Tower for example—the horizontal dimensions of each separate tubular unit are not so large as to require additional interior supports and the tubes themselves carry both wind and gravity loads. In a "double-tube" structure like the Brunswick Building the floor area has been increased so that a single girder can no longer span from wall to wall. A second tube, acting as a shear-wall core, has been introduced to sustain a portion of both the gravity and the wind loads transmitted to it by the floor slabs. Even larger buildings, such as the John Hancock, employ rows of interior columns to sustain part of the gravity loads; all wind loads are resisted by the diagonally-braced exterior walls.

Yet another system, proposed by Khan, replaces the interior columns with a series of trusses, spaced 20 stories apart, which act as transverse girders connecting and stiffening the tube walls. If such trusses are several floors deep, the favorable relationship of their depth to width of span results in an economical use of materials. The space they occupy can be used for specialized functions, such as housing the building's mechanical equipment. These trusses would also support either groups of floors stacked above them or suspended below them. Certain intermediate floors would be column-free, while the column spacings of the other floors could be varied to meet different functional requirements. Story heights and facade construction could also be varied within the limits set by the primary load-bearing structure. In 120- to 130-story buildings of this type, the transference by the trusses of all vertical loads to the exterior walls would increase the structure's resistance to deflection and overturning.

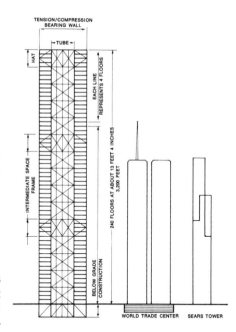

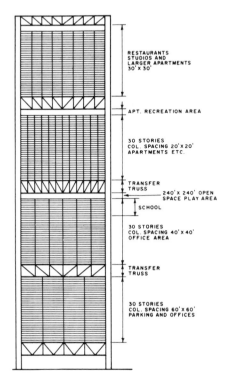

150 Story Superframe Building in Steel
1969 (project)
I.I.T.: Third Year Student Project
Alfred Swenson, faculty advisor

A multi-use prototype structure was developed as a theoretical replacement for Chicago's congested and outmoded city center. Such a building would have a gross floor area of about 6 million ft.^{2} (557,400 m^2). Offices occupy 80 floors, with apartments 47 floors, 18 floors for mechanical equipment and five for lobbies, restaurants and commercial spaces. Fifty of these 1,656 ft. (505 m) tall towers, placed 4 mi. (7 km) apart along an expressway/rapid transit corridor would contain enough rental space to replace the downtown area.

In a building of this height an economical structural solution for resisting wind loads should bring as much of the vertical load as possible to the building's perimeter to resist overturning. As much structural material as possible should be brought to the perimeter to resist deflection.

The solution chosen was a large-scale steel skeleton, or superframe, consisting of two elements: a double-layered cage of large steel tubes, or supercolumns, wrapped around the outside of the building; and a series of eight trussed superfloors set 207 ft. (63 m), or one superstory, apart, and supported by the supercolumn cage. The superfloor trusses are two floors deep and the space between them is occupied by mechanical equipment. A superstory contains 16 office floors or 20 apartment floors carried by two subframes. The subframe carrying the upper half of the floors is suspended by columns in tension from the superfloor above. The subframe carrying the lower half is supported by columns in compression from the superfloor below. The floor in the middle of the superstory is thus left free of columns and can be used for auditoriums, exhibit halls or commercial space.

The subframes resist the local wind and gravity loads in their respective sections of the building. These loads are then transferred through the superfloor trusses to the supercolumn cage which carries the gravity loads to the ground and provides the overall wind stability for the building as a whole. This system brings 100 percent of the building load to the building perimeter and 65 percent of the structural material to the perimeter supercolumns.

Two methods would be used to fireproof the building. The hollow steel tubes of the supercolumn cage contain water. In case of fire the water is circulated by pumps for cooling. The superfloor trusses and subframes are fireproofed with conventional asbestos plaster. The expansion due to the temperature difference between the exposed cage and the insulated sub-

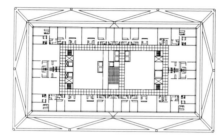

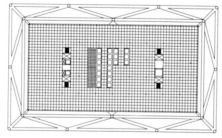

FLOORS 98 - 147 · APARTMENTS AND OFFICE STORAGE

FLOORS 62 - 98 · OFFICES

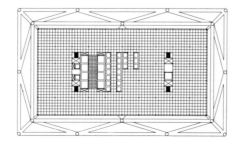

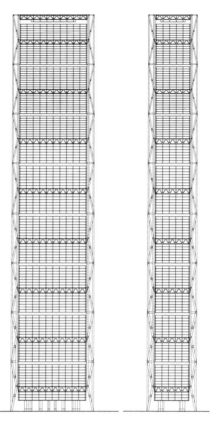

frames is taken up by the expansion joints located at the column-free floors in the middle of each superstory. The building would have a central air-conditioning system and the facade would be sheathed in tinted mirror glass to reduce cooling load and sky glare.

116-Floor Square Tower 1970 (project)
Robin Hodgkison
Advisors: Prof. Myron Goldsmith,
   Prof. Fazlur Khan
Dept. of Arch., I.I.T.

After a series of preliminary studies, this square tower with 216 ft. (66 m) sides was developed along lines similar to the design of the World Trade Center in New York.

In addition to the entrance floor, 108 office stories and six mechanical levels in the areas of the six tension braces are provided. The optimum angle of the diagonal bracing of the tubular diaphragm is 45 degrees. The diagonals are meant to cross at the junction of column and spandrel beams.

Behind the horizontal tension bracing are ceilings of greater height, necessary for the installation of the mechanical equipment, likewise for the location of "sky lobbies." In the topmost floor—a tall area—the intermediate level which would be modularly expected can be dispensed with. In order to reduce the dead load as much as possible, lightweight concrete is used for floor beams and slabs. For the tube walls and the tubular construction of the core, reinforced concrete of normal bearing ability is employed.

The horizontal ductwork of the air conditioning is passed through the standardized openings in the floor beams, which have a 46 ft. (14 m) span.

Space taken up by diagonal bracing accounts for the loss of two windows on each floor, yet without these diagonals an intolerable sway factor of 1:300 would result. In addition they permit a reduction in the dimensions of the vertical columns, since the latter are no longer required to resist bending. As the core elements are stepped back in relation to the building's height, the column-free floor area around them in-

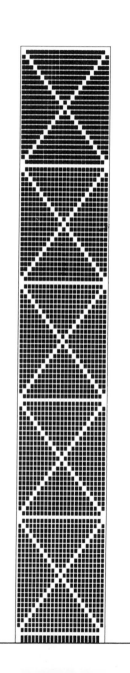

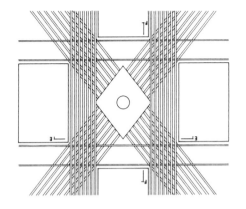

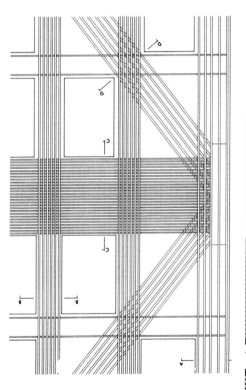

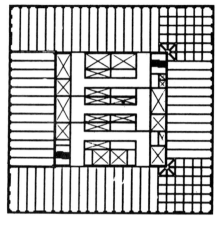

creases from 46 ft. to 59 ft. (14 m to 18 m), creating even greater flexibility. In addition a large part of the vertical loads is concentrated on the exterior walls, in order to strengthen the stability of the tube wall.

In the proposed high rise, some 25,000 office workers could be employed, but the results of the concentration of people on mass transit, parking, etc. would have to be carefully investigated. As a possible location for this project, Hodgkison chose the Illinois Center site, for which, at present, a much denser grouping of lower buildings is planned. In addition to three office buildings, he proposed four Y-shaped 100-story apartment towers, ca. 800 ft. (265 m) high, for some 25,000 residents, as well as a series of public facilities in an open sunlit arrangement.

Reinforced Concrete Hollow-tube Megastructure 1973 (project)
Fazlur Khan
Dept. of Arch., I.I.T.

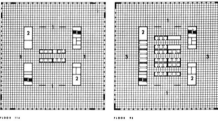

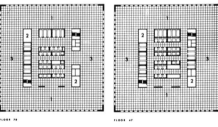

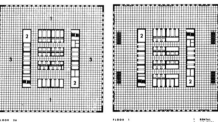

One difficulty resulting from the requirement in very tall buildings for natural light in all peripheral rooms, especially if they are to be used as dwellings, is the maintenance of a sufficiently shallow building depth to permit such light to penetrate into the interior.

Because the sway factor—defined as the ratio of horizontal deflection to total height—is also influenced by the relation of building height to the dimension of the shortest side, a further limit to the minimum permitted building depth must be observed.

Khan proposed overcoming these limitations by a restructuring of the apartment or office floor plan into a circular arrangement with a hollow center. The ring of floors rests on radial

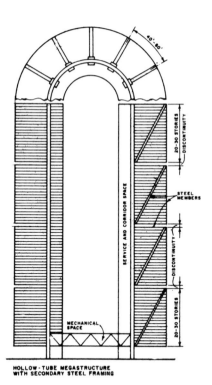

HOLLOW-TUBE MEGASTRUCTURE
WITH SECONDARY STEEL FRAMING

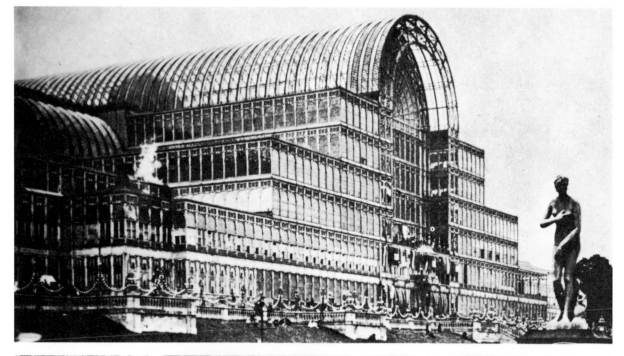

Machinery
Hall

cantilevers projecting from a 200 ft. (60 m) diameter reinforced concrete cylinder constructed by the slip-form technique. This secondary floor structure, also possible on the interior of the tube, could be of either steel or prefabricated reinforced concrete elements rigidly secured to the primary hollow tube after its completion.

Large Spans

The historical development of exhibition halls in our times goes back to the building of the Crystal Palace in London in 1851. There new structural processes on a large scale were given their first practical trial. For the first time so huge a building was erected

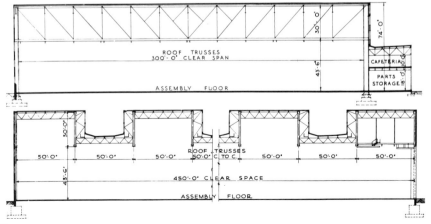

structural rigidity of lamella domes were the reasons why this system was selected for the Houston Astrodome. The engineers for the dome were Kiewitt and Bass of Roof Structures Inc. The largest geodesic steel dome built is the dome in Baton Rouge, Louisiana, by Buckminster Fuller. It has a 384 ft. (117 m) diameter and serves as a regional tank car repair and maintenance depot for the Union Tank Company. It is a double-layer structure, having a spacing of 4 ft. (1.2 m) between the outer and inner hexagonal grids.

Concert Hall 1942 (project)
Mies van der Rohe

As early as 1942, four years after his arrival in the United States, Mies van der Rohe attempted to emulate the "anonymous" industrial architecture of America in some of his spatial and architectural concepts. To present his idea for a grand, column-free concert hall, he chose to use a photograph of Albert Kahn's Glen Martin Aircraft Assembly Building at Baltimore, one of the largest clear span buildings in existence at that time and one of the most splendid industrial buildings of our century. Kahn's hall of 1938 measures 300 x 450 ft. (91.50 m x 137.25 m) with a floor to ceiling height of 43 ft. (13.12 m), and is spanned in the shorter direction by ten 30 ft. (9.15 m) high steel trusses. These trusses are set 50 ft. (15.25 m) apart and the spaces between are developed alternately as light wells, so that the free height varies. Below this roof structure, Mies placed a number of free planes by which he created the space for a concert hall. Within such a clear span structure, maximum flexibility in the placement of functional elements is possible. Mies showed here that this is really a multi-functional space. Implicit in the idea of a

which, in principle, consisted solely of iron and glass. The exhibition hall covered an area of 800,000 sq. ft. (72,000 m²), and was constructed in barely four months. The vaulted hall reached the fullness of its expression in the Machinery Hall of the World Exhibition in Paris, 1889, by Contamin and Dutert, which spanned a width of 375 ft. (114 m). For nearly 2000 years, until the construction of the Machinery Hall, the largest span was that of the Pantheon in Rome; its 142 ft. (43 m) span represents the approximate limits of masonry. The Machinery Hall of 1889 remained the largest span until the recent 720 ft. (220 m) clear span concrete shell exhibition hall, Centre National des Industries et Techniques, built in Paris in 1960, and engineered by M. N. Esquillan. It consists of three corrugated double shell intersecting barrel vaults forming an equilateral triangle in plan, and the three abutments 720 ft. (220 m) apart are tied together with cables.

The largest clear span steel building in the world up to a few years ago was that of the Astrodome, which covers the Harris County Sports Stadium in Houston with a clear span of 642 ft. (195 m). The low cost and remarkable

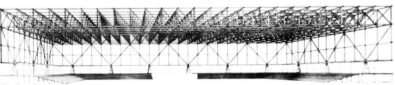

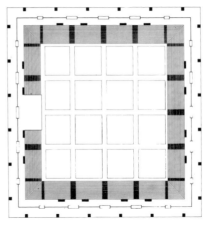

As of early 1977, New York City has expressed serious interest in building Mies's 1954 Convention Hall project.

concert hall was the possibility for accommodating nearly any function relative to the magnitude of the structure. This project expressed the concept of "universal space," one of the major aspects of Mies's philosophy.

Convention Hall 1954 (project)
Mies van der Rohe

Mies van der Rohe's project for the Chicago Convention Hall was developed in 1952–54. A preliminary version, prepared at the request of the South Side Planning Board, was published early in 1953. The definitive version was prepared as a Master's Thesis in Architecture at Illinois Institute of Technology under Mies's direction. The students who developed this joint thesis were Pao-Chi Chang, Henry Kanazawa and Yujiro Miwa; all of whom also worked on the preliminary version. Frank J. Kornacker, a Chicago engineer, gave valuable advice on the development of structural concepts for the project.

The program for the preliminary version required a hall to accommodate conventions of up to 50,000 people and exhibitions of heavy industrial machinery. Mies made a conceptual proposal for a column-free hall 700 ft. (214 m)

square, spanned by a system of two-way trusses. Inverted tripod supports were spaced 100 ft. (30 m) apart around the building perimeter, leaving 100 ft. (30 m) cantilevers at the corners. An aerial view collage of the version showed the hall facing a large open plaza, flanked by low auxiliary buildings. The project was located on a site proposed by the South Side Planning Board, bounded by Cermak, King Drive, 25th Street and Michigan Avenue. Another interior collage showed the roof trusses meeting an un-articulated marble wall, with the inverted tripods not shown.

In the definitive version, a hypothetical site with direct access to a highway and public transportation was chosen. Again, the size of the main hall was taken as about 500,000 sq. ft. (46,450 m²), to seat 50,000 people. Underground parking was provided for 20,000 cars as well as direct truck and railroad access to the floor of the hall. The hall itself was a major element in a larger convention complex, which included a spacious plaza, a hotel, and a smaller auditorium, exhibition and conference building.

The structure of the final version also used a two-way system of Pratt trusses, spaced 30 ft. (9.14 m) apart and 30 ft.

(9.14 m) deep, creating an enormous column-free space 720 ft. (220 m) square and 90 ft. (27 m) high. All the truss members were steel wide-flange sections from the 14 in. (35.9 cm) series, which provided a wide range of cross-sectional areas to meet varying loads economically, and yet permitted simple welded connection details. The horizontal chord members of the trusses increased in area towards the middle of the roof span, while the vertical and diagonal members increased in area towards the edges of the span; this reflected the stress variation in the two-way system. The purlins supporting the roof deck ran in opposite direction in alternate panels of the structure in a basket-weave pattern; this arrangement placed equal loadings on all the trusses.

In the preliminary version, the lateral stability of the roof was provided by the inverted tripod supports, which also carried the gravity loads to the ground. In the definitive version, a more sophisticated support system was developed, which kept the load-bearing and lateral bracing elements in flat planes, eliminating the interior projections of the tripods. The gravity loads of the roof were carried down to concrete piers on each side by vertical steel columns 60 ft. (18.2 m) high, bolted directly to the pier tops. There were six piers on each side, spaced 120 ft. (36.4 m) apart with a 60 ft. (18.2 m) cantilever at the corners. The preferred solution would have carried the steel columns down to the ground level in a simple, direct manner. However, the Chicago Building Code required all structural members to be fireproofed up to 20 ft. (6 m) above the floor. Instead of wrapping the last 20 ft. (6 m) of the column in fireproofing, it was decided to support it on a structural concrete pier. The connections of the columns to the roof trusses were rigidly welded after the roof had deflected, thus effectively eliminating bending moment in the columns themselves. The building was braced against lateral movement in the vertical plane by diagonal members in the walls. In the horizontal plane, stability was provided by four edge bands of cross bracing, two panels wide, around the perimeter in the bottom chords of the roof trusses. The building wall was further stiffened at the bottom by a horizontal edge truss 30 ft. (9.14 m) wide, partly suspended by hangar rods from the roof above. This edge truss formed the ceiling of the recessed promenade around the building.

The enclosure of the Convention Hall was carefully studied in a series of drawings and models. It was decided to place the thin enclosure skin at the center of the structural members, which allowed the structural frame to be expressed on both the interior and exterior of the building. A pattern of vertically oriented 5 x 10 ft. (1.52 x 3.04 m) panels was chosen as the spacing of the enclosure mullion system. Although glass would have given a sense of delicacy and lightness to the structure, it was set aside as a major facade element for reasons of environmental control. Air conditioning was essential in such a building, and glass would add to the heating and cooling loads. Also, the hall would be used for a wide variety of activities, and would provide a neutral, unchanging backdrop for them. However, clear glass was used for the inner wall of the recessed promenade; it helped to give a sense of lightness to the huge opaque volume of the building above it. Schemes using two or three colors to define the triangular structural elements of the facade were studied. Two of these schemes were selected as alternatives to the final solution, one using dark green and black marbles with white veins, and one using black, brown and tan granites. A third alternative was selected for the final solution, using dark and light grey anodized aluminum. These studies showed that color not only helped to express the structure, but gave a sense of richness and vitality to a building of this monumental scale.

From the three alternatives, the metal scheme was chosen as the final solution. The building's multi-purpose function, accommodating numbers of people, had a social significance that required it to be neutral and objective, leaving little room for subjective expression. The neutral quality of the metal enclosure seemed not only to be in agreement with the metallic character of the structure itself, but also to express the anonymous character of its function.

In 1956, Ludwig Hilbersheimer said of this innovative design: "In this hall the proportions are uniform, and in complete agreement with the structure. The square ground module occurs everywhere in the building. The proportions are made clear in their new objectivity. The rational consistency, which unites interior and exterior, leads to mathematical harmony and objective order." And in 1968, A. James Speyer, curator of twentieth century art at the Art Institute of Chicago, said: "The heroic scale and the powerful structure of the Convention Hall are without equal in the architec-

Airplane Hangar

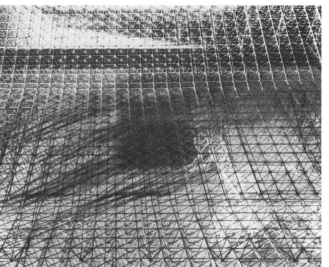

ture of the twentieth century. It is an unexcelled statement for buildings with large spans. It is in the grand tradition of the engineering building of the nineteenth century, as exemplified by the works of Thomas Telford and Richard Turner, of Henri Labrouste and Gustav Eiffel. That aphorism of Viollet-le-Duc, the father of structural rationalism, is directly illustrated: 'Toute forme qui n'est pas ordonnée par la structure droit étre repoussée.' "

Airplane Hangar 1953 (project)
Konrad Wachsmann

In the early 50s, Konrad Wachsmann developed a tubular space frame system for building cantilevered hangars of large size. The project was undertaken at the behest of the U.S. Government, and was completed with a stunning model as part of its final presentation. At the time, Wachsmann was teaching at the Institute of Design, and the model was constructed with the assistance of students from that school.

The structure was ingeniously made of prefabricated parts, so that it could be easily dismantled, transported and re-built in a different location. The overall dimensions of the cantilevered roof were 787 x 380 ft. (240 x 115 m), which provided a floor area of approximately 300,000 sq. ft. (27,881 m^2). The cantilever projected 164 ft. (50 m) in two directions. The main connection point for the interlocking steel tubes was brilliantly worked out; it could be fixed or taken apart by the use of a hammer. The total structure had eight major supports, each of which consisted of three individual supports in its own right. Wachsmann's hangar was a technological tour-de-force. Though never built, it has had considerable influence on a number of major contemporary architects.

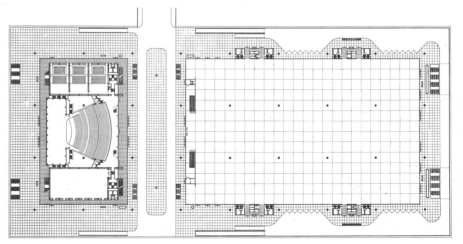

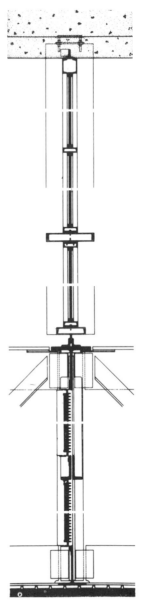

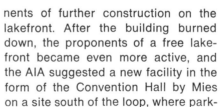

**McCormick Place 1971
Lakefront and 23rd
C. F. Murphy Associates
(Gene Summers)**

On January 15, 1967, the first McCormick Place, built on the lake front in 1960, went up in flames. This rude and rather tasteless structure was unpopular, mostly because of an inefficient interior communications system. At the time of its construction, concern about its possible enlargement was being expressed especially among the opponents of further construction on the lakefront. After the building burned down, the proponents of a free lakefront became even more active, and the AIA suggested a new facility in the form of the Convention Hall by Mies on a site south of the loop, where parking places for 10,000 cars could be built in a two-story underground structure over a railway. This site, with its direct access to mass transit, was in accord with the city planning prerequisites which Mies wanted to incorporate in his Convention Hall; he had there-

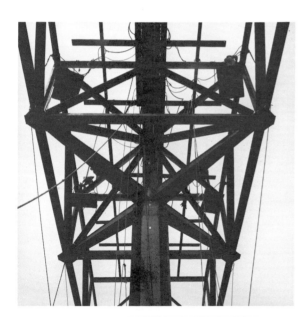

fore planned it for an urban renewal area west of the present location of McCormick Place.

But since Chicago is America's most important convention city, the political authorities of Chicago—under pressure from the business world—decided on the quickest and easiest solution, namely reconstruction on the same site on Lake Michigan. Construction was begun in May of 1968 and in September, 1971 the building was opened.

Though the second design was universally preferred to the first (indeed though it is all the more remarkable in view of the fact that the entire substructure of reinforced concrete had survived as a platform and had to be reused for the new building), criticism of the location persisted.

The architects attempted with all available means to make the best of the site forced on them, both by producing a markedly open design and by

adjusting the building and base to the green landscape of the lakefront. Although the new structure is one-third larger than its predecessor and contains almost double the space under a roof area of 871,000 sq. ft. (80,960 m^2), it gives a lighter appearance. A parking garage for 2,000 cars was laid out underground and fully landscaped south of the structure. On the lake side a continuous shoreline promenade was laid out and a bicycle path was added that

now stretches along the entire Chicago lakefront.

While the Convention Hall of Mies van der Rohe was to contain merely a large convention hall, the program for McCormick Place was considerably more differentiated in its extension and rearrangement of the facilities which the old structure had contained; all sorts of large and small conventions, film and theater presentations, automobile shows, garden shows and product exhibits take place there. Moreover, on the south end of the installation, Arie Crown Theater with its 4,350 seats, plus a full stage with fly loft and hydraulically operated orchestra pit for 100 musicians, were added. It is the largest theater auditorium in Chicago. Three rehearsal theaters, each with 345 seats, are situated on the lower level. Simple materials—structural steel elements painted black, exposed concrete block and brick—establish a human scale, but all diverting decor is avoided.

A common roof connects the theater portion with the great convention hall; between the two glazed cubes is an open space that connects city and lake. Its 180 ft. (54.90 m) span is immensely impressive.

This mall acts as a continuation and conclusion of 23rd Street, and constitutes the main entry to the building. Here a bus stand provides present access to mass transportation, but plans call for a rapid transit train station, to be reached by a pedestrian tunnel.

The great train stations of the previous century created a similar impression. Robert Cuscaden commented on the exposition space: "The architect in this case . . . works from a background that included 16 years in Mies's office. Little wonder, then, that despite its incredible size and complex diversity Summers' McCormick Place is an object lesson in discipline and logic. There is a control and ordering of space and detail here that is awesome. This is especially true of the main exhibit area, a vast room of some 300,000 square feet (27,900 m²) and yet one that contains only eight columns. Here, indeed, one finds the Van der Rohe concept of 'universal space' triumphantly carried out. Here, truly, is a space so unencumbered with specific spatial elements that it can remain forever

universally responsive to functional needs."

The 1350 x 750 ft. (411.75 x 228.75 m) roof construction, which lies 115 ft. (35 m) above the surface of the lake, has a total weight of 24 pounds per sq. ft. and is carried by 9 x 4, (i.e. 36 reinforced concrete supports sheathed in steel). The support spacing of 150 ft. (45.75 m) in both directions is a multiple of the 30 ft. (9.15 m) column spacing present in the basement, also of new supports which have been footed in the middle of the 30 ft. (9.15 m) bays in order to disrupt the existing foundation as little as possible. The supports, with a cruciform cross section of 5 ft. (1.52 m) are a further example of the suitability of this support form for structures with square support grids. The roof, cantilevered 75 ft. (22.75 m) on all sides, extends over exterior rows of columns which stand outside the glass walls. The 10,000 ton roof construction of McCormick Place, with its height of 15 ft. (4.58 m) and a module of 30 ft. (9.15 m), forms a space frame made of

Industrial Hall

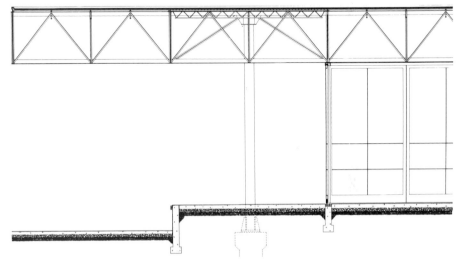

truss girders crossed at right angles. Because of the advantageous cantilevering on all sides, the span widths are reduced and, incidentally, the dimensions of the bearing members as well; the fascia beams intended for the Convention Hall could be dispensed with.

All interior and exterior unclad steel construction elements, including the sheet steel sheathing of the columns and the window frames, were painted flat black. For the 7 x 10 ft. (2.14 x 3.24 m) panes, gray tinted, heat absorbing glass was chosen and the concrete base was given a sheathing of metallic gray glazed brick.

Before Gene Summers planned the hall construction on the existing base in the form carried out, he had investigated two other projects. In the first he envisioned two separate structures—a larger exposition hall and a smaller structure which would have housed the theater; in the second, he combined both elements into a single unit—however, under a giant suspended roof that spanned 1200 ft. (366 m) in the long direction. It was, in effect, a bridge construction, which took into account the long, narrow site.

Industrial Storage Hall 1967 (project)
Paul Zorr
Advisor: Prof. Myron Goldsmith
Dept. of Arch., I.I.T.

Paul Zorr completed this thesis proposal for an Industrial Hall at about the same time McCormick Place was conceived. The roof structures of both works are composed of two-way space trusses. They differ in method of erection and in detail of support. Unlike McCormick Place, which was built piece by piece above the ground, Zorr's thesis project could be assem-

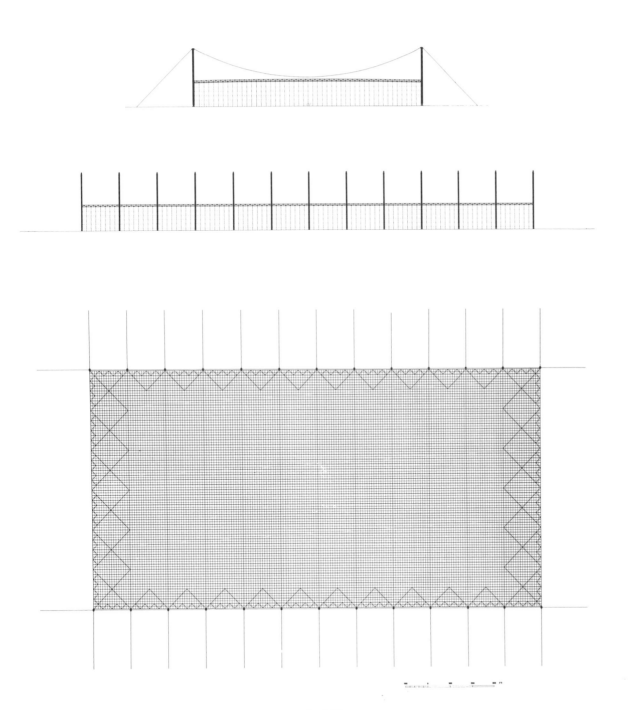

Roof Plan

bled entirely on the ground and then raised to its final position. This method featured a tension connection between roof and columns, as opposed to the compression system utilized at McCormick Place.

**Exhibition Hall for Chicago 1969
      (project)
Peter C. Pran
Advisors: Prof. Myron Goldsmith
          Prof. Fazlur Khan
          Prof. David C. Sharpe
Dept. of Arch., I.I.T.**

Some of the greatest changes accomplished in architecture in the nineteenth and twentieth century occurred in the forms and construction of large halls. The use of the suspension principle for these halls has great potential. For large spans the cable supported roof structure is very economical when compared with other proposed or existing structures. However, bridges have taken more advantage of the system than have buildings. Of the many suspension bridges built since the early nineteenth century, the largest is the recently completed Verrazano-Narrows Bridge in New York, a product of the engineering firm of Ammann and Whitney. Its main span, 4,260 ft. (1298 m), is also the longest span of any structural system in the world. This shows the immense possibilities of the suspension system applied to large span structures.

In this Exhibition Hall for Chicago, the cable supported roof structure was chosen as the most efficient and most economical structure for the large clear span. The building has a clear span of 1,000 ft. (305 m), and is 2,000 ft. (610 m) long in the other direction divided into 12 bays of 166 ft. 8 in. (51 m) span each.

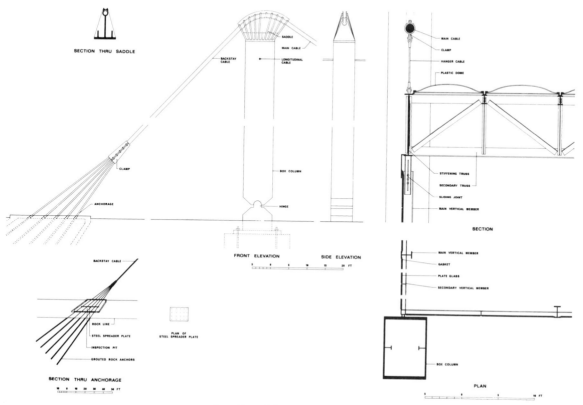

SECTION THRU SADDLE

BACKSTAY CABLE

CLAMP

ANCHORAGE

BACKSTAY CABLE

ROCK LINE
STEEL SPREADER PLATE
INSPECTION PIT
GROUTED ROCK ANCHORS

PLAN OF
STEEL SPREADER PLATE

SECTION THRU ANCHORAGE

SADDLE
MAIN CABLE
LONGITUDINAL
CABLE

BOX COLUMN

HINGE

FRONT ELEVATION   SIDE ELEVATION

MAIN CABLE
CLAMP
HANGER CABLE
PLASTIC DOME

STIFFENING TRUSS
SECONDARY TRUSS
SLIDING JOINT
MAIN VERTICAL MEMBER

SECTION

MAIN VERTICAL MEMBER
GASKET
PLATE GLASS
SECONDARY VERTICAL MEMBER

BOX COLUMN

PLAN

Details of Structure

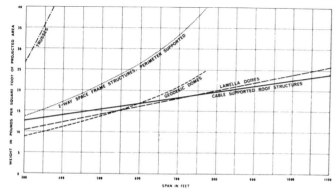

COMPARATIVE WEIGHTS OF LONG SPAN STEEL STRUCTURES

This is a research project worked out at Illinois Institute of Technology. The structural system is worked out as a general solution to clear span exhibition halls of spans from 300 to 1200 ft. (91 x 365 m), or more, as well as a specific solution to the problem of the 1,000 ft. (305 m) span for large exhibitions and conventions.

From comparative structural studies, it is apparent that for spans of over 800 ft. (245 m), no other system can compete in weight with a suspended roof structure. The weight curves show that

the geodesic dome can compete only up to 500 ft. (152 m), and that the lamella dome can compete up to 800 ft. (243 m). The comparison made between the suspension system and traditional truss systems, whether one-way or two-way or space frame, suggests that for spans over 200 ft. (61 m), the suspension system weighs less. In terms of cost it is concluded from the studies that the suspension system is more economical for all spans over 400 ft. (122 m).

The Convention Hall by Mies has a square roof of 720 x 720 ft. (220 x 220 m) with a two-way steel truss system 30 ft. (9.2 m) high. While it is an excellent somewhat high steel weight of 34 psf (pounds per square foot), while the cable supported roof structure in the Exhibition Hall for Chicago, for the same span of 720 ft. (220 m), has a weight of 17 psf. Using the suspension system to cover the same floor area—about 500 x 1000 ft. (152 x 304 m)—the weight would be 15 psf.

The Exhibition Hall for Chicago has a window wall 100 ft. (31 m) high. The economically practical sag to span ratio varies between 1/9 and 1/6. From the main cable, the hanger cables are connected down to a stiffening truss, which goes from column to column. The stiffening trusses and the secondary trusses between them constitute the roof structure. The columns are hinged at the base, to take care of temperature movements in the structure. The backstay cable goes down to the ground at a 45 degree angle, and is anchored into a suitable anchor block. Lateral stability in the building in the other direction is secured by a long cable on each side connecting the top of all the columns together, and anchored into the ground at each end. Plexiglas domes, 10 x 10 ft. (3.2 x 3.2 m), cover the roof.

Union Station 1968 (project)
Lawrence C. Kenny
Advisors: Prof. Myron Goldsmith
Prof. Fazlur Khan
Prof. David C. Sharpe
Dept. of Arch., I.I.T.

In this gigantic hall glassed in on all sides, 600 ft. (183 m) wide, 900 ft. (275 m) long and 75 ft. (22.5 m) high, the various private railways which converge on Chicago would be combined. The design proceeds from the assumption that the tracks—as in the case of the present train stations in Chicago and New York—are located on a plane under the street level. On both sides of a broad distribution zone arranged in the center, escalators lead from the street and entrance level down to the train platforms. The tracks open up in an inner court visible from all sides, and a distribution passage at street level with access from all directions surrounds these depressed areas inside the glass walls of the train station hall. On the track level some 25 ft. (7.65 m) lower there are also taxi and bus stations with direct entrance and exit as well as baggage handling and technical installations. On two low stories under the openings above the tracks, there are parking places for 2,000 passenger cars.

The impressive roof construction consists of six segments, each with four supports, which is separated by expansion joints. A square field of 150 ft. (45.75 m) lateral length—inciden-

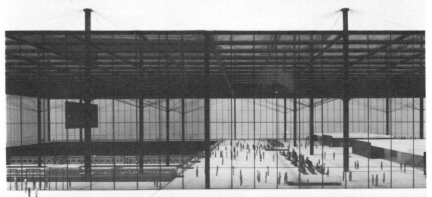

tally, the support width of McCormick Place—is penetrated in the middle by a 2 ft. (61 cm) square steel column made up of 1 in. (2.5 cm) steel plates, which juts out 25 ft. (7.65 m) over the roof surface. The module is further subdivided by main beams into square fields of 30 ft. (9.15 m) and again subdivided by secondary beams into fields of 10 ft. (3.05 m) lengths. The weather proof roof skin of the plastic domes extends over these small fields. From each column head 36 cables spread out, which are fastened at the cross points of the main beams; their diameter lies around 1 in. (between 2 and 3 cm). From these cross points, cables are also connected to each column below the roof plate; 20 cables of approximately ¾ in. (2 cm) diameter are connected from points 25 ft. (7.65 m) below the roof to the supports with points at the periphery of the modular system. They are employed to provide horizontal stiffening and to prevent the roof from shifting upward as well as stiffening of the supports themselves. The roof plate is only 16 in. (40 cm) high.

First the main columns, measuring a height of 115 ft. (35.10 m) or 90 ft. (27.45 m), are to be mounted on their foundations; the roof will then be put together in segments lying on the ground, the upper cables attached and the roof hoisted up by hydraulic jacks. The cables are pre-tensioned and cut to the proper length; small variations of length are inconsequential because of the flexibility of the system.

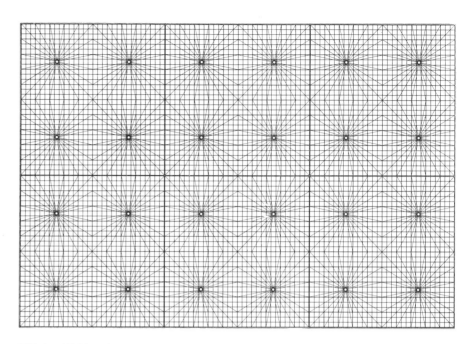

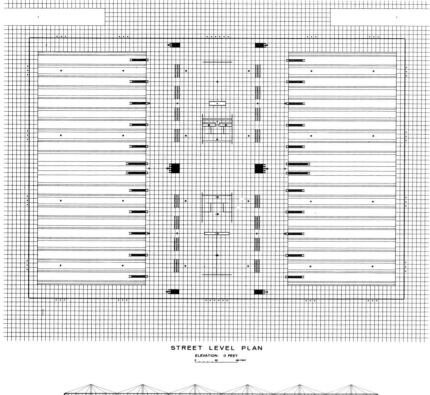

STREET LEVEL PLAN
ELEVATION: 0 FEET

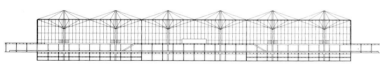

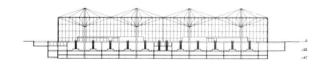

A result of this design on a smaller scale was the work which SOM (Myron Goldsmith) submitted for the competition of the American pavilion in Osaka in 1970. A flat roof plate was also here supported from above and below from six steel columns. The main floor with 20 open small film theaters was to lie under the entrance level jutting out on all sides as a semi-story, which was to serve as holding room for waiting customers.

Thus it was once again demonstrated how a convincing construction principle can be applied to various problems with equal functional justification. The weight of the roof construction with 4.82 pounds per sq. ft. is amazingly small and shows that this construction system is far superior to all other solutions. Even an extension of the spacing between supports from 150 ft. (45.75 m) to 300 ft. (91.50 m) would have resulted in an increase to only 5.3 pounds per sq. ft. The inside of the train station hall is a grand vision of refined steel structure and light; it reveals how the development of structural possibilities has progressed from the impressive train shed which Solon S. Beman built for the Grand Central Station in Chicago in 1889.

Baxter Laboratories 1975
Central Facilities Building
Skidmore, Owings & Merrill
  (Bruce J. Graham, design partner
  Fazlur Khan, structural engineer
    partner
  John Turley, senior studio architect
  Phil Thrane, technical coordinator)

Since the first edition of this book, the principle of the cable suspension roof has been realized in an actual building, designed by Skidmore, Owings & Merrill for a Chicago client, Baxter Laboratories. As of this writing (early 1976) it is unique in the world for its size and scale.

Construction of a large complex housing Baxter's corporate headquarters was completed in 1975 on a 90-acre tract near Deerfield, Illinois, 25 miles north of Chicago. Four pavilion office buildings, all steel framed, surround the Central Facilities Building, which contains a cafeteria and kitchen on the upper level and, below grade, a training school, auditorium, executive dining room and reception facilities. It is this last unit which features the cable suspension roof. Seen most readily from the Illinois Tollway to the east, at a distance of several hundred yards, its exterior is dramatic enough: a great horizontal wall of glass, 288 ft. (87.8 m) long, 48 ft. (15.6 m) high and clad in white-coated aluminum, is dominated by two powerful columns that rise to a height of 35 ft. (10.6 m) above roof level. Both rest on 80-ft. (24.4 m) caissons. Each is made of poured concrete in its lower extension. Above the cafe-

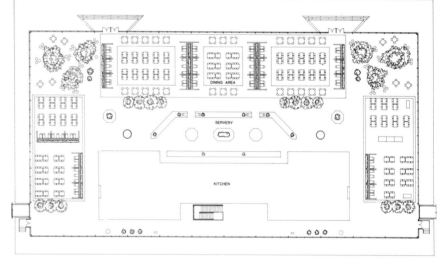

teria level it is a steel shaft 6 ft. (1.8 m) in diameter, tapering to 3 ft. (.9 m) 9 in. (.22 m) at the top. The 48 cables which are suspended from each mast, descending to the roof and to the roof's edge, are 1⅜ in. (.03 m) in diameter.

A closer view of the building is more impressive still, not only because its system of support is so enormous, but because its basic functional principle is so utterly evident, even to the lay-

man. Beyond the obvious fact that the roof is hung from the cables, there exists an extraordinarily complex and subtle pattern of details without which that support could not be successfully provided. Herein lies a major difference between the Baxter building and the Kenny thesis to which it otherwise owes so much in concept. Only a firm with the size, scope and facilities of SOM could carry out the computa-

tions and systems analysis necessary to solve intricate problems like roof edge deflection and roof torsion in so large a building.

What the viewer does not perceive then, is the mathematical delicacy brought to bear so that temperature changes affecting the cables are accommodated; so that the roof will meet the glass wall without breaking the wall; so that the roof will not twist out

of line.

To increase the stiffness of the roof system, an additional 24 cables secure the roof grid from its underside. They are exposed on the inside of the building, running diagonally from their respective masts to nodes on the underside of the roof frame. Another 36 cables ⅝ in. (.015 m) in diam. run vertically at 24 ft. (7.3 m) intervals around the building perimeter. They are at-

tached at the top to the perimeter nodes of the roof frame, at the bottom to the building foundation. The vertical cables are concealed in every fourth curtain wall mullion. Movement between the roof and curtain wall is accommodated by vertical slip joints.

If exterior mast cables alone had been used, variations in temperature and wind/precipitation loading would have allowed the roof to move up and down in excess of 3 in. (.073 m). Tensioning with the underside cables reduced this movement to a manageable 1½ in. (.036 m), making the connection between roof and curtain wall feasible. The total weight of the steel roof structure, including the cables, is 6.50 pounds per sq. ft.

Grant Park Concert Hall Shell 1970 (project)
Randolph, Lake Shore Drive, Monroe, and Columbus Drive
C. F. Murphy Associates (Gene Summers)

This handsome steel shell structure, with accommodations for 3,000 seats, was proposed for a Grant Park site. Additional seating for 7,000 to 9,000 would be provided on sloping grass areas. An underground parking facility would have stalls for 3700 cars. The shell was never constructed, but hope remains that another site will be found for it.

Structurally the acoustic shell is a two-way space truss combining an arching and cantilevering action spanning 300 feet at its widest point and rising a maximum of 60 feet. This open lattice is infilled with transparent acrylic plastic. Supporting facilities are integrated into the underground parking garage and pedestrian circulation ties directly into that of the neighboring Illinois Center Development. (Although Felix Candela's most influential buildings were designed before he moved to Chicago in 1971, and cannot be considered Chicago buildings, reference might be made here to his pioneering structural endeavors in concrete shells, like the vigorous shell structure of his 1958 nightclub in Acapulco.)

Urban Planning; Transportation; The Development of the Suburbs

Though the fame of the Burnham Plan has contributed greatly to Chicago's reputation for pioneering efforts in urban design, the fact is that the city has been shaped for the most part the way almost all American metropolises have: more by fate than by forethought.

Its surface is laid out in the form of a grid, an arrangement historically traceable to the Land Ordinance of 1785, which divided all of the young United States beyond the original 13 colonies into one-mile-square sections. As a planning device, the grid has the virtues of simplicity and clarity, while suffering the drawbacks of monotony and lack of differentiation. It is well suited to a densely built-up business area like the Loop, whose regularly-spaced streets and intermittent alleys allow for a balance of pedestrian and vehicular traffic as well as for facility in the delivery and pickup of materials essential to business functions. In residential areas, however, the grid uses land simplistically. It is just not a very flexible means of accommodating the wide range of human activity—from residential to industrial, from commercial to recreational—that is normal in large cities.

In Chicago, a number of proposals have been advanced to ameliorate the rigidity of its format. Most of them involve plans which would restrict the grid to those commercial precincts where it makes generally good sense, while providing residential areas with a wider variety of layouts, ungeometric and asymmetrical ones included. Park land between neighborhoods has likewise been suggested as a way of concentrating green space which otherwise, in the grid system, remains

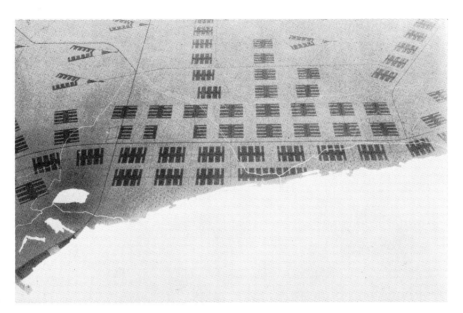

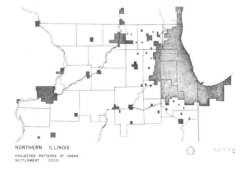

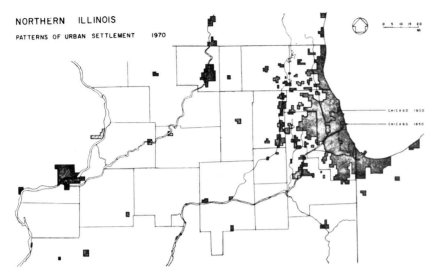

NORTHERN ILLINOIS
PATTERNS OF URBAN SETTLEMENT 1970

CHICAGO 1900
CHICAGO 1850

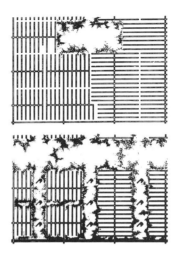

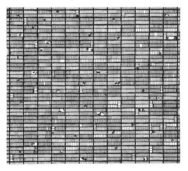

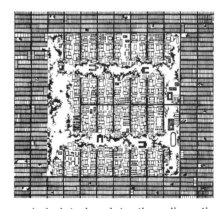

scattered, often lost to streets, to automobile traffic and to parking. Motor cars could be required to move for the most part circumambiently to neighborhoods, with limited access to the interiors of residential areas.

City Planning and the Grid System
Ludwig Hilberseimer, David Haid

One solution to problems created by the grid system was suggested by Professor Ludwig Hilberseimer of the City Planning department at I.I.T. Beginning with a typical street pattern in Chicago —this one happened to be near Marquette Park—he showed that merely by interrupting streets, a traffic-free pedestrian route could be opened to the park. Thus the park could be brought into closer contact with the residential area, and schools might be built in the new strips of open land. Pedestrian safety would be assured and the percentage of land pre-empted by streets and alleys would be greatly reduced.

The problem of density prompted architect David Haid to seek an alternative solution to the practice of placing low-income families in forbidding high-

rise apartment towers. Taking Professor Hilberseimer's Marquette Park scheme as a point of departure, he investigated the idea of building atrium houses as condominium dwellings, with financing placed within reach of lower-income families.

As a first stage small groups of such houses could be built, followed by the redevelopment of what Haid conceived as a typical city unit. One hundred and forty-five atrium houses could be built on lots formerly occupied by 72 single-family residences. The new units would be grouped around shared courtyards connected by attractive pedestrian walkways. These public spaces would be used by vehicles only in emergencies.

Haid's plan contains a further possible step: the redevelopment of a typical square mile in Chicago. Through streets would be reduced in number, as in the Hilberseimer proposal, thus opening free area for parks, pedestrian zones, schools and business. In the large landscaped areas along the periphery of the atrium house groups high-rise apartments could be constructed. If such redevelopment pro-

ceeded lot by lot, the disruptive process of mass re-settlement could be avoided. At the completion of the plan only 15 percent of the available land would be taken up by vehicular thoroughfares and parking.

Schools and stores would be within walking distance of the residences, moreover along routes free of traffic. A density might be achieved which would be far more socially tolerable within the circumstances of the environment than is the standard today.

Neither of these plans, nor several others of comparable intelligence, has been realized. There is a traditional American aversion to large-scale public design and long-range government planning; private enterprise has been a sacred legacy. Nevertheless, its more or less unregulated application in the development of cities has produced one of the most painful communal ailments of modern times: the urban-suburban sprawl.

The term sprawl implies movement, which suggests in turn that the question of community planning is inseparable from that of transportation. Chicago developed into an immense city primarily because its location at the southern end of the Great Lakes, within a canal's length of the Mississippi River waterway system, was critical to overland transportation. Similarly, within the city as it grew, transportation was vital to the access its citizens had to their places of employment.

In the earliest days, the horse-drawn omnibus provided the chief means of public movement for common folk, while railroads enabled wealthier people to live in outlying areas that eventually became suburbs. As the nineteenth century progressed, cable streetcars and electrified modes of surface and elevated transit led to a widening of the city's diameter, and an increasing density of population within it. Chicago thus witnessed its first urban explosion in the years prior to 1900.

Its second, which continues today, involves the suburbs as well as the city proper, and is essentially a phenome-

non of the post-World War II period. Its central component is the automobile, which has allowed people of average means to live at considerable distances from their job locations.

Meanwhile, a movement of industry from the core to exurbia has likewise occurred, more or less simultaneously and for many of the same reasons. A research report produced at the University of Chicago in 1966 had this to say: "After the Second World War it became apparent that industrial concerns were abandoning the core areas of America's large cities. As a result of this exodus, once highly productive land was less and less utilized. Empty, deteriorating industrial buildings quickened the collapse of the inner cities and the newest waves of immigrants were deprived of employment opportunities in their own neighborhoods."

The proximity of job and home which had done so much to vouchsafe the early immigrant's survival in Chicago, can no longer be counted on today.

At the same time, the massive settlement of the suburbs has only heightened the need for better transportation between the city and its periphery, partly to service suburbanites who work in the city and partly to help city dwellers reach jobs in the suburbs. But the response to this need has not been a carefully planned and regulated public transit system. Instead, consonant with the psychology of the automobile age, super highways have been built. They have been cut through pre-existing neighborhoods, many already ailing and all further disrupted by the great concrete gulches. Still, the volume of traffic and the time required to commute from one place to another continue to increase. The result is a form of transit sclerosis.

During the 1960s attempts in various forms were made to attract industry

Illinois toll station by Charles Genther

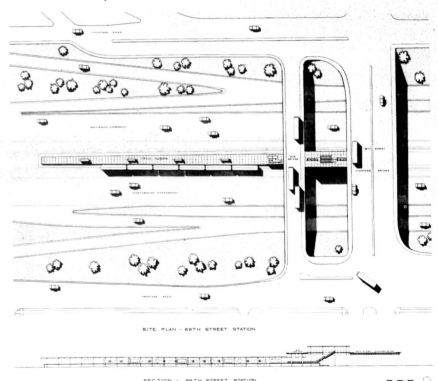

SITE PLAN - 69TH STREET STATION

SECTION - 69TH STREET STATION

back to areas of the inner city it had already departed. In fact, the super highways themselves were conceived as a means of encouraging this. The highly controversial **Crosstown Ex-**

pressway, proposed as a north-south artery on the far west side of the city, was meant to be a good deal more than another enormous traffic trough. Its proponents held that if proper zoning

111

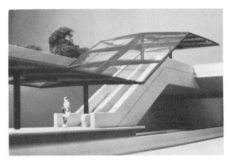

could be insured, low-cost housing could be constructed along the roadway and new industry built in a broad corridor between its two traffic lanes. Included in the package would be improved facilities for both private and mass transportation, holding out the hope of shorter commuting distances for the people living adjacent to the roadway. (What Crosstown hoped to achieve in the architecture of mass transit facilities has been accomplished with the functional yet elegant **CTA Rapid Transit stations** in the median strip along the Dan Ryan and Kennedy expressways, designed by **SOM with Myron Goldsmith, design partner and Pao-Chi Chang, senior architect.**)

Crosstown has been one of the most hotly debated issues of the late 1960s and the 1970s. Its opponents maintain, that despite intentions to create a viable new community, it would amount to little more than another violation of an old one. Its destiny at the present time remains uncertain.

So, for that matter, does the question of planning for the city as a whole. Urban design in Chicago and its environs is a matter either of isolated, fragmented—and qualified—successes in the past, or speculative proposals for the future. Two examples of isolated success, albeit in the outlying regions of Chicago, are Riverside and Pullman.

Riverside

Aesthetically speaking, the finest of the nineteenth century Chicago suburbs is Riverside. It was designed by the premier American landscape architect of his day, Frederick Law Olmsted, in collaboration with Calvert Vaux, the same Englishman who had earlier helped him lay out New York's Central Park.

The two men came to Chicago in 1868, with a view to planning a new settlement on a plot of land nine miles west of Chicago and connected to the city by the Chicago, Burlington & Quincy Railroad. There, on gently sloping terrain covered by a forest in full growth—features rarely found in the prairie surrounding Chicago—they set about creating that ideal of late nineteenth century urban man: a community with the convenience of the city but a minimum of city harassments, with the ease of the country but little of rural isolation.

Olmsted's design included plans for village greens and commons, as well as a variety of playgrounds, sheltered park benches and other facilities calculated to promote outdoor social contacts. For the banks of the Des Plaines River, which ran through the town, he envisioned a public walk, boat docks, terraces over the water and rustic pavilions from which regattas could be viewed. The amiable, curving roadways of his street plan represented a consciously-designed alternative to the grid.

Like many such plans before and after it, the Olmsted-Vaux scheme for Riverside was never realized to its creators' satisfaction. Conflicts with the sponsoring development company led both men to retire from the project in 1870. Still, Riverside as completed was something of a jewel. Vaux himself designed a number of its most impressive residences. William Le Baron Jenney built a home for himself there, and erected a water tower which later became the town's symbol. The several houses Frank Lloyd Wright put up in Riverside are among his finest works. Even today Olmsted's spirit is in great degree preserved in the appearance of Riverside, and the Supreme Court of Illinois has reconfirmed public domain over the town's spacious parklands. A remarkable number of early buildings have suffered only minor alterations.

Pullman

Pullman, a south side suburb, was founded in 1880 by railroad car builder George M. Pullman as a model industrial community. At least such was his lofty intention.

On a narrow trapezoidal site of roughly 4,000 acres (1,600 ha) along the western shore of Lake Calumet, architect Solon S. Beman and landscape

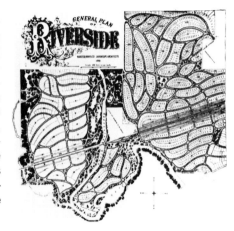

architect Nathan F. Barrett planned an entire company town. The first 100 dwelling units were completed by the summer of 1881. A hotel, a church and The Arcade (a multi-purpose building containing stores, a post office, a bank, a library and a theater) were constructed near the Illinois Central Railroad's Pullman station. To the north

were the shop buildings of the largest railroad car works in the world.

Pullman and his associates invested nearly $8 million in the project, and they believed, in keeping with the standards of the time, that they were achieving a philanthropic goal. They had seen to the creation of a whole town where all public services and

113

facilities were accommodated, and where each of the 1,400 dwelling units to be rented to company employees was planned for single-family use, with good light, sound ventilation, modern sanitation and access to a private yard.

At the same time, everything in Pullman—houses, parks, schools, shops—was owned by the Pullman Company, which maintained and supervised its property with determined paternalism. In 1898, four years after a bloody strike by Pullman workers was broken by federal troops, the Illinois Supreme Court denied the company the right to own and operate a town. George Pullman's dream was ended, but the town itself has survived a period of neglect, and is being restored and maintained as a national landmark.

If Pullman was its founder's failure, it was its architect's extraordinary success. Beman designed the whole complex, endowing it with an expressive unity all the more remarkable for the assortment of styles it embraces. Stylistically, the larger and more public buildings are indebted mostly to Rich-
114

ardson, and if they lack his customary monumentality, they possess a consistent friendly liveliness throughout. The workers' row houses are understandably humbler, but surprisingly various in manner, with vernacular intimations of the Stick Style, the Shingle Style and Queen Anne prevailing.

Among the most notable of the Pullman buildings was the rather grand Arcade, 256 ft. (78 m) long, 146 ft. (44.5 m) wide and 90 ft. (27.4 m) high, constructed of red brick with light stone trim, and featuring a broad iron-and-glass roof over a central passage lined with offices and shops. Comparably memorable elements of the whole are the expansive Florence Hotel and the Greenstone Church, a bright little neo-Romanesque structure that remains one of the most charming houses of worship in the Chicago area. In its prime the community was dominated by a 195-ft. (59.4 m) high water tower

which contained "the largest water tank in the world." The water was pumped up by the famous Corliss Steam Engine, which had earlier driven the machinery at Philadelphia's Centennial Exposition of 1876.

Chicago 21

Chicago, we have affirmed, has had no dearth of grand designs. If anything, it has been notably more lacking in the means to achieve them. They have tumbled from official-sounding agencies one after another down through the years, usually accompanied by great professions of hope and almost as standardly followed by failure. By now when they appear, they seldom elicit more than a vast civic yawn.

The reason for such indifference is that the citizens of Chicago recognize two central facts about large community enterprise here: first, it is highly unlikely to succeed without the sup-

port of the local power structure, which consists of big business and City Hall; second, those two groups cannot be directly moved to action by any group outside themselves.

But what if they should elect at last to share the endorsement *and* the implementation of a major plan for the city? The theoretical answer is, it might work, depending, however, on still other variables over which they themselves may have insufficient control.

There is, in any case, such a plan, with such an endorsement and the expressed intention to implement it. Unsurprisingly, it has been publicized more widely than any comparable project since Burnham's. Also unsurprisingly, it has been greeted with as much wariness, and even opposition, as enthusiasm. Nevertheless, it possesses enough ambition and suggests enough potential to warrant comment here.

"Chicago 21"—a title which implies its completion by next century, a little more than a generation away—is a plan to revitalize the central area of the city in general and downtown in particular.

In the early 1970s, studies which the City Planning Department had already initiated—with a view to resuscitating the ailing central districts—became bogged down for want of money. Thereupon a group of leaders of the city's major business corporations—known as the Central Area Committee—agreed to fund the completion of the studies. The CAC, however, stipulated a condition: that the city government cooperate by giving highest priority to the Planning Department's studies and any large design they might lead to. City Hall consented. Review committees representing both the CAC and the municipal government were named, and the architectural firm of Skidmore, Owings & Merrill was commissioned to produce a master plan.

Gradually a two-fold objective emerged: first, the regeneration of several neighborhoods now bordering the downtown area in an arc from the north counter-clockwise on the map to the southwest; second, the construction of a whole new neighborhood south of downtown, on railroad yards presently in virtual disuse. It was presumed that this idle railroad land might be bought cheaply. With such purchase in mind, a limited dividend corporation—the Chicago 21 Corporation—was formed. A comparable strategy was devised relative to land along the Chicago River in the aforementioned older neighborhoods: this might be similarly acquired, and transformed from its current tawdriness into a handsome riverbank precinct.

Thus old sections might be rehabilitated while new ones were being created, all in the anticipation that today's population of 160,000 in the central area would be eventually doubled. The fact that suburbia is beginning to experience environmental miseries of its own in the wake of its largely unregulated growth has added hope that significant numbers of people might be attracted back to a city which could offer the advantages of easier, improved transportation as well as proximity to business and entertainment districts.

The fulfillment of such hopes, however, is contingent on several highly problematical factors. What guarantee is there for adequate public schools in the area? Would the high density necessary to provide new areas with desirable urban facilities like affordable housing and good public transportation also spawn a lot of the brute high-rise structure notorious for working hardships on families with small children? Even given satisfactory an-

Above, South Loop new town; *below*, mall on downtown State Street

swers to these questions, would the resultant, presumably salutary, urban milieu be enough to reverse the flight to the greener suburbs by citizens who like the automobile life—with all its attendant problems—better than any other?

These are only some of the issues on which the ultimate success of Chicago 21 depends, and each of them has stimulated hot debate.

The proponents of the plan prefer the metaphor of an antiseptic dressing to that of a segregating moat. They argue that since the city's deterioration has spread outward like an infection from the core, its healing rehabilitation might be expected to work the same way: a benevolent cycle might replace a vicious one. They likewise claim to be working diligently on a variety of methods—some distinctly unconven-

tional—of insuring a higher quality of schooling and child care.

The fairest summary of Chicago 21's prospects, then, is that they are uncertain and unpredictable. That is not a very helpful conclusion, yet all other views seem to be so tinctured by the optimistic or pessimistic bias of the viewer that they cannot be accepted as fully reliable at the present time.

Dwellings

One of the attributes of a metropolis, its variety, has traditionally been considered among the qualities that make city living attractive to civilized man. Some critics have observed, however, that what was once variety has become more nearly chaos in the modern city. The arguments on behalf of this view are persuasive; some of them have been cited elsewhere in this text. Urban planning remains the greatest single problem facing contemporary architecture.

Within it, no issue is more vexing than housing. Yet for all that is unsolved and unresolved in this realm, the spectrum of modern dwelling design is vast, and its quality at times impressive by any architectural standards. It is hard to imagine how we could call that society substantially better than our own which does not provide its citizens with the freedom to take advantage of as wide a range of housing design as we possess. The downtown high rise is as comfortably suited to some residents as the single-family suburban home is to others. Chicago and its environs contain virtually all the major types of contemporary residential design. The better examples are not only among the best anywhere, but in many cases reflect the traditional formal concerns of the Chicago school.

Haid House

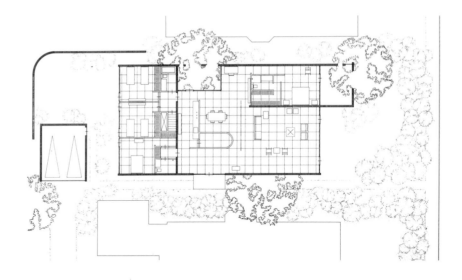

Single-family Houses		Walgreen House	1974
		Lake Forest	
Lewis House	1940	Clarence Krusinski	
Libertyville			
Frank Lloyd Wright		Freeark House	1975
		Riverside	
50′ x 50′ House	1951 (project)	John Vinci, Lawrence C. Kenny	
Mies van der Rohe			
		Pran Residence	1975 (project)
Geneva House	1952	Wilmette	
Geneva		Peter C. Pran	
Jacques Brownson			
Rose House	1957	**Single-family Houses**	
A. James Speyer			

Collins Residence 1963
Libertyville
James Hammond and Peter Roesch

With the obvious exception of Wright and the Prairie School, Chicago's accomplishments in the design of the single-family residence have received relatively little attention from the historians. Such indifference, whether conscious or unconscious, is probably traceable in large part to the overshadowing reputation of the city's commercial and industrial building.

Vacation House 1969 (project)
Alfred Swenson

Haid House 1971
Evanston
David Haid

Lurie House 1974
Evanston
Laurence Booth and James Nagle

Otherwise, it is not justified by the facts. Even as early as the development of the balloon frame in the 1830s, the city played a significant role in American residential architecture.

Studio-Exhibit Pavilion 1974
Highland Park
David Haid

Geneva House

Lurie House

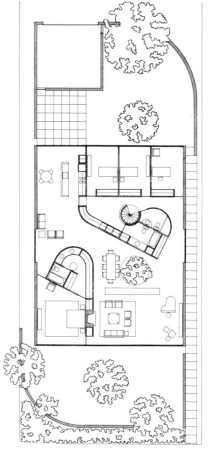

Moreover, the later contributions of gifted eclectics like Howard Van Doren Shaw and David Adler, to name but two, have been underestimated for the very reason that eclecticism has had something of a bad name during the last several decades. These men are still in the process of being reevaluated by the critics, for the most part affirmatively.

Meanwhile, the merits of the Chicago single-family residence can be suggested even within the confines of work produced after World War II by architects of the second Chicago school.

Here again, the influence of Mies van der Rohe is a central fact, and his Farnsworth house the chief source of ideas. The prismatic form and exposed rectilinear steel frame of that structure, enclosing large areas of glass on the exterior and an open, essentially flowing space within, have their echoes in all the houses illustrated here.

Nevertheless, there are variations of these themes among them, as well as passages indebted to other Mies works. The Rose house of A. James Speyer in Highland Park is an L-shaped building with a black-painted steel

frame. One wing of the L features glass walls and an open-plan interior, while the other is divided into more cubicular interior spaces and faced with wood. Brick, on the other hand, is the material which alternates with glass in most of the other structures: The Collins House of Hammond and Roesch in Libertyville, the Freeark house of Vinci and Kenny in Riverside, the Walgreen House of Clarence Krusinski in Lake Forest, the Lurie House of Booth and Nagle in Evanston and the houses designed for themselves by David Haid in Evanston and Jacques Brownson in

Geneva.

Each of these various works has its own identifying aspects. Krusinski's Cor-Ten steel frame is an unusual residential device, but one not out of harmony with the Walgreen House's forested setting. In both the Collins and Freeark houses, a glass front is set back between two end walls of brick, though the former is a low, strict, one-story structure while the latter has two floors and a strikingly free curve to its glass facade. Curves also enliven the interior of the Lurie House—together with oblique wall angles—all recalling

Pran Residence

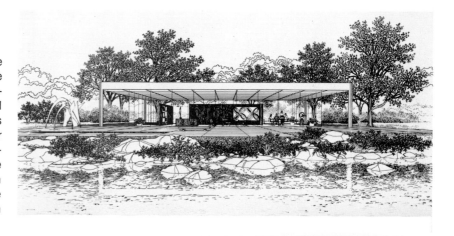

the famous plan of Mies's court house of 1934. The overhead beams of Brownson's house are comparable with the plate girders of Crown Hall.

The David Haid House turns inward to make maximum use of its small site. Although situated between two closely adjacent large old residences, its four enclosed courtyards afford private outdoor spaces off various areas of the house. The Rose House is in a wooded, unimpeded area rather like the one proposed for the Pran Residence. The last of these is surely the most transparent of all these post-World War II projects. Its glass walls recall Mies's 50′ x 50′ House; its frame, on the other hand, is a white, almost velvety translation into residential terms of the structural form Mies used in his Berlin Museum. Swenson's Vacation House project shows another variation of an

Rose House

Studio-Exhibit Pavilion

50′ x 50′ House

all-glass house, raised on four columns to adapt to a rocky landscape.

The studio pavilion of David Haid (in Highland Park) is not strictly speaking a house, but it is residential in the sense that it is an adjunct to a house, and is used for a variety of leisure purposes like receptions and family avocational pursuits. Most of the time it houses the owner's collection of antique autos. Like all the other buildings in this residential section, it is based on Mies's concept of multi-functional space.

Lewis House

Freeark House

Vacation House

Atrium Houses 1961
1370 E. Madison Park
Y. C. Wong

Atrium houses, as a compact dwelling form, descend from the early urban civilizations in Greece, Italy, Spain and Japan. In the 1930s, Mies van der Rohe returned to this form for some of his residential work in Germany. The first of these projects was defined by masonry walls ranging from true enclosures to space-organizing planes extending freely beyond the roof slab. Mies's later designs for a complete atrium house complex and a residence for the Hubbe family were denied building permits by the Nazi government.

In this group of eight atrium houses located in Chicago's Hyde Park, Y. C. Wong has carried forth his teacher's concepts. A long central court divides the complex in half; this is used by adults as a common yard and by children as a playground. Each dwelling has an entrance from here as well as from the street. Within the tan-colored brick walls each house has a private courtyard garden, unseen from and undisturbed by the street outside. With the exception of the kitchen and bath, which are lit by skylights, all rooms face the courtyard and become spatially unified with it.

The atrium house provides an independent and flexible environment without resorting to the uneconomical suburban alternative of separate but crowded dwellings on narrow lots. Although these units appear identical from the street, each tenant has freedom to order the internal space. As an inward-turning residential environment, this project is the antithesis of the Farnsworth House, which Y. C. Wong worked on as an employee in Mies's office. Yet both are realized with the precision and directness characteristic of the second Chicago school.

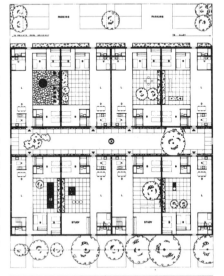

Row Houses 1967
Hyde Park
Y. C. Wong

This ensemble of eight 2-story row houses is located in the vicinity of the same architect's Atrium Houses. From the exterior both projects present smooth brick walls broken only by doors. Within the row houses is a two-story dwelling unit with a floor area of 1,900 sq. ft. (180 sq m). The two-story glass rear wall overlooks a private courtyard and the second floor is set

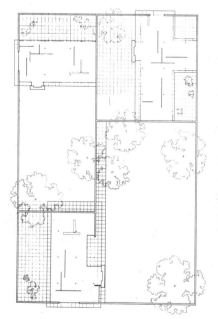

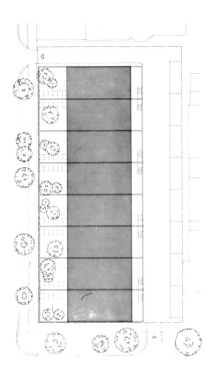

veloped in his urban court house projects; a compact and private sphere is created despite the density of its surroundings.

Noble Square Development 1970
Noble & Division
Perkins & Will
(Lawrence Perkins, partner in charge
Philip Kupritz, project designer
James Caron, project architect)

This is a privately developed residential community located on an 8.8 acre (3.5 ha.) cleared urban renewal site. The project consists of handsomely clustered groups of one-, two- and three-story low-rise living units and a single 28-story high-rise tower with one- and two-bedroom apartments. A plaza and a community service pavilion have been placed in front of the existing church, thus forming a focus for the community. The existing elementary school and high school remained on the site. The exterior of the low-rise units is made of face brick with accent walls of stucco and aluminum sliding sash, and the roof top sun decks have treated wood planks: the structure is of simple masonry bearing walls.

back from the glass to create a two-story space in part of the living room. This last device, which has the effect of visually increasing the size of the room, was used by Le Corbusier in 1948 in his Marseille Unité apartments.

The row or town house, common in the Eastern seaboard cities and in Europe, is realized here in a manner which recalls the concepts Mies de-

Kedvale Square Project 1970
1860 S. Karlov
Louis Rocah

Of the various small-scaled urban renewal projects constructed in the city during the last few years, Kedvale Square is one of the most carefully worked out. On a site of only 4.7 acres (1.9 ha) a total of 116 dwelling units were placed within two types of three-story buildings. There are eight individual structures in all, so placed that two large landscaped areas have been created between them. Two playgrounds are near the outside of the site, and parking is permitted only along the perimeter, with the parking spaces acting as a buffer zone against the street traffic. The bearing wall structure is expressed in the brick facades by means of projecting piers on the end facades. Filler panels are in stacked bond, while floor slabs are indicated by double courses of soldier bricks. Even the sidewalks, lamps and refuse containers are marked by a precision of detail that is unusual for a project built with modest means.

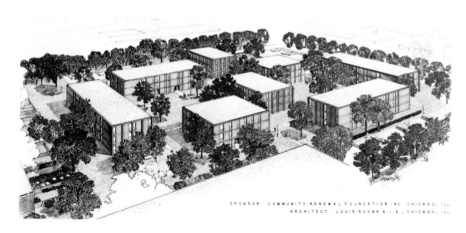

Greenwood Park Apartments 1971
East 47th Street
Harry Weese & Associates
(Ben Weese, design partner
Ezra Gordon and Jack M. Levin,
associate architects)

Ten years ago the area along 47th Street near the lake consisted of rapidly decaying residential and commercial buildings. The combined efforts of private and public institutions later succeeded at least in beginning a reversal of the course of the neighborhood. Pleasant environments for hundred of families were provided. As part of the Lake Village Redevelopment, 15 two- and three-story row houses were built, containing a total of 122 dwelling units. Residences of varying size and amenities were made available to families of different income levels. Especially successful are the scale and grouping of the units and the overall landscaping of the site.

0   5   10   20

SECOND FLOOR PLAN - BUILDING A

KEDVALE SQUARE

0   5   10   20

SECOND FLOOR PLAN - BUILDING B

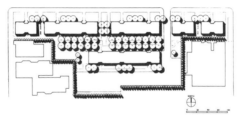

123

Terrace Townhouses 1975 (project)
Fujikawa, Conterato, Lohan
(Dirk Lohan, partner in charge
Melvin Wilson, senior architect)

The Terraced Townhouses of the office of Fujikawa, Conterato, Lohan (formerly the office of Mies van der Rohe) is surely among the most arresting designs to emerge from that firm during the present decade. It was conceived as an alternative to—more precisely, a compromise between—the two types of residential structures standard to the large modern city: the high-rise multi-unit apartment building, whose typical advantages are efficiency and economy, and the low-rise townhouse, with its equally customary virtues of privacy and intimacy.

Dirk Lohan, partner in charge of the project, has designed two 560-foot-long parallel structures, each consisting of five levels of two-story-high duplex units staggered from the street, in terraces. Both structures thus thrust diagonally upward to a height of 105 ft. (32 m), but toward each other, so that the resultant section of the whole is trapezoidal. The space between the two major volumes, each a parallele-piped in effect—is given over to a concourse mall of shops, restaurants, banks and a movie house. That space may or may not be roofed over, but either way it would function as a kind of vast interior—a galleria—for which there is more precedent in Milan and Naples than in Chicago.

All the units would have private terraces on the exterior, and access on the interior to corridor balconies overlooking the concourse below. Coming from the Mies office, which has otherwise been so closely associated with the rectangular prism, the Terraced Townhouses are a surprisingly offbeat concept, although the precision of detailing is familiar, and the huge glass

wall enclosing the ends of the two units —topped as it is by a vigorous steel truss girder—is a structural enuncia-tion fully consonant with the Miesian rationale.

The townhouses have been proposed for a west side area neighborhood somewhat comparable sociologically with Uptown. The site is a full city block bordered by Kedzie Avenue, Madison Street, Albany Avenue and Warren Boulevard. The budget is modest, with a view to accommodating lower- to middle-income tenants.

Hyde Park Redevelopment 1955–on
47th Street to the Midway, Washington
Park to Lake Michigan
I. M. Pei, Loewenberg and
Loewenberg, Harry Weese &
Associates

Following World War II the processes of urban change—aging buildings, "converted" dwellings, absentee landlords—contributed to the deterioration of the once prestigious suburbs of Hyde Park and Kenwood. Later attempts by neighborhood groups to arrest this decay soon made it apparent that only extensive programs of rehabilitation, clearance and redevelopment, paid for with massive investments from the public and private sectors, would have any salutary effect. By 1955 basic plans for renewal were drawn up, and by 1959 construction was begun on the Hyde Park Townhouses and the University apartments.

The three-story townhouses by Harry Weese were either faced inward to form small squares, or extended along existing streets. Privacy was insured by placing the principal rooms on the second floor and high-windowed bedrooms on the third.

The twin-towered University Garden Apartments (1959–61) occupy a site

Dorchester Apartments 1967
5825 S. Dorchester
Skidmore, Owings & Merrill
(Bruce Graham, design partner)

In this project a 15-story apartment tower has been so skillfully combined on a small site with seven atrium houses, that any feeling of mutual encumbrance is avoided and a sense of openness is maintained.

The cross-shaped reinforced concrete tower is cantilevered out from twelve concrete pylons and a central core. The exposed concrete of the tower, exceptional in its workmanship, differentiates the tall structure from the face brick facades of the low residences grouped on three sides of the central court from which the tower rises. The fourth side provides access to the street, from which ramps lead to an underground garage on the basement level.

As an example of the successful combination of varied housing types within a small site, this project could well serve as a prototype for similar future construction.

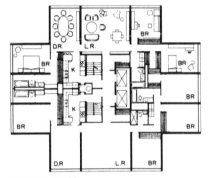

TYPICAL FLOOR

defined by the separated lanes of busy 55th Street. Of reinforced concrete construction, these two structures were among the first to employ load-bearing screen walls, a system wherein a bearing wall of slender columns and shallow spandrel beams transmits wind and gravity forces directly through transfer girders above the first floor arcade to the columns and footings. Designed by I. M. Pei and Loewenberg and Loewenberg, and engineer August E. Kommendant, the buildings stand on either side of a landscaped court, well related with the flanking rows of the townhouses described above.

125

Carl Sandburg Village 1960 onward
Clark, LaSalle, Division and North
L. R. Solomon and J. D. Cordwell and Associates

The convenient location of the Carl Sandburg Village site—just west of the Gold Coast and south of Lincoln Park—insured a steady demand for the middle and upper income housing that was finally constructed there. The city acquired the land with federal aid and turned it over to private developers. Little resettlement was required during clearance; the site had been occupied

mainly by stores, commercial buildings and small run-down hotels. Sandburg Village's high-rise apartment towers, townhouses grouped around small courts, artists' studios, plazas, playgrounds and exhibition areas brought variety to the area and acted as an impetus for the continued private reha-

bilitation of the surrounding neighborhood.

During the competition for the commission of Sandburg Village, the firm of **Brenner, Danforth, Rockwell** submitted a particularly handsome proposal for the Carl Sandburg Village development.

I.I.T. Campus: Student and Faculty Residences 1953–55
31st, Michigan, Wabash and 33rd
Mies van der Rohe

The earliest impetus for the renewal of the near south side was the decision of Armour Institute of Technology (later Illinois Institute of Technology) to remain at its south side campus. The first new residential facilities on the campus were built after World War II by Skidmore, Owings and Merrill, but the most significant architecturally were three reinforced concrete apartment buildings designed by Mies van der Rohe when he was still director of I.I.T.'s architecture department. The nine-story towers for married students and faculty share the same structural expression as Mies's landmark Promontory Apartments, built in 1949. Columns and spandrel beams are unclad concrete; spandrel panels are buff-colored brick. As in all of Mies's residential high-rise structures, the recessed glass walls of the ground floor lobby form an arcade on all sides of the building.

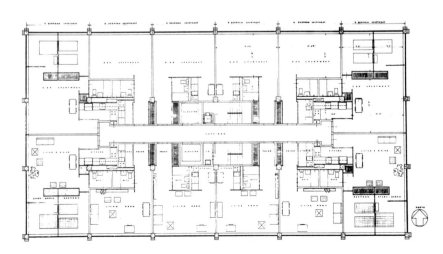

Lake Meadows 1950–60
31st, King Drive and 35th
Skidmore, Owings and Merrill

Lake Meadows was the first extensive residential urban renewal project financed by private resources. The decision of I.I.T. and Michael Reese Hospital to remain in their traditional locations and to help rebuild the blighted neighborhood around their facilities led to the formation of the South Side Planning Board. A broad plan was drawn up and the New York Life Insurance Company was induced to invest more than $35 million in the construction of ten high-rise apartment buildings containing 2,033 units of racially-integrated middle-income housing. A 100 acre (40.5 ha) site was acquired and cleared with the use of public funds. It was likewise "written-down," so that its cost was competitive with that of land in outlying areas. The municipal government took charge of relocating former residents, changing streets, and rezoning land use. The school board and park district installed educational and recreational facilities. The first of the buildings was completed in 1953, and the project was completed by 1960. Three types of buildings are sited on only 9 percent of the available land; the remainder is landscaped as a park.

Commonwealth Promenade
Apartments 1955–58
330 Diversey
Mies van der Rohe with Pace
Associates

2400 Lake View Apartments 1961–62
Fullerton at Lake View
Mies van der Rohe with Greenberg
and Finfer

While to the casual observer Mies's apartment towers may appear identical, a comparison of the two aluminum-clad projects overlooking Lincoln Park suggests the considerable variations possible within a given architectural concept.

The Commonwealth Promenade was originally meant to be a four-tower complex; the unfortunate death of Herbert Greenwald, Mies's friend and client as well as the project's developer, prevented that intention from being carried out.

In siting, plan and materials, the Commonwealth towers are almost identical to the two buildings comprising the 900 Lake Shore Drive Esplanade. Built at the same time, both

of four plumbing stacks within the apartment floor areas limits the ease with which individual dwellings may be altered in size. The lower nine floors contain one- and two-room units. Three-room units are located in the middle stories and on the top 12 floors, four- and five-room units. This allocation concentrates traffic in the lower stories, so that only one elevator is required for the upper 19 floors.

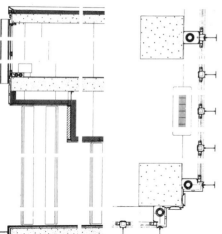

Prairie Shores 1958–62
2801–3001 King Dr.
Loebl, Schlossman and Bennett

The success of the I.I.T. campus expansion and the Lake Meadows redevelopment project resulted in a private investment of some $27 million in the Prairie Shores project adjacent to the Michael Reese Hospital. Five high-rise apartment buildings with over 1,200 dwelling units, plus a local shopping center and recreational facilities, occupy a site acquired and cleared with $6.2 million of public funds. The increased tax revenue of the renewed area will more than make up for that outlay.

groups are of flat-slab concrete construction. They were considered daringly tall for their time. In the lower floors rolled steel sections rather than rods were used for reinforcement. A special fabricating plant was built to produce the then-revolutionary aluminum facades, anodized in natural color at Commonwealth and in black at 900 Lake Shore Drive. Sections one column bay wide and one story high, complete with window frames and hardware, were transported to the sites, hoisted into place, and glazed.

By the time 2400 Lake View was built, techniques had advanced to the point that the entire 28-story skeleton could be built in conventional reinforced concrete construction. There the facade is of natural-color anodized aluminum and gray-tinted sun-control glass.

The rectangular column bays and nearly square floor plan in 2400 Lake View result in a U-shaped central corridor around an elevator/service core. Although partitions can be placed at any curtain wall mullion, the presence

Marina City 1963
300 N. State
Bertrand Goldberg

Like Harry Weese, Bertrand Goldberg is one of Chicago's leading architectural independents and, like another, Walter Netsch, he has developed a rather conscious and coherent, albeit personal, theory of architecture. Though as a young man Goldberg studied with Mies van der Rohe at the Berlin Bauhaus, he long ago abandoned the Miesian affection for the rectilinear frame in favor of organic shapes and curvilinear massing. Concrete is the medium in which he has done his most memorable buildings.

Yet in the best publicized of these, Marina City—not to mention in most of his other recent endeavors—Goldberg insists his working principle was the capacity of contemporary building technology to produce nearly every conceivable constructive form. Thus he claims identification with the Chicago tradition of technologically-derived architecture. Needless to say, in view of what looks like rhapsodic handling of form at Marina City, Goldberg's self-estimate is disputed by many Miesians, but just as obviously, Marina is a remarkable exercise in concrete structure, and it clearly takes its form, as Goldberg says it does, from the system that holds it up.

The system, as evident in the two cylindrical apartment towers that dominate the multi-part Marina complex, consists of a central concrete core in each tower, from which 60 circular floors are cantilevered outward and partially supported by a ring of peripheral columns. The lower elevation of each tower, equal to a height of 18 stories, is given over to a continuous helical ramp which serves as a parking garage for the occupants of the 40 stories of apartments above. (The remaining two stories house utilities.)

At the base of the towers is a plaza of several levels which features a marina, a shopping center, a skating rink and a restaurant. Directly adjacent is a ten-story structure housing offices, a bank and recreational facilities. A large theater building containing two cinemas and a television studio rounds out the Marina City complex.

These various components testify to the original purpose of Marina City, which was to provide a kind of residentially self-sufficient mini-city in the heart of downtown Chicago. Built on the north bank of the Chicago River at State Street, the project is eminently central and strikingly dramatic in its situation—both to the Loop pedestrian looking across the river at its spectacular towers, and to the apartment dweller who gazes out of them at a splendid panorama of surrounding Chicago.

Surely, Goldberg's effort is structurally daring enough to fall within the Chicago engineering tradition. The two apartment buildings were the tallest cylindrical structures ever erected at the time of their completion, 1962, and several of the functional advantages of their forms are worth recounting. The cylindrical plan implies a small building perimeter, a minimized wind load and consequent savings in materials costs. On the other hand, the wedge-shaped plans of the apartments have inspired complaints about an awkwardness in the allocation of parts. Marina's decor likewise has been criticized on grounds of an occasional tawdriness not necessarily excused by the low budget it otherwise so admirably exploits in structural aspect.

Raymond Hilliard Center 1964–66
South State and Cermak Road
Bertrand Goldberg

Built by the Chicago Housing Authority on a site most recently occupied by decayed housing and junk yards, the Hilliard Center is a grouping of five reinforced concrete structures. They house both elderly residents and younger families with children. The two 16-story towers, connected by a one-story community center, have compact wedge-shaped apartments reminiscent in plan of Marina City, a project designed by the same architect. The scale and layout of the Hilliard apartments, none of which is more than a few steps from the elevators, make them well suited to elderly dwellers. The two 22-story structures are composed of round-ended rectangular units arranged in a gently-curving arc.

The curved surfaces and oval window openings are expressions of the nature of reinforced concrete; the curves provide increased rigidity while the oval openings reduce the stresses around the punched voids.

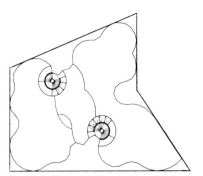

Glasshouse project, Mies van der Rohe, 1922

Lake Point Tower 1968
505 N. Lake Shore Drive
Schipporeit-Heinrich Assoc.
   (Graham, Anderson, Probst and
      White, associate architects)
   (William Schmidt and Assoc.,
      structural engineers)

The direct antecedents of this widely-acclaimed apartment tower are two projects for glass-walled buildings by Mies van der Rohe: a 1919 office building intended for Berlin's Friedrich-strasse, and a 1920–21 30-story sky-scraper, meant for a theoretical site. Both proposals were similar in con-cept: they were multi-storied flat-slab structures, non-rectangular in plan, and completely sheathed in glass. Mies discovered, while experimenting with glass models, that the play of re-flections, as opposed to the effect of light and shadow, could be a compel-ling formal device. Thus the prismatic facade of the first project was replaced by the curvilinear form of the second.

At the time Mies's proposals ap-peared, they were considered more revolutionary than prophetic; nearly 50 years passed before George C. Schip-poreit and John C. Heinrich—two young Chicago architects who had studied with Mies at I.I.T. before work-ing in his office—applied his concepts to a 70-story apartment structure.

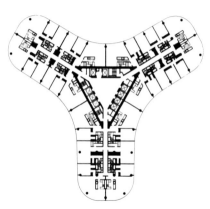

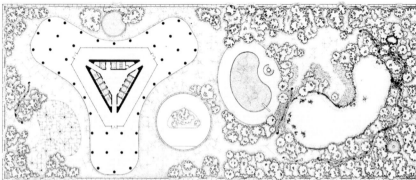

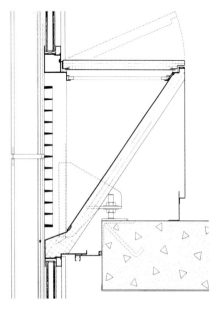

At the time of its construction, the 645-ft. (196 m) tower was the tallest apartment building as well as the tallest reinforced structure in the world. At its center is a triangular service core containing elevators, stairs and mechanical shafts. This core, which functions as a vertical tubular cantilever, has reinforced concrete walls varying in thickness from 4 ft. (1.20 m) at the base to 12 in. (30 cm) at the 59th floor. It absorbs all wind forces, and its triangular plan offers greater rigidity than would a rectangular section would in resisting horizontal bending and shear loads transmitted to it by the floor slabs. All vertical loads are sustained by the core, together with the round columns on the building's periphery.

On the bronze-anodized aluminum curtain wall, the spandrel panels are fitted with intake grills for the individually-controlled heating and air-conditioning units in each apartment. Continuous I-section mullions frame double-glazed windows with exterior panes of bronze-tinted sun control glass.

The building's three wings set on a 120 degree axis make it impossible for residents to look into neighboring apartments. Another consequence of this three-lobed floor plan is that no more than six apartments open onto a single hallway; the long corridors of conventional high-rise apartment buildings are eliminated. Each of the 880 dwelling units can be easily altered in size in the event of changing demands in the housing market.

The tower rises from a block-long, three-story base sheathed in dark brick, which contains public spaces, lobby and parking for 700 cars. A landscaped entrance to the lobby is placed beneath a circular light well that is open to a superbly-planted garden (designed by Alfred Caldwell) on the garage roof.

Although Lake Point Tower has been criticized for its siting on land that might otherwise have been entirely reserved for public use, the project is nevertheless a spectacular addition to Chicago's lakefront. On a clear evening, as each successive window bay of the undulating facade is lit by the rays of the setting sun, the building is transformed into a gleaming column of gold.

131

Edgewater Beach Apartments 1974
5555 N. Sheridan
Solomon, Cordwell, Buenz &
  Associates, Inc.
  (John Buenz)

This elegant apartment building, located on North Lake Shore Drive about eight miles from the Loop, is indebted to Lake Point Tower in both its shape and appearance. The architects, having packed the core with mechanical facilities and public spaces, decided to let the glass line of the surrounding dwelling units reflect the triangular core shape. An optimal outside view from all apartments is thus made possible. The handsome living-dining rooms of the two bedroom units are situated at the round tower corners. Two additional identical towers close by are planned for the near future.

Boardwalk Apartments 1974
4343 N. Clarendon
Stanley Tigerman

Several other intelligently designed projects of very recent vintage attest to the optimistic view of Chicago's residential future. The Boardwalk Apartments of Stanley Tigerman and Associates is situated on the edge of Uptown, a north side neighborhood which became, during the 1950s and 1960s, one of the more notorious dumping grounds for many of the city's poor displaced by the frequently disastrous urban renewal projects of those decades. Boardwalk is aimed at middle-income tenants, a fact indicative of Uptown's gradual revival in the early 1970s. At a cost of $15.96 per gross square foot, the building is a model of economy, a fact reflected aesthetically in a simple but sensitively proportioned modular reinforced concrete frame. Distributed over 28 stories are 450 dwelling units as well as a 270-car garage, commercial spaces, a restaurant, a swimming pool with bathhouse, a tennis court and a landscaped plaza deck.

Newberry Plaza 1975
State Street and Oak Street
Ezra Gordon and Jack M. Levin

Gordon and Levin are the designers of another multi-use residential and commercial complex in the heart of Chicago's near north entertainment district along State and Rush streets. The program included residential requirements that would satisfy families, young couples and singles, as well as mature couples desiring larger apartments. The solution took the form of a 56-story apartment reinforced concrete "point block" tower composed of 620 dwelling units, with the upper 12 floors allocated to larger, luxurious units. A base component was developed which comprised 60,000 sq. ft. of self-contained commercial office area around a three-story interior garden atrium with restaurants. Above a four level garage, a landscaped plaza with pool, sun deck and 15 three-story family townhouses completed the project. The structural system for the high rise is clear. Its exterior "punched hole" concrete frame, which is brought down via transfer girders and large columns over the lower floors, is reminiscent of the Brunswick Building.

Two blocks away on 100 East Walton Street the firm of Dubin, Dubin, Black and Moutoussamy has erected an apartment building which is a structural variation of the Newberry Plaza's closely spaced exterior column system.

Schools, Colleges and Universities

Philosophically, the architects of the first Chicago school were deeply rooted in the American democratic tradition. Louis Sullivan, in a sense the spokesman for the group, expressed the conviction that "if democracy could not produce a good architecture and art, it could not create a good life for its citizens." Sullivan believed the act of building carried profound moral implications. In this context, he considered it the goal of the democratic architect to "create community in which all men can live in dignity, freedom and the enjoyment of human brotherhood."

At the end of the nineteenth century, Chicago had—as it still has today—a large immigrant population. Ethnic groups from all over the world came here; many were obliged to settle in poor areas scattered throughout the city. It was only through their children that some minorities finally began to enter the mainstream of American life.

In theory, the public education system in America was organized on democratic principles of the highest order, and Chicago architects made a notable effort to design school buildings which reflected these values. Thus, instead of the austere and authoritarian institutions common to the old century, children were offered learning environments that were markedly more open, more humane and scaled more to the needs of the young.

Dwight H. Perkins
Born: 1867—Memphis, Tenn.
Died: 1941—Lordsburg, N.M.

Chicago's reputation as the American metropolis with the most progressive school buildings was established some 70 years ago, largely through the efforts of Dwight H. Perkins. In 1888, following two years of study at Massachusetts Institute of Technology, Perkins came to Chicago and joined the firm of Burnham and Root. He was placed in charge of that office from 1891 to 1893 when the senior partners were busy with preparations for the Columbian Exposition. In the year the Fair opened, he established his own practice.

In 1905, the Chicago Board of Education, which at that time was responsible for both the building and operation of the city's schools, appointed Perkins its chief architect. Although he held this position for only five years, he designed approximately forty new schools and additions during that period. In this work, his singular imaginative powers as an architect were revealed for the first time.

Carl Schurz High School 1909
3601 N. Milwaukee
Dwight H. Perkins

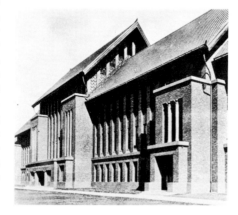

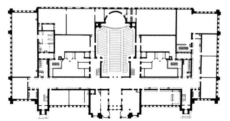

The Carl Schurz High School is Perkins' masterpiece. It was also one of the most modern schools of its time. Instead of compressing the plan into the rectangular shape of the traditional school, Perkins designed the building from the inside out. The result was a structure with two long wings on diagonal lines. Also novel was the architect's attempt to make the school a neighborhood center as well as an educational institution—a concept that is widely embraced in school design today.

Although relatively simple in organization and free of superfluous decoration, the exterior of the Schurz School is both dramatic and bold. Strong vertical piers, narrowly spaced, are counterbalanced by horizontal string courses and finally stopped by the wide eaves of the high pitched roof which dominates the entire structure. Equally striking is the color scheme: burnt red brick walls with light stone trim, topped by the softer red tile and green copper highlights of the roof. The building is also distinguished by its generous use of glass.

Grover Cleveland Elementary School 1910
3121 W. Byron
Dwight H. Perkins

Smaller in size than the Carl Schurz High School, the Grover Cleveland Elementary School is also more sober in appearance. Its exterior design is simple and powerful; basic forms are emphasized by subtle patterns in the brickwork. The composition is again based on the interplay of verticals and horizontals, although the points of juxtaposition are less dramatic here. Worthy of note are the parabolic capital blocks which produce an effective transition from the vertical pilasters to

the high horizontal parapet while at the same time echoing the string course between the first and second floors.

Perkins planned this school in the form of a short-stemmed T, thus providing maximum light and ventilation for each of the three nearly identical wings. The structure is also characterized by large window areas.

Crow Island School 1949
1112 Willow Road
Winnetka, Ill.
Eliel and Eero Saarinen; Perkins, Wheeler and Will

In both concept and form, the Crow Island School of Winnetka—a northern suburb of Chicago—marked a turning point in the city's history of school building. On the premise that a maximally comfortable atmosphere could promote the learning process, the architects created what was to become the prototype for the suburban pavilion school. Their point of departure was the individual classroom, designed so as to be usable for all grades and in various forms for different teaching methods. This flexibility was highly compatible with the school's new educational program, itself based on a departure from traditional methods of instruction that confined pupils to rigid rows of desks and stressed learning by repetition and memorization. In an effort to meet not only the emotional and intellectual, but also the physical

needs of children, the ceiling height was lowered from the standard 12 ft. (3.66 m) to a more intimate 9 ft. (2.74 m).

The building itself is a long, rectangular structure with three wings of classrooms extending from a central core of common facilities. Separate outdoor play areas are shared by pairs of classrooms.

The exterior design is exceedingly simple; interest is provided by the warm colors and contrasting textures of brick and wood and by the glazed ceramic sculpture set at intervals in the walls. Its child-oriented scale gives this school a unique and charming quality.

Public Buildings Commission

In 1968, the Chicago Board of Education turned the responsibility for school building over to the newly formed Public Buildings Commission and began leasing facilities from this organization. The Board was forced to take such a step because of its inability to solve the problems imposed upon it by the system of financing schools in America. Under this system funds for construction and operation of schools in a given area are derived from that area's real estate tax income. The inequities which this arrangement has produced are obvious. The central

cities have suffered from a reduction in tax revenues due to the flight of higher-income families to the suburbs. During recent years, the real estate tax income in Chicago rose 22 percent while school operation costs increased 123 percent.

The PBC, in conjunction with the Chicago Park District, set up a master plan for 26 school projects calculated to accommodate 38,000 pupils. The entire program was to be completed in a period of five years, and for the most part this timetable was adhered to. The total cost was approximately 200 million dollars. The project was an outstanding accomplishment in organization, planning and financing on a large scale—and its success made Chicago a noteworthy example to other large cities with similar school problems.

Jacques Brownson, chief designer of the Chicago Civic Center, was the PBC's head architect until early 1973. He took considerable pains to see to it that all new buildings avoided the rigid atmosphere so typical of older American schools. He sought to do this by replacing traditional cubicular classrooms with large spaces that could be organized in various ways by means of easily movable room dividers.

All school buildings designed as part of the PBC plan were done by private architects working within a framework

of common standards outlined by the Commission in a series of guideline documents. Special emphasis was placed on adjustment to the universal module of 5 x 5 ft. (1.52 m x 1.52 m). Maximum flexibility was another important requirement. In line with this, a realization of the concept of "The Lighted Schoolhouse"—that is to say, the school that also serves the community in the evenings as a neighborhood center—was an auxiliary goal of the program. The new schools were situated almost exclusively in marginal zones of the inner city.

If the PBC assignments were confining to the architects who received them, they were also challenging opportunities to create the kind of open "democratic" architecture called for by the leaders of the first Chicago school. The most striking result of the program as a whole, and a direct outcome of the Commission's decision to employ private architectural talent, was the multiplicity of solutions developed for basically identical problems. Although almost all the individual projects contain similar groups of units —usually a school building in conjunction with a sports center and/or various other specialized structures—stylistically they are separate and distinct —and often ingenious. Despite economic limitations, common standards and other constraints, some significant architecture grew out of the PBC program.

Almost from the time of its inception, there was debate between the proponents of compact multi-storied school buildings for the PBC program and the defenders of the suburban pavilion type with its large ground space requirements. The latter group argued that it was socially degrading to deny already underprivileged city children the advantages of landscaped suburban

schools.

The PBC's response to this argument over space requirements was to propose a plan which combined school building and park renovation. By constructing schools on public park land, it would be possible to avoid the removal of dwellings or the use of undesirable sites on traffic arteries. The Commission argued further that parks which had degenerated into unkempt and unsafe conditions might be upgraded by new schools that would also serve as community centers. Finally, they conceived provisions by which new "vest pocket" green areas elsewhere could be incorporated into the park system, so as to make up for land given over in older parks to school parking lots.

Despite such arguments in behalf of the use of traditionally untouchable free space for the new school building program, and despite the most significant argument, namely the right of children from low-income families to instruction in an optimal environment, the PBC proposal sparked a legal battle, waged on citizen initiative against the construction of schools in parks.

This issue went all the way to the Illinois Supreme Court. A set of guidelines was laid down under which the construction of schools might indeed be permitted on park land. As it turned out, three of the PBC projects were built in parks.

Sojourner Truth Primary School 1971
1409 N. Ogden
Fox & Fox

The first school opened under the PBC program was the Sojourner Truth Primary School, designed for 1,100 children. Added to it is Chicago's first pre-school facility for three and four year olds. The two units are in sepa-

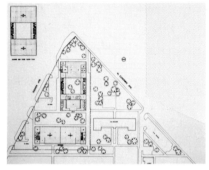

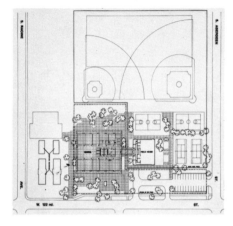

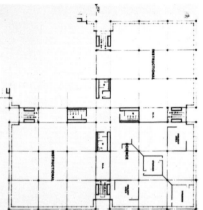

rate buildings situated on adjacent sites of 14,000 sq. ft. (1300 m²) and 9,100 sq. ft. (815 m²).

Both buildings are rectangular. The three-story primary school has a landscaped inner court; common facilities are located at the center of the long exterior walls. The nursery school is housed in a single story structure with core areas on the short sides. In both cases, the interior spaces can be variously arranged by means of dividing walls.

The steel skeleton construction of these buildings is fully revealed in the exterior design. Details are kept simple; good material coordination and the contrast between the black steel skeleton and the light filler panels of concrete block gives the structures distinction. This early project incorporates all the essential aims of the PBC plan.

Edward H. White Elementary School 1971
1130 W. 122
James A. Cronin & Associates

This small school, containing a kindergarten and eight grades for 300 children, is situated on the south edge of the city. An enclosed walkway connects the one-story school building to a gymnasium which is also available for public use. The architects have placed the common facilities in a central hall surrounded by large, variable instruction areas.

Left, Sojourner Truth Elementary School; *above,* Edward H. White Elementary School; *right,* Walt Disney Magnet School

Walt Disney Magnet School 1972
4140 N. Marine
Perkins & Will

The Walt Disney Magnet School is a center for educational experiments in the city. Although planned within the PBC guidelines, this three-story, L-shaped building has an innovative floor plan reminiscent of English university building models. Large square areas of approximately 8,000 sq. ft. (750 m²) are separated by perpendicular additive modules, 15 ft. (4.60 m) wide, which contain stairways, toilets and special rooms.

Dyett Middle School 1972
555 E. 51
David Haid

Because of its intended location in one of the old public parks laid out by Burnham, the Dyett Middle School was a source of controversy. It was strongly opposed by I.I.T. professors David Sharpe and Daniel Brenner, as well as by architects Harry Weese and Douglas Schroeder. (Weese and Schroeder had earlier developed a proposal for the rejuvenation of park areas by means of recreational facilities not connected with schools.) The PBC defended its position on grounds previously discussed plus the argument that the designated building site was occupied for the most part by an abandoned park road and dead trees. The school was eventually built there.

In a conscientious effort to design a complex which would use as little park land as possible, architect David Haid first explored the possibilities of multi-storied structures. He concluded, however, that high buildings would visually overwhelm the park. His final plan consisted of an instruction building, one and a half stories high when seen from the exterior, connected by an underground passageway to an adjacent athletic facility. By means of this hidden connection, Haid avoided the danger of fragmenting the park with too great a stretch of low-rise construction.

The Dyett Middle instruction building is 357 ft. (109 m) long and 240 ft. (73.40 m) deep with two interior courts from which its full two-story height is visible. The upper level contains the general instruction areas, labs and administrative offices; on the lower floor are the library, various special project facilities and faculty rooms which also serve as cafeterias. The main floor is completely column-free and can be subdivided into conventional classrooms or other desired space groupings, by means of easily movable dividers. Because the two stories were designed with identical support modules and ceiling heights, these same dividing walls can be used on the lower level. The courtyards are also available for nature study, conferences and discussions.

Haid organized the instruction building into four "learning houses," among which a total of 1,500 pupils is divided into smaller groups of 375. The school's team teaching program, which involves instruction by several teachers simultaneously and in varying group sizes, is ideally accommodated by the flexible floor plan.

The building itself is a large span structure. Its steel roof rests on columns, also of steel, which are located directly in front of the exterior walls and which straddle the reinforced concrete construction of the lower floor.

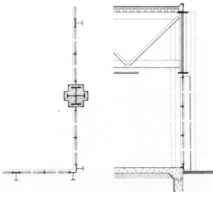

All heating, cooling and ventilating installations are located on the roof. The entire instruction building is equipped with a sprinkler system so that the size of class areas is not limited by fire code regulations.

The adjacent athletic building is divided into three areas along the lines indicated by the main interior columns. The gymnasium is in the central section, adjoining the entryway. This section also contains toilets and peripheral traffic areas. On one side are a grandstand, dressing rooms and showers; on the other, a grandstand and dressing rooms plus a swimming pool and sun terrace. After school hours, these facilities are made available to the community through an independent entrance.

The athletic building is also a large span construction. It has a height of 23 ft. (7.02 m) and is spanned by four plate girders with a support width of 70 ft. (21.35 m) and cantilevers of 30 ft. (9.15 m) on each side. Perpendicular to these lie truss girders of equal height and a 100 ft. (30.50 m) span width. Only the eight massive main columns had to be clad in concrete.

This cladding was made with irretrievable form work of sheet steel—an external expression of the internal structural material.

The two buildings of the Dyett Middle School are identical in module and detail. Their dark, well proportioned, fully glazed facades have a quality of transparency that allows them to fit unobtrusively into the restored park landscape.

Transition

Two PBC schools by the Mies van der Rohe office, designed after Mies's death in 1969, are characterized by a clear expression of skeleton construction. Both the new Roberto Clemente High School and the new Orr High School have steel frames clad in concrete. Both likewise feature square

structural bays. The columns are painted flat black; between them are unrecessed brick panels of varying heights and steel framed windows with relatively small panes. The frames of these schools and their terse expressive austerity place them closer to the earlier Miesian manner of the I.I.T. buildings, 860–880 Lake Shore Drive and the Promontory Apartments.

Orr and Clemente are identical in concept. Each has a compact instruction building of relatively great depth and a separate athletic building which is shared with the public. The floor plans are firmly fixed in comparison with those of the PBC schools previously discussed. Classrooms are concentrated in the exterior zones with a maximum depth of 30 ft. (9.15 m); the central area contains commonly shared facilities and small special rooms.

Roberto Clemente High School 1974
Division & Western
Fujikawa, Conterato, Lohan
   (Dirk Lohan, partner in charge)

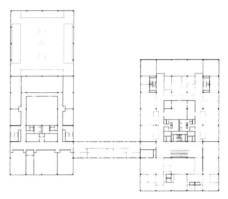

Like the Dyett Middle School, Roberto Clemente High School sparked public controversy. Its nine-story instruction building, designed to accommodate 3,000 students and still leave open space on the site, was regarded by some as much too tall for a high school.

Since West Division Street transects the Clemente site between the instruction and athletic buildings, the two structures are connected by an elegant steel bridge of open web trusses. The bridge is two stories high and has the width of one complete bay—30 ft. (9.15 m)—with service rooms on one side. Additional instruction space was provided in the athletic building in the form of an upper story which contains classrooms and other special rooms.

The ground floor of the instruction building is taller than the other stories. It corresponds in height both to the first floor of the athletic building and to the dimension necessary for bridge clearance over West Division Street. Thus, the structures are organized into a clearly scaled group by a device which at the same time enhances the appearance of the taller building.

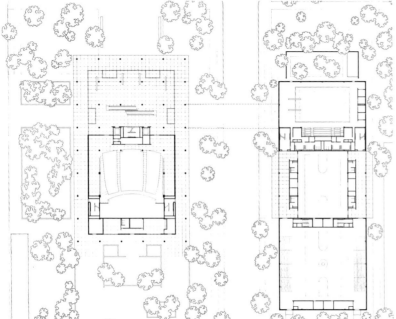

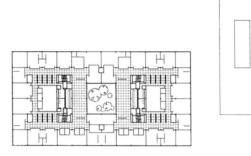

Above. Roberto Clemente High School; *right,* Orr High School

Orr High School 1974
750 N. Pulaski
Fujikawa, Conterato, Lohan
  (Dirk Lohan, partner in charge)

The new Orr High School, which houses 2,000 students, is a smaller, three-story structure connected to a separate athletic building only at the lower level. The ground floor of the instruction building is used entirely for interior facilities, with an auditorium and two music rooms in the central area. Above this section on the top floor is a small inner courtyard.

The new Orr High School reveals a close affinity with the philosophy which lay behind I.I.T. This is most noticeable in the relationship of the buildings to each other, and to the open space provided around them.

Farragut High School (Addition) 1971
2345 S. Christiana
Wendell Campbell and John Macsai

The Farragut High School addition is a single volume attached to an already existing structure. Prior to its renovation, old Farragut was a rather typically antiquated Chicago school, its earliest parts dating from 1894 and 1907. These portions were demolished to make room for the new building, which is connected by a two-level light bridge to the one remaining older element, constructed in 1927. Space, or the limitation thereof, was thus a factor in suggesting the compactness of the new unit. Property lines to the north, east and west, not to mention a modest budget, necessitated a simple, four-story prism, which is organized nonetheless to accommodate a wide range of functions. The auditorium, gymnasium and music department on the first floor share a common lobby, which likewise features an independent entrance meant to serve the community. Since the auditorium and gymnasium require a two-story height but only a portion of the floor plan, the balance of the second floor is given to lounge and dining facilities. The latter in turn are related to dining areas located in the bridge and oriented toward both the new and the old buildings. The third and fourth floors consist of academic spaces, a learning resource center and student lounges. The entire package is enclosed in a modular steel frame, stern but well-proportioned, and structurally characteristic of the majority of new Chicago school buildings.

Whitney M. Young Magnet High School 1971
211 S. Laflin
The Perkins & Will Partnership

The Whitney M. Young Magnet High School is one of the more architecturally dramatic efforts to upgrade educational facilities in the inner city. It sits on a two-square-block site split by Jackson Boulevard, a little less than two miles west of the Loop—in other words, in an area that has suffered mightily from the acute urban miseries of the past decade. The architects, Perkins and Will, have filled this area with a fine arts unit to the south (adjacent to parking and green space) and a pair of structures on the north, one devoted to academic activities, the other to physical education. A facility equal to the needs of 650 hearing-impaired students (from among the total student body of 2650) is located in the first floor of the academic unit, while the comparable level of the fine arts building is devoted to music, theater, painting, sculpture and the graphic arts. Such priorities of function are considerably more daring than traditional among schools in the poor areas of big cities.

Young is no less forceful in its architectural aspect: its three steel-framed structures are connected by enclosed truss bridges that lend a powerful scale to exterior and interior alike. This boldness is echoed in the massive, exposed girders that roof over the swimming pool of the physical education building. To all this it is worth adding that Young reflects the long connection between the latest chapter in the history of school design in Chicago and one of its more celebrated earlier ones. The Perkins and Will partnership can be traced back to Dwight Perkins, architect of the Schurz and Cleveland schools.

Percy Julian High School 1975
10330 S. Elizabeth
Skidmore, Owings and Merrill
   (Myron Goldsmith, design partner
   David Sharpe, senior architect)

Visibly related to the Young School in both plan and scale is Percy Julian High School on the far south side, a product of SOM, with Myron Goldsmith in supervising capacity. Again, three box-like units there are divided among athletic, arts and academic functions. One of the most distinctive architectural features of Julian is the three-story lobby of the academic building: a vast and generous space whose great glass wall vividly reveals the steel frame which unifies the constructive form of the whole complex.

Wendell Smith Elementary School 1974
744 E. 103
Arthur Takeuchi

Compared with these three multi-part schools from the 1970s, Arthur Takeuchi's Wendell Smith Elementary School is simpler and more direct in design, but easily the equal in quality of any structure erected during the eight year history of the PBC program.

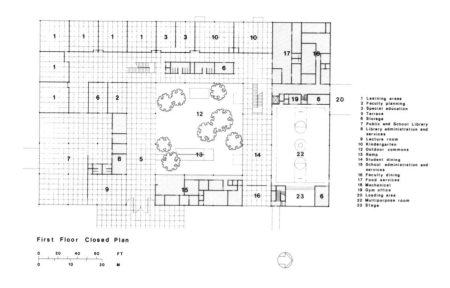

First Floor Closed Plan

```
0    20    40    60    FT
0     10        20     M
```

1 Learning areas
2 Faculty planning
3 Special education
4 Terrace
5 Storage
6 Storage
7 Public and School Library
8 Library administration and services
9 Lecture room
10 Kindergarten
11 Outdoor commons
13 Ramp
14 Student dining
15 School administration and services
16 Faculty dining
17 Food services
18 Mechanical
19 Gym office
20 Loading area
22 Multipurpose room
23 Stage

New Waller Elementary School 1976 (project)

W. Armitage and N. Burling
James Mitropoulos
Advisors: Prof. Peter C. Pran
        Prof. George Hinds
            with assisting advisors
        Lecturer Peter Roesch
        Prof. Louis Rocah
Dept. of Arch., Univ. of Illinois,
Chicago Circle

This proposal for a new near north side elementary school for 750 students, shows a discipline in its design as well as a richness in its spatial approach. While a 30 x 30 ft. (9.14 x 9.14 m) bay steel structure, with round columns, is used systematically throughout, the entries, walkways, interior courts and classrooms are treated in an informal and gentle way which would make it a pleasant place for smaller children. A 45-degree wall opens up the main entry and leads people in, while another opening to the north connects the interior court with a public park.

It is a single long, two-story prism with immense amounts of horizontally paned wall glass laid between wide bays. The construction consists of a unified system of steel truss girders and joists supported by standard fire-resistant pipe columns. In the center of this ground-hugging box is an open court, which functions as both a thoroughfare and an arena for outdoor activity. Its most arresting formal feature is a hairpin ramp which connects the lower with the upper level. Like the rest of the building, it is a model of open frame steel construction, which Takeuchi has used to dramatize the leanness and lightness of his overall design. All the customary components of an urban grade school—plus a branch of the Chicago Public Library—are economically contained within this simple format.

Transition: Colleges

In view of ever-increasing educational expectations, rising birthrates and the growing significance of trade schools offering intermediate degrees as alternatives to today's overcrowded universities, many new colleges for various age levels have appeared in Chicago and its environs during the past decade. These have been built either on a community basis, by the counties or the state of Illinois or else on private initiative. In the city of Chicago, the public colleges are operated by the "City Colleges of Chicago," a corporation in its own right.

Malcolm X College 1971
1900 W. Van Buren
C. F. Murphy Associates
(Gene Summers)

Malcolm X College is located two miles west of the Loop on a spacious site along the Eisenhower Expressway. This training institution, operated by the state of Illinois, includes a two-year junior college program with optional hygiene and child care courses. In addition to a child care center, speech and theater courses, sporting events and career-oriented evening courses are offered to the population of the surrounding area.

Such an extensive program—designed for 10,000 students—had to be housed in a single compact block if open space was to be provided on the site. Two interior courts located on the third level also provide areas for recreation. The auditorium, sports facilities, library and student community rooms are made available to the public outside of school hours.

The project demanded a thoughtful planning and execution in both interior layout and exterior design. The

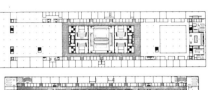
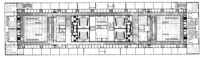
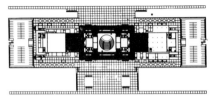
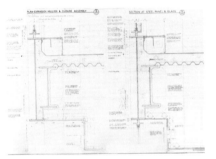
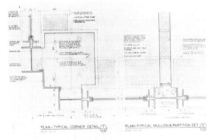

facades consist of a novel, uninsulated curtain wall made of seamless welded steel sections. These run evenly past the columns lying behind them. The building reveals its structure in the rows of columns encircling the ground level.

All steel structural elements are painted flat black; the spaces between these are of brick masonry. The scale of the building is unbroken—consist-

143

ent to the last detail. Its uniformly organized structure and horizontal emphasis may seem forbidding at first; yet the arcades surrounding the ground floor, the articulation of outdoor spaces and entry areas, and the two interior courts produce a pleasant and inviting atmosphere.

The Loop College Competition

In 1969 the Loop College hired The Office of Mies van der Rohe and J. W. Sih & Associates, engineers, to develop a proposal for a new facility. A site at the corner of Wabash and Lake was selected, for which a 20-story new Loop College building was designed by Dirk Lohan, partner in charge at the Mies firm. The land was bought in 1971, and the design presented publicly in November 1972. But the state government had decided to freeze capital expenditures from the fall of 1972. No money was made available for the new Loop College until 1974. Early that year Governor Daniel Walker's administration announced its own plans for a new Loop College and a state office building, with the intent to use these buildings to revitalize the Loop. In June 1974, the Capital Development Board invited 150 real estate developers, architects, and citizen groups to propose sites for the new Loop College. From the different suggestions that were received, five were chosen for the final selection. These included the schemes by **Solomon, Cordwell, Buenz & Associates** for a block bounded by Congress, State, Jackson and Plymouth Court; **Dirk Lohan**'s project at the corner of Wabash and Lake; the **Chicago Chapter, AIA**'s proposal for recycling the Old Colony Building and adding the new building at State and Congress (**Walker Johnson,** designer); **Stanley Tigerman**'s riverbank proposal; and the **Landmark Preservation Council**'s sug-

Above from top, Office of Mies van der Rohe, Stanley Tigerman; *right from top,* Chicago Chapter, AIA, Landmark Preservation Council, Solomon, Cordwell, Buenz

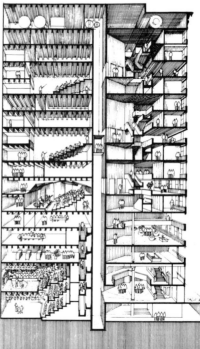

gestion to renovate and use the Marquette Building (**Thomas Welch,** designer). In January of 1975, Mayor Daley with City Colleges Chancellor Oscar Shabat and the State Street Council, announced that the City of Chicago had selected the first-mentioned of these sites. Later, the CDB announced that they also preferred that site, and then proceeded to choose **Solomon, Cordwell, Buenz & Associates** as the architects for the new Loop College.

Du Page College 1974
22nd & Lambert Rd.
Glen Ellyn, Ill.
C. F. Murphy Associates
(Stanislav Gladych)

Although Du Page College (unlike the inner city projects above) is located in a prosperous suburban area, the architects had a similar goal of integrating college with community by means of shared facilities. The library, athletic facilities, theater and meeting rooms are all open to the public.

The school's program includes a wide variety and scope of instruction, including trade courses, a two-year junior college, adult education classes, job counseling and cultural activities. A building program was developed based on a maximum of 12,000 to 13,000 students. Construction began on a 272 acre (110 ha) site in 1973, with a classroom building, teaching center and administration building rounding out the first of these phases. The second phase, scheduled for 1978, will feature a college center and athletic building. The last phase, in 1980, will include an additional classroom building and a theater. The execution of the later stages can be adapted to actual needs and financial conditions prevailing at the time.

Murphy's design concept, while based on current trends in university planning, is more specifically determined by Du Page's particular situation. In order to meet the requirement of extensive interaction between the various teaching areas, the campus has been laid out according to function rather than academic departments, with great importance laid on flexibility in the use of the individual buildings. In the center of the grouping are the classrooms and laboratories, with a direct connection to the six variously-sized lecture halls in the teaching center and to the dining hall, stores and student lounges in the College Center. The theater and the athletic facilities, easily reached by the general public, as well as a small administration building, are also placed within direct access by means of the covered pedestrian passage in the ground floor. Above this are the individual buildings, each perceptable as a separate structure, but connected by interior courts. Emphasis is placed on ease of communication between students and faculty and among the students themselves, so in addition to lounge areas for use during breaks, the faculty offices, in groups of six sharing an adjacent workroom, are dispersed throughout the school.

Since the school is situated in a suburban residential area, massive, institutional-appearing buildings have been avoided and care has been given to the integration of the structures into the park-like surroundings. The athletic building has been sunk into the ground to minimize its considerable size, and parking places for faculty have been provided on the ground floor of the connector buildings. Student parking, necessary because of the absence of mass transit facilities, is placed sufficiently far from the school buildings to avoid traffic disturbances.

The buildings themselves, above the ground floor connector structure, are all to be of self-oxydizing Cor-Ten steel with gold-toned sun-screen glass. This highly reflective glazing will mirror the surrounding landscape, further increasing the integration of structure and site.

Thornton Community College 1971
50 W. 162
South Holland, Ill.
Fitch, Larocca, Carington, Jones
**   (Michael Gelick, design director)**

This project was first of a two phase building program for a community college located on a Midwestern prairie site, which will serve a total number of 5,000 day and 10,000 evening students.

The community college maintains the following educational programs: academic, general, occupational, adult and continuing education as well as community service. The design solution is a concentrated continuous structure linked to the site with berms and ramps. Its linear form makes additions possible at both ends. Special functions can be added along the east or west face. The main artery of interior circulation is an undulating student street which links the library, lecture halls, counseling center, student center, engineering, technology and physical education facilities at the lower levels with classrooms, laboratories, and offices at the upper levels.

The structure is an exposed reinforced concrete frame (poured in place) with 3 ft. (1 m) post-tensioned beams running in the east/west axis, and concrete slabs running in the north/south axis. The bay is regular in the north/south axis with a span of 17 ft. 4 in. (5.3 m) and varies in the east/west axis from an exterior dimension of 26 ft. (8 m) to an interior dimension of 52 ft. (16 m). Structural supports, mechanical shafts, vertical circulation and rest rooms are contained in alternate bays, thus insuring flexibility in

the interior lofts. Cantilevers of 8 ft. 8 in. (2.6 m) can be built on either east/west or north/south edges.

U.S. Navy Technical Training Building
**   1975 (project)**
Great Lakes
Holabird & Root
**   (Jerry Horn)**

This well-planned school building has a highly refined exterior expression adjusted to the functional and technical requirements of the program. The Technical Training Building is divided

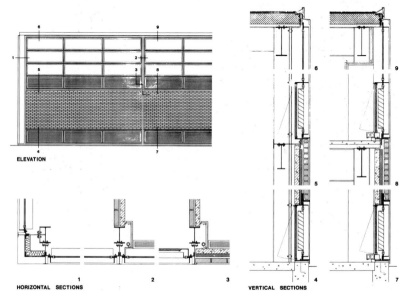

ELEVATION

HORIZONTAL SECTIONS

VERTICAL SECTIONS

into two schools, Radar (OS) Training and Engineman's (EN) Training. The separation of the two schools—a requirement specified by the Navy—is achieved by a common corridor on the first floor. Both schools are organized on a 5 x 5 ft. (1.5 x 1.5 m) module with full-height demountable partitions functioning as room dividers. Rooms are made flexible, varying from 20 ft. (6 m) to 50 ft. (15 m) in width. The building corridors are set up in a closed loop configuration to provide optimum flexibility of the modular walls. Lighting and air supply systems are arranged in an even pattern which allows adequate light and air supply in various rooms without requiring the rearrangement of fixtures or air boots. The exterior cladding is a shop fabricated demountable steel frame system with over-sized brick or glass infill. All louver areas on the exterior are operable for natural ventilation, allowing the exterior mechanical zones to be shut down during certain months of the year.

U.S. Marine Training Center 1952–54
Great Lakes
Skidmore, Owings & Merrill
(William Priestley)

William Priestley, who worked with Mies in Berlin during the 1930s, was the supervising architect of this facility. It is a school building of steel long span construction that suggests comparison with some of Albert Kahn's industrial factories. All structural elements here disappear behind a translucent curtain wall of blue-tinted heat absorbing glass. On the long facade the load-bearing members project slightly, clearly indicating bay size. On the short facade it is not the bay size but the stiffening members of the free-standing facade that are discernible. Such detailing of a facade is closer to

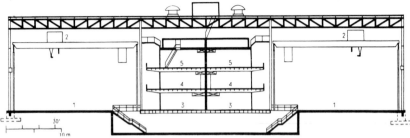

that employed by Kahn's office during the 1930s than to the strong emphasis on expression of structure found in Mies's early facades at I.I.T.

Universities

Northwestern University

The first building on the Northwestern Campus, dating from 1855, was a frame building with six classrooms, a chapel, a museum, two auditoriums, some dormitory rooms and a bell tower. Various structures in a variety of styles followed, dominated by the neo-Gothic common to the Ivy League schools of the East.

In the early 1960s the University determined that it could expand its lakeshore campus only by means of landfill; to have acquired ground in the prosperous residential neighborhood

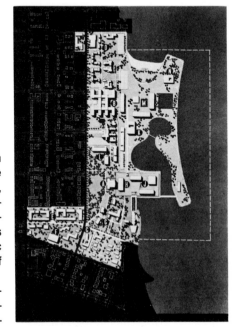

to the west would have removed more property from the community's tax roles, and would have been prohibitively expensive.

Skidmore, Owings and Merrill received the commission to create a master plan for the new land in 1961. Although SOM did erect several individual buildings, their total concept for the area was unfortunately not followed.

Lindheimer Astronomical Research
Center 1967
Skidmore, Owings and Merrill
(Walter Netsch, design partner)

Built at the northeast corner of the new landfill, this structure achieves a commendable unity of expression despite considerable diversity of individual components.

A white-painted tetrhadral framework of steel tubing supports two observation domes. A two-story bridge connects these domes to each other and to the elevated instrument rooms below. Within the sheet metal cladding of the elevators and stairways leading up through the open framework to

these rooms are the separate concrete foundations for the telescopes themselves.

The framework offers the least possible surface for wind load and a minimum expansion and contraction due to temperature change.

Core and Research Library 1969
Skidmore, Owings and Merrill
(Walter Netsch, design partner)

Grouped around a plaza and connected to old Deering Library, the pavilions of the Core and Research Library reflect in their form the radial arrangement of the book stacks within them. Both units make use of the same

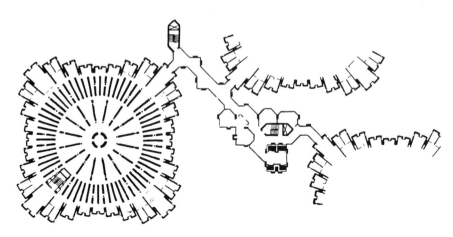

The University of Chicago

By a national standard, Chicago's colleges and universities are young. Among the schools here with substantial academic standing, only Northwestern University and Lake Forest College are older than the University of Chicago, which was founded as late as 1892. Under the leadership of its first president, William Rainey Harper, and aided by $5 million in capital, the

catalog, administration and circulating desk facilities, but each contains collections for specific academic disciplines. In turn, each discipline has its own central reading area and study carrels.

The exterior architectonic expression of the interior function has been the subject of much discussion. Built before Netsch fully developed the "field theory" underlying some of his later buildings at Chicago Circle Campus. This library complex is generally regarded as functionally efficient, although some architectural critics have held that it lacks the unified plasticity of his later work.

School of Social Service
Administration 1963–64
Mies van der Rohe

Though nearly concealed by the thick foliage of the Midway, this low-lying structure contrasts impressively with its rather pretentious neighbors.

Its interior spaces, organized into split-level floors with a strong axial focus, contains classrooms, a library, seminar and office spaces in addition to a multi-purpose entrance area of unusually elegant proportions. This centrally-placed one-and-one-half story space, with a clear ceiling height of 18 ft. (5.80 m), can accommodate 300 to 400 people for meetings, assemblies and exhibitions. A central core, panelled in walnut, separates this hall from the library, and on either side stairs

University of Chicago quickly achieved a reputation for progressive education that it maintains today.

The campus, designed at the time of the 1893 World's Fair by Henry Ives Cobb, was based on English prototypes. The limestone buildings in neo-Gothic style were grouped around large quadrangles. Individually, these edifices tend to be rather pedestrian; as a whole, however, they possess an admirable unity of mood and scale.

After World War II style was abandoned, and a series of new buildings was erected, most of them on the south side of the Midway Plaisance (site of the Columbian Exposition's amusement park). Commissions were granted to various architects of note. The result was a kind of architectural gallery similar to that found at Harvard and Yale. But with the possible exception of a single building by Mies van der Rohe, none of the structures achieve the high standards found on those two East Coast campuses.

lead up and down to the mezzanine floors.

Cruciform steel columns, of four wide-flange welded sections, are subtly differentiated on the facade from the mullions of like section, in that the mullions stop short of foundation and fascia rim. Large expanses of glass maximize visibility from within and without.

University of Illinois at Chicago Circle
1965
Mostly by Skidmore, Owings & Merrill
(Walter Netsch, design partner)

This is one of the few completely new urban university campuses in the country, and it is built from one bold, innovative and unifying concept. Comprising 106 acres (ca. 43 ha) with an academic core of some 40 acres, the intensively developed complex is situated just southwest of Chicago Circle —the junction of the Kennedy, Eisenhower and Dan Ryan expressways. Such a site, possible only with the intervention of municipal land clearance and public funds, offers ease of access by car and by public transportation.

In the first two phases of construction, buildings were designed to serve functions rather than disciplines. Within this concept, specific classroom buildings, laboratory buildings, and high-rise office buildings were constructed, rather than the more traditional mixed-use buildings. This permitted maximum flexibility in the reassignment of spaces, especially in view of rapid initial expansion of faculty and student enrollments, and tentative educational programs.

Undergraduate instructional facilities which generate mass movement of students in short periods between classes, and are therefore not adaptable to elevator traffic, were located

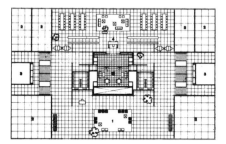

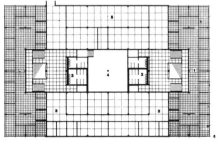

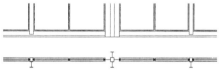

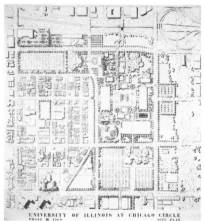

UNIVERSITY OF ILLINOIS AT CHICAGO CIRCLE
PHASE III 1969 SITE PLAN

in three- and four-story walk-up buildings. Faculty studies, administrative offices and other facilities generating a smaller and more evenly distributed flow of traffic were housed in high-rise buildings. The tallest structure is the dramatic 28-story administration building, University Hall, which offsets the strong horizontal thrust of the overall plan.

In the third phase of construction, three mixed-use, interdisciplinary buildings were constructed: the Science and Engineering Research Center, south of the campus core; the Behavioral Science Building, west of the faculty office building; and the Edu-

cation and Communications Building, northwest of the central campus.

Each of these new centers is linked to the central campus area by extension of the raised walkway system. At Circle Campus, common facilities shared by all departments are located in a tightly-knit center, thus encouraging social interaction among people from all disciplines, with more specialized facilities remaining at the perimeter. At the hub of the campus is a raised plaza, connected by a central amphitheatre to the Lecture Center below. The latter, which contains 21 lecture halls, is flanked by the Library and the Student Union Building.

Walter Netsch's "field theory" approach was used in the Architecture and Art Building, the Behavioral Science Center and the Science and Engineering Research Center. These "fields" are generated by superimpos-

ing one grid on another at a 45 degree angle and then developing spaces from that module.

The geometry of these Circle Campus buildings is highly disciplined and

the resultant forms and spaces have both variety and beauty. Within the fields the structural grid is clearly worked out.

Skidmore, Owings, and Merrill, Chicago, were the architects/engineers for the following Chicago Circle Buildings: lecture center, library, science and engineering laboratory building, staff office building, architecture and art laboratories, classroom buildings, science and engineering research center, behavioral sciences building and plant research building.

Other architectural firms and their involvements include: Harry M. Weese and Associates, the Physical Education Building and the Education and Communications Building; C. F. Murphy and Associates, the Student Union Building; Epstein and Company, the Physical Services Building.

An Urban University 1967 (project)
Dorman D. Anderson
Advisors: Prof. Myron Goldsmith
Prof. Fazlur Khan
Dept. of Arch., I.I.T.

This is a study in the architectural ordering of the spatial requirements for an urban university. The single structure is planned to contain 6¾ million square feet (627,320 m²) of academic and support facilities and is intended to serve between 37,500 and 45,000 students, depending upon the proportion of graduate students and the curriculum offered.

The value of such a large institution is the extensive range of programs and personnel which are readily accessible to the students and faculty. This project was developed on the basis that a university should be a unified academic community, not a grouping of departments housed in separate buildings. A compact single structure would allow pedestrian circulation between

the extreme edges of the "campus" within 10 minutes.

As the scale of a university grows, clear organization of the campus becomes increasingly important in order to assure physical accessibility. In this project the circulation system is an ordered hierarchy of spaces which converge on the central exhibition space. A large, glass-roofed volume is the focal point which provides the needed visual orientation within the university.

The structural system is a series of 120-foot-square (36.5 m square) bays spanned by a two-way, post-tensioned concrete grid. The project is planned for construction in three phases.

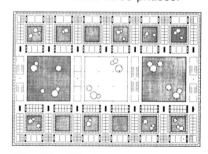

Architecture in the Chicago Region

Until World War II the industrial and commercial architecture built in the region immediately around Chicago was almost uniformly lackluster and thoughtless. Exceptions to this generalization—Solon S. Beman's Pullman shops, the several factories of Albert Kahn, plus some anonymous vernacular architecture (bridges, grain elevators and the like)—only serve to underscore the truth of it.

It remained for designers associated with the second Chicago school to produce a significant number of distinguished structures in the outlying districts. A number of these are worthy of comparison with the best works downtown.

O'Hare International Airport
1963 and on
C. F. Murphy Associates
  Terminals (Stanislav Gladych)
  Restaurants (Gertrude Kerbis)
  Hotel (John Novack)
  Garage (Stanislav Gladych)

Control Tower
I. M. Pei & Associates
  (James I. Freed)

The year 1963 marked the opening of O'Hare Airport, later O'Hare International Airport, a facility which Chicago constantly, proudly—and accurately—boasts is the world's busiest. Principally the product of C. F. Murphy and Associates, O'Hare is a vast enterprise comprising dozens of structures large and small alike, virtually every one of them designed in homage to the Chicago, specifically the Miesian, tradition. At the time of its opening, Mies's influence was at its crest, and O'Hare's ubiquitous rectangular frames, expressed in steel, concrete and glass, attest vigorously to this.

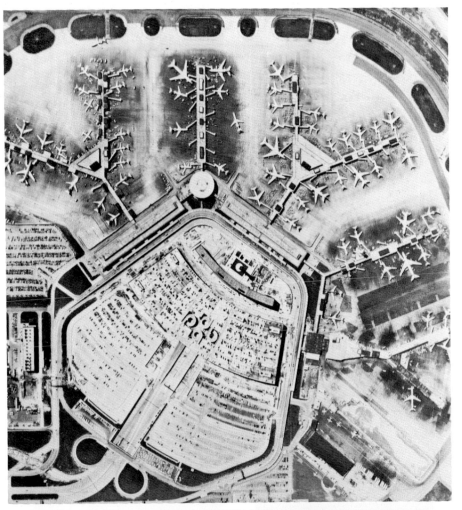

The original Murphy plan is mostly though not yet fully realized. It is meant to consist eventually of three long rectangular domestic terminal buildings ranged in a half-hexagon around a parking area, a portion of which is to be occupied by a hotel and a parking garage. The terminals will be linked by a pair of cylindrical restaurant buildings. A new international terminal is scheduled to replace the present one, which in turn will give up its location to one of the domestic terminals. Two tubes of the Chicago subway will be carried out to O'Hare, running directly beneath the Kennedy Expressway.

Among all these components, those remaining to be built are one of the domestic terminals, one of the restaurant structures, the subway extension and the international terminal (the last of these is intended for the northeast corner of the airport). Just about all the rest of O'Hare is constructed by now, and to the eye the master plan is nearly as readable as it is coolly logical. It is meant to be trafficked by pedestrians, and hardy ones at that; flight connections require traversal on foot rather than reliance on the shuttle bus systems common to most other large airports. This fact has been reasonably cited as a drawback at O'Hare, although it is counterbalanced by a clarity of traffic patterns and a freedom from the frequent capriciousness of shuttle transportation.

The architecture of the airport is clean, spare, simple and, in its best passages, as admirable as anything achieved by the second Chicago school. The domestic terminal interiors, long, wide, high and column-free, are rather magnificent spaces, and the deference to Miesian principles which is evident throughout the rest of the airport makes for an impressive cohe-

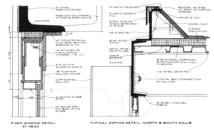

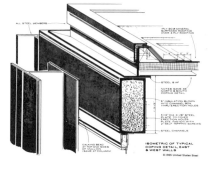

United Airlines Education & Training Center 1960–70
Elk Grove, Ill.
Skidmore, Owings & Merrill
(Myron Goldsmith, senior designer; Bruce J. Graham, partner in charge)

"On a raw industrial tundra northwest of Chicago, a few miles from O'Hare Field, the low sweeping frame of the new United Airlines headquarters building stands, white and calm and powerful, its great grid effortlessly spanning 66-foot bays with tremendous horizontal emphasis. This impersonal monument of (post-tensioned) concrete belongs to its own epoch with the same rational confidence as the jets flying overhead. It could have been created at no other time, and perhaps in no other place: its plain, virile strength springs from the vigor of Chicago today." Allan Temko in *Architectural Forum,* May 1962

The impression created by the buildings could scarcely be better described today. It was Goldsmith's and Graham's task, with designer James Ferris

siveness among the various parts. The gently concave hotel facade, nine stories high and 720 ft. (220 m) long, has the grace and elegance appropriate to its function as a hostelry, while the heating and refrigeration plant nearby is a maximally simple celebration of the immense machinery within it. Yet structurally the two buildings are broth-

ers, just as the frankness of expression in the alternating bands of concrete and steel that mark the exterior of the massive, 7000-car parking garage keep that building in the same stylistic family.

Stanislav Gladych was the chief designer of the terminals, the heating and refrigeration plant and the garage. Ger-

trude Kerbis was principally responsible for the restaurant buildings and John Novack for the hotel.

The handsome, sculptural control tower was designed by another architectural firm, I. M. Pei of New York, with James I. Freed as partner in charge of design.

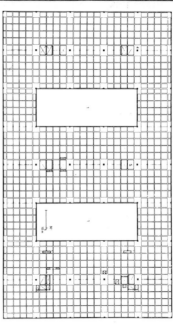

assisting, to provide a maximally economical and flexible office space for one of America's largest airlines. They managed this task so well, both functionally and visually, that within the following eight years SOM received the commission for two large extensions to the project.

The site, in the midst of a suburban sprawl of residential and light industrial development, is park-like in its landscaping. The first building phase included a two-story, 700 ft. (213 m) long administration building and a two-story training center. At the end of the 1960s an eight-story high rise for the training of stewardesses and management personnel was added, while a two-story annex to the administration building was erected across an access road and connected by means of a second story bridge. The depth of the first

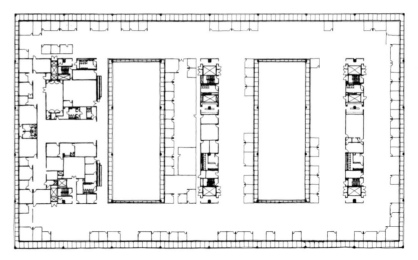

administration building, with its immense 66 ft. (20.12 m) bays, made necessary three interior light courts, to provide natural illumination. Here, as on the exterior, the glass facade is placed well back from the columns. The floors and roof, of coffered flat-slab construction, have post-tensioned ribs at intervals of 12 ft. (3.66 m). A modular ceiling is suspended from the slabs and carries the movable interior partitions. The white concrete skeleton, white ceiling, and coordinated gray partitions create a calm, orderly, yet not austere, atmosphere. The transparency of the exterior and courtyard walls permits a visual connection between site and courtyard planting.

In his *Architectural Forum* article (May 1962), Allan Temko further writes: "UAL's principal designer is 43-year-old Myron Goldsmith of SOM's Chicago office, an architect/engineer who may well prove to be the master of his generation. Goldsmith indeed may be one of the first of the artist-scientists foreseen by Pier Luigi Nervi as the 'builders of a new physical order of civilization': men who have so mastered structure that they can express it intuitively, as poets do language."

**United Airlines Reservation Center
1971–72
Elk Grove, Ill.
Graham, Anderson, Probst and White**

The internal arrangement of this reservation control center evolved from a careful analysis of the interaction between personnel and communications equipment. Because the Center is located in a flood plain, communications modules were installed in the second story around a core containing a control center office, conference room and toilets. The ground floor contains administration offices, employees cafe-

Project by Mies van der Rohe, 1945

teria, telephone vaults and mechanical equipment.

The entire building is double-glazed: the set-back facade of the ground floor features clear glass, while on the second floor the outer panes are heat-absorbing glass tinted gray. The exterior of the steel skeleton is clad with ⁵⁄₁₆ in. (8 mm) steel cover plates over sprayed-on fireproofing. The white-painted frame, repeating the horizontal emphasis of the SOM-designed Education and Training Center nearby, is in itself an elegant and direct expression of the large span.

Factory 1965 (project)
David Haid

The complete absence of columns in this 83,000 ft.^{2} (7,700 m^2) industrial building allows total flexibility in the placement of manufacturing equipment and interior mezzanines. In spanning the required area, economy dictated the use of as few but as nearly identical structural elements as possible. The system chosen has twelve exterior columns spread over the long facades of the building. This limitation in the quantity of columns would reduce the number of foundations required in comparison to those of a structure of similar size employing conventional column spacing. Supported by the columns are six overhead trusses from which is suspended a roof plate of transverse secondary trusses, perpendicular to the main trusses and cantilevered 17 ft. 6 in. (5.40 m) at either end. Half of each main truss and all of each secondary truss section would be prefabricated in the shop, thus reducing the assembly time required at the site. Ducts and utilities could be installed in any direction within the depth of the secondary trusses, from where connections would be made to manufacturing equipment below. From finished floor to under side of roof would be a clear height of 24 ft. (7.50 m), dictated by the maximum reach of fork-lift trucks in stacking the lightweight products manufactured here.

Villa Park Trust and Savings Bank 1966
Villa Park, Ill.
James Hammond and Peter Roesch

One of the structural concepts that interested Mies van der Rohe was the roof plate suspended from overhead trusses. He investigated it with his students at I.I.T., discussed its applications and employed it in a 1945 project for the Cantor Drive-in restaurant in Indianapolis.

Many years later architect Peter Roesch, who had studied and worked with Mies, began designing a suburban bank. Poor soil conditions at the site made it uneconomical to use a structural system requiring numerous foundations. The overhead trusses, with only four column footings, seemed an appropriate solution, and they were employed here in an actual building for the first time.

Two 10 ft. (3.05 m) deep trusses span the long direction of the 140 x 90 ft. (42.70 x 27.45 m) roof plate. The trusses are welded to wide-flange columns. All steel structural elements are painted black, and the sharply-defined frame provides a moment of order and clarity, in the midst of a haphazard suburban shopping district.

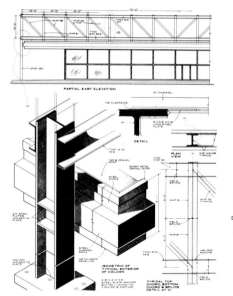

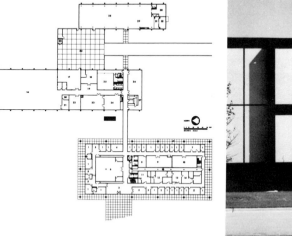

Top left, details, Villa Park Bank; *remainder,* Inland Steel Building

Inland Steel Corporation:
  Metallurgical Research Laboratory
  1968
East Chicago, Ind.
Skidmore, Owings & Merrill
  (Myron Goldsmith, design partner
  Frank Weisz, senior designer)

This group of buildings in a park-like setting is an innovative combination of research laboratories and workshops for the production and testing of new materials and techniques in the steel industry. The requirements of the client—flexible office and laboratory spaces with large spans and column-free workshops—provided the architects with an ideal opportunity to demonstrate the possibilities of steel as a building material.

The structures, of unclad steel, are grouped independently of each other along a connecting track. Though based on similar construction systems, they employ different span and facade details, and contain different mechanical and technical equipment.

The main entrance is in a two-story office and laboratory building, with the sun-control glazed facade set back from the cruciform columns. The center building is a column-free one-story

structure with the facade directly behind the columns; it contains a model workshop, cafeteria, kitchen, and mechanical and toilet rooms. In the third structure, the shop for the construction of full-scale mock-ups, the columns again stand directly before the facade. A traveling crane on the interior traverses the entire structure on its own separate row of supports, and the high ceiling permits the introduction of a mezzanine on the south wall.

In its total conception as well as in the execution of its details, this industrial complex is one of the outstanding works of the second Chicago school of architecture.

Container Corporation of America:
Folding Carton Plant 1968
Carol Stream, III.
Skidmore, Owings and Merrill
(Bruce J. Graham, design partner
Michael Pado, senior designer)

The 30 acre (12 ha) site of this production facility is located in a gently rolling terrain some 24 mi. (39 km) west of Chicago; careful placement of buildings with well-conceived landscaping of access roads, parking and loading areas have helped maintain the rural character of the setting.

The complex contains a one-story, square factory building, 565 ft. (172 m) on a side, connected by a glassed-in bridge with a two-story, 148 ft. (44 m) square administration building. A second building group of almost identical layout, construction and detailing was erected nearby for the production of packing materials. Differentiated by a three- rather than two-story administration building, it was put up under the supervision of Container Corporation's own planning office.

Because of the large dimensions of the factory building, the selection of

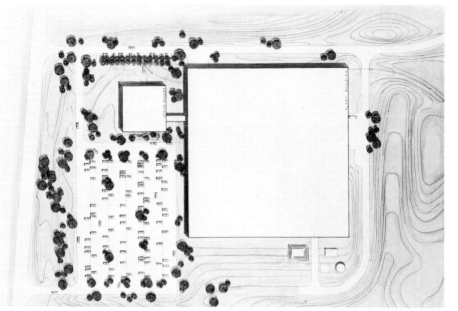

the most economical structural system was a primary concern. The architects developed a number of alternate proposals which were precisely worked out in terms of cost. Various steel and pre-cast concrete systems and bay sizes, and six facade-types, were investigated.

The proposal chosen for the factory, a steel skeleton with 40 ft. (12.20 m) square bays, employed a truss and steel decking roof system and a facade of precast concrete panels.

The character of the administration building is determined by the 30 x 30 ft. (9 x 9 m) bays and coffered roof

slabs in white concrete. The dark gray sun-control glass of the facade is set back within the structure, thus emphasizing its scale.

Skil Factory 1968
Wheeling, III.
C. F. Murphy Associates
(Gene Summers)

The first phase in the construction of this electrical hand-tool plant was the erection of a factory structure and an adjacent building housing mechanical equipment. Still planned are a design and research building and a centrally located administration building, both of which would be serviced by the already built mechanical unit.

With the exception of the cafeteria and administration areas presently housed in the factory building, all walls are without windows; the interiors are electrically lit and fully air-conditioned. Between the exposed cruciform columns of the facade are filler panels of gray-white flecked glazed brick, laid up with gray mortar. Two modules are of sheet steel. The truck dock doors are cut into them.

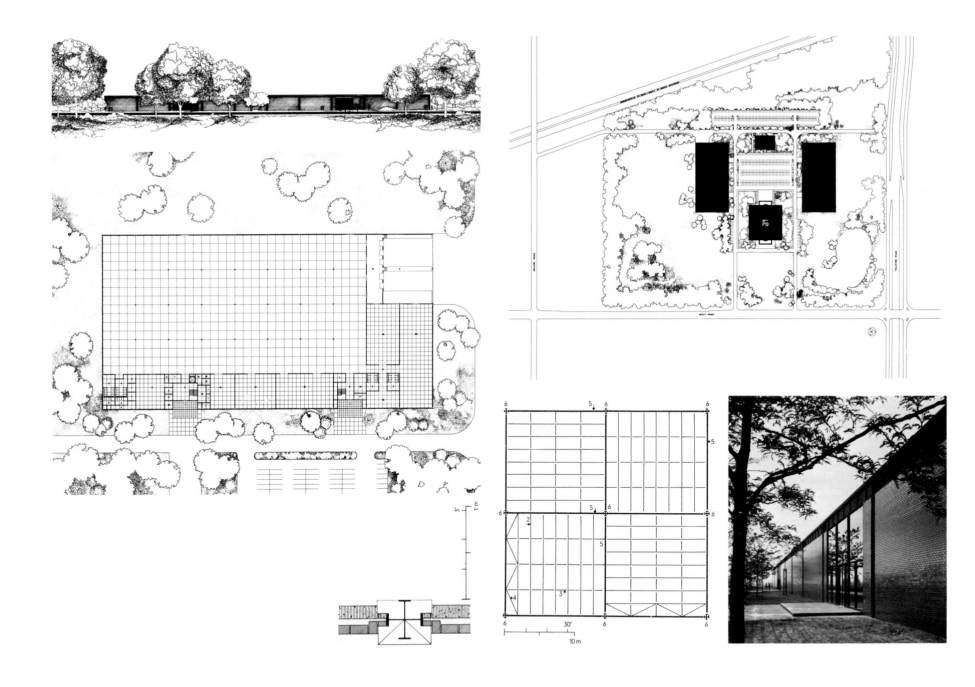

Far left, Skil Factory; *left top,* Cedergreen Frozen Food Plant; *left center,* floor plan, Cedergreen Frozen Food Plant; *below,* Plastofilm Corporation.

The buildings, though not inexpensively constructed, are at first glance rather understated. They represent an unusually high standard for industrial structures. Noteworthy are the choice of materials, careful attention to scale, and pleasant landscaping.

Cedergreen Frozen Food Plant 1973 (project)
Northbrook, Ill.
Peter C. Pran and Chris Cedergreen

The structural system of this project is similar to that of the Skil Factory. A 40 x 40 ft. (12 x 12 m) bay system with cross-shaped columns was used throughout. Only the production hall and the office area were enclosed by exterior glass walls, while the large frozen food storage area was completely enclosed by brick walls. The non-bearing infill walls were of blue glazed brick, while the steel was painted white and the machinery inside bright yellow, to emphasize its sculptural qualities.

Plastofilm Corporation 1968–71
Wheaton, Ill.
David Haid

A factory/office building for a plastic package manufacturer brings together administrative, sales, and production functions under one roof. Because of constantly changing manufacturing techniques and processes, and a continually increasing variety of products, a building of maximum flexibility was required. Structural steel framing was used to span large areas with a minimum of columns, and a 24 ft. (7.30 m) clear interior height permitted efficient fork-lift stacking of relatively light products, as well as the introduction of a mezzanine for tool and die shops.

The office area is on two levels: reception and exhibition area, plant offices and employee facilities on the ground floor; executive and sales offices on a mezzanine. The exposed steel skeleton is painted black, and on the north and south facades gray glare-reducing glass is set above masonry spandrel panels. The east and west facades are of masonry except for the

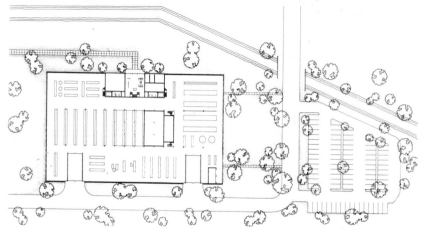

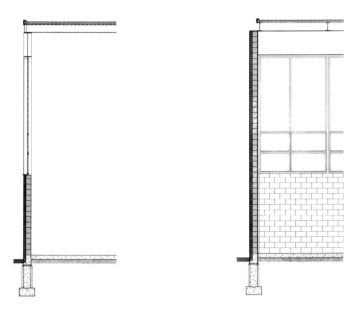

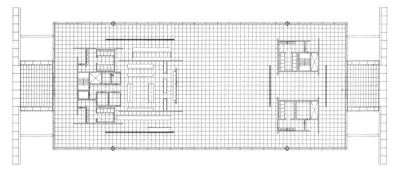

Abraham Lincoln Oasis 1968
South Holland, Ill.
David Haid
(Wiesinger-Holland, structural engineers)

Building an expressway restaurant as a bridge across traffic lanes was a novel yet logical design approach. The facility is equally accessible from both directions; one structure suffices in place of the usual two.

The structural skeleton here is of self-oxydizing Cor-Ten steel, and has since gained a warm, rust-brown tone that blends nicely with the nearby wooded landscape. The construction system is of plate girders acting as spandrels supported by cruciform columns at point ⅕ of the total span. Both the diminishing separation of the girder ribs and the reinforcement near the window axes give clear expression to the load-bearing function of the construction. Here the logic of construction is translated convincingly into architectural form.

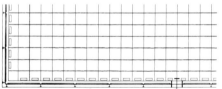

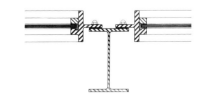

floor to ceiling glazing in the office area on the east.

The simple, almost reticent design shows the great attention paid to both overall scheme and detailing. A meaningful solution is presented to the problem of finding a convincing architectural expression of structure and function.

Top left, details of Plastofilm Corporation; *bottom left,* Plastofilm Corporation in construction; *right,* Abraham Lincoln Oasis

The glazing of bronze-tinted sun control panes, is in frames of specially-rolled Cor-Ten sections, and the building is fully air conditioned. The interior space is divided by white-plastered cores at each end of the building. They contain rest rooms, a gift shop and a kitchen. Cafeteria and snack bar counters are screened by low partitions of bottle green laminated glass. Exposed structural elements are painted in dark hues, and brightly-colored silk drapes in the dining space define the "in service" areas. English oak panelling clads free-standing storage units. The architect has succeeded in avoiding austerity and anonymity through the choice of warm natural materials.

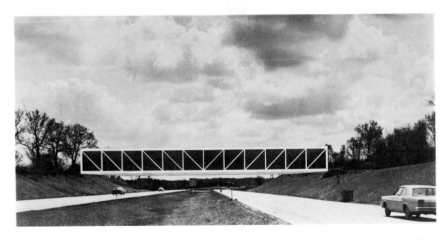

Edens Expressway Restaurant 1967
   (project)
Peter C. Pran
(Advisors: Prof. Daniel Brenner,
         Prof. Fazlur Khan
Dept. of Arch., I.I.T.)

In this expressway restaurant project two trusses of floor-to-ceiling height extend the entire length of the building. With this clear span structural system, the steel weight and construction cost are approximately the same as those of the Abraham Lincoln Oasis Restaurant.

Environmental Awareness Center 1974
   (project)
Rich Potokar
(Advisors: Prof. Michael Gelick
            Prof. Fred Wiesinger
Dept. of Arch., Univ. of Illinois,
   Chicago Circle)

A truss system was used in similar manner here, in order to bridge the 225 ft. (68.5 m) over the Eisenhower Expressway. Within this 45 ft. (13.7 m) high exhibition hall, floor levels can easily be removed or added according to use requirements.

These three projects, the Abraham Lincoln Oasis, the Eden Expressway Restaurant and the Environmental Awareness Center, utilize expressway air-rights while providing easy pedestrian access on both sides of the thoroughfare.

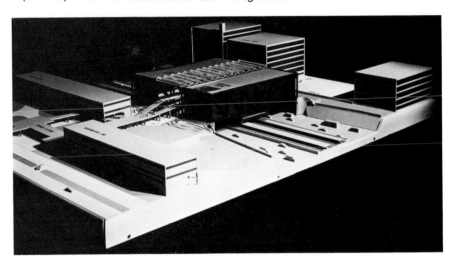

Northbrook Public Library 1969
Northbrook, Ill.
James Hammond and Peter Roesch

The large, unimpeded spaces of this suburban library facilitate subsequent functional rearrangement while affording both users and personnel a broad overall view of the facilities. Space is provided for 127 adult readers using 80,000 books and 200 periodicals. Also available is a conference room seating 18. The children's library accommodates 58 readers and contains 19,000 books. A multi-purpose area seating 108 is provided with a kitchen, and is used for film and slide shows for the entire community. The library also of-

fers a phonograph record, film and slide lending service.

The large upper floor is reached via a broad stairway. Two cores containing workrooms and conference room form spatial divisions. Careful coordination of furnishings, carpeting and equipment creates a pleasant and inviting atmosphere.

The architects originally intended to support the upper story by a two-way truss with two supports on each side. Finally, a rectangular bay was employed, in a 3 x 5 bay arrangement.

In contrast to the bronze-glazed upper floor, the lower floor is almost completely closed; the set-back walls provide covered parking space and a patio in front of the children's library. Since the building is sited in a slight depression, viewers on the main floor look directly into the surrounding park-like landscape.

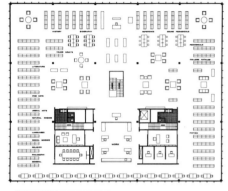

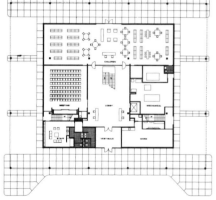

Above, Northbrook Bell; *right,* Fourth District Courts Building

Northbrook Bell Equipment Building
1973
Holabird & Root
(Jerry Horn)

Few recent buildings convey the aesthetic rationale of Chicago architecture more persuasively than this one. Its purpose is to house equipment for the switching of long-distance telephone signals over much of northern Illinois. Increasing population in that area renders future expansion of the facility likely. Indeed the topmost of its three floors has already been transformed from office to equipment space.

Hence the simple boxlike form and modular layout of Northbrook Bell, both of which make vertical and horizontal additions possible without altering the building's fundamental visual character. The same view to expand-

**Fourth District Courts Building 1976
Maywood, Ill.
C. F. Murphy Associates
(Helmut Jahn)**

ability led the architects to locate a microwave tower, with four receiving and transmitting horns, on the side of the main structure rather than on its roof, which would have been the standard place for such an appendage.

This is the functional program, and it is responsibly carried out. Yet what results aesthetically is an uncommonly handsome article of solid geometry, smooth, hard and precise, as elegantly understated as black velvet. The painted steel frame carries panels of dark gray glass. The tower echoes the structural candor of the principal mass next to it, but its network of pipes and platforms and its bright red quartet of horns together effect a striking contrast of form and color. Further relief of the prevailing rectilinearity is afforded by the four cylindrical exhaust stacks situated on the north side of the building. Northbrook Bell is all utility, yet no less pure as a piece of architectural sculpture.

The Chicago Civic Center emphatically established a precedent of freedom from the allusion to historical styles which had guided the hand of court building designers since the nineteenth century. The Fourth District Courts Building in Maywood is conceived with that same freedom in mind. The two structures are products of the same office, and although they were supervised by two different architects—Jacques Brownson at the Civic Center and Helmut Jahn in the Maywood project—a kinship of expressive motive is unmistakable.

The Fourth District Courts Building recalls another recent structure: Northbrook Bell, by Holabird & Root. Both of these works bear an outward resemblance to each other in the sensitivity of their proportions and smoothness of transition from steel frame to window panels, likewise in their rigorous reliance on the modular grid. The suggestion of expandability that results from

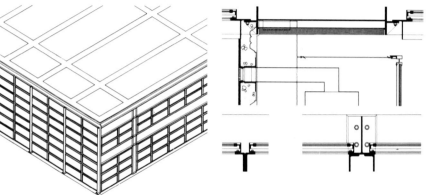

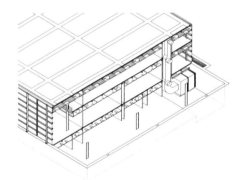

that grid system is yet another feature common to them.

The plum-colored Fourth District Courts Building houses two basic functional elements within its three levels and 185,000 sq. ft. (17,300 m²) of interior space: a judicial complex of ten courtrooms with office and auxiliary areas and an administrative complex. The areas enclosed within the two 50 ft. (15.2 m) bays are for the most part public spaces. Offices are consigned to the peripheral spaces created by 20 ft. (6 m) cantilevers which extend beyond the bays to the outer wall. The building is equipped with a complete sprinkler system which permitted elimination of fireproofing on the steel.

Woodfield Office Building 1973
Schaumberg, Ill.
James Hammond and Thomas Beeby

Located close to the gargantuan Woodfield Shopping Center, this structure is unusually elegant for a suburban office building. A typical area-per-story of 16,500 sq. ft. (1,550 m²) contains an off-center service and elevator core plus transverse bay spacing which affords optimally flexible accommodation of small and large tenant layouts. A recessed ground floor with high ceilings provides space for large commercial-institutional service organizations. The exposed poured concrete building

frame is sand blasted. Ground floor lobby walls are travertine and the floors, terrazzo. The building is surrounded by generous landscaping.

Far left, Fourth District Courts Building; *left*, Woodfield Office Building; *below*, Manufacturing Building Expansion

Manufacturing Building Expansion
1973
Pre-Finish Metals, Inc.
Elk Grove, Ill.
Clarence Krusinski

During the first phase of this complex project, a manufacturing building 500 ft. (152 m) in length and 35 ft. (10.6 m) high was constructed. Within its column-free space, a system of overhead cranes was installed to transport materials. A materials storage building similar in volume was added two years later. Finally, a structure housing the company's executive offices was erected. Careful planning permitted construction with a minimum disruption of the ongoing manufacturing operations. The most successful part of the manufacturing building is the interior, notable for its precise and well proportioned steel frames and space.

Arco Filling Station 1973
Mount Prospect, Ill.
Laurence Booth and James Nagle

Another adventurous solution to a building problem that is all too commonly surrendered to cliché is the Arco Filling Station by Booth and Nagle, located at the junction of Illinois Rte. 83 and Rand Road, in Mount Prospect. This compelling 1972 design originated with the client's decision to sell gasoline at very low prices—hence his demand for a minimally appointed facility: pumps, overhead shelters, an attendant's booth, two small comfort stations, and nothing else.

What the architects in collaboration with the designers from CARD came up with is in notably imaginative contrast to the modesty of the program. The three shelter truss-arms radiating outward from the cylindrical booth are functional responses to the traffic patterns engendered by a triangular corner site, yet aesthetically they are brilliant realizations of the formal possibilities of revealed structure. The steel modules of the cantilevered canopy are based upon the triangular motif of the plan, and produce a vigorously declarative system of visual forms. The pump columns are uncommonly large —thirteen feet high—partly to carry a portion of the load of the canopies and partly to provide an unmistakable target to customers. The graphics which record sale prices and gas totals are likewise exceptionally readable, since they are situated apart from the pumps and directly in the driver's line of vision.

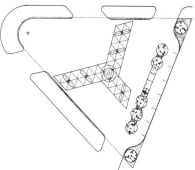

Influence outside Chicago

by Peter C. Pran
and Franz Schulze

Is the best Chicago architecture in Chicago? One question leads to others before yielding an answer: by Chicago architecture do we mean a building principle? a stylistically identifiable genus of structures? or simply works by Chicago-based designers?

Apropos the last of these categories, many critics believe that Louis Sullivan's finest buildings were put up outside Chicago. These might include not only the famous Wainwright and Prudential Buildings, respectively in St. Louis and Buffalo, but the series of exquisite banks Sullivan did in Midwestern towns like Owatonna, Minnesota and Grinnell, Iowa.

Similarly, **Mies's Seagram Building** in New York, together with its splendid and revolutionary plaza, is widely regarded as the premier tall building of the second third of the century. Certainly that architect never achieved any hall structure in Chicago more monumental than his **New National Gallery in Berlin,** a late work of majestic scale and meticulous detail. If one adds just a few of **Frank Lloyd Wright's** far-flung accomplishments (e.g., Falling Water, **Johnson Wax** in Racine, the Imperial Hotel in Tokyo, Taliesin West) to the above short list, a reasonable if debat-

Johnson Wax

able case can be made that Chicago designers erected their most memorable work outside Chicago.

However, this is not quite the same as saying that Chicago building in concept or type has been exported better than produced at home. If we think of skeleton frame construction as one of the hallmarks of the city's architecture, it did indeed become the norm for commercial buildings early in the twentieth century. But the Beaux-Arts costuming of such New York skyscrapers as Cass Gilbert's Woolworth Building or Ernest Flagg's Singer Building is hardly consonant with the idea of candid structural expression, which is central to the efforts of the first Chicago school. The fact is, the early Chicago Commercial Style did not exert any powerful influence on either American or European building immediately subsequent to it.

Eclecticism pretty much took over in the U.S. after 1910, just as Sullivan said he feared it would. And when a strong belief in structural expression once again became widespread, it was, as we have already observed, more a response to Europe's International Style than to any native American movement. Nationally speaking, the first Chicago school was hallowed later rather than followed earlier.

Nevertheless, a comparison of New York's Park Avenue just north of Grand Central Station with the Chicago Loop is enough to substantiate the view that Chicago builders of the past quarter-century have managed better than the designers of any other city in the world to develop a convincing *school* of architecture.

Mies's architectural method became as popular as it did, we are often told, because it was so easily taught. This may be true, but there is a large difference between the look of his work, which is readily learned, and the principles behind it—not to mention the taste—which are not. The blockish anonymity that characterizes so much of Park Avenue is little better than a caricature of Miesian "purism."

The Loop, on the other hand, more properly the good post-World War II buildings in the Loop—and the point is that there is a host of them—testify to the fact that second Chicago school architecture is devoted to immeasurably more than Miesian cosmetics. It is rather, as we have emphasized here, based upon organic derivation and rational expression of structure and space together with the conscious search for a unity of technology and aesthetic form. These elements comprise the fundamental lessons which younger Chicago architects have learned from Root, Sullivan, Wright and Mies as a company. They not only

count for far more than surface appearances, but help to account for the exceptional ambience of downtown Chicago, where buildings relate with striking coherence to each other and to the space they fill. Viewed this way, from the standpoint of a whole environment, the best Chicago architecture is indeed located in downtown Chicago.

As to influences beyond the city, then, that seems more confined to major individual works by individual architects. Further, it has been more decisively felt in the last several decades than in the early twentieth century. Among the American designers who have been singularly moved by Mies during various phases of their careers are Philip Johnson, I. M. Pei, Kevin Roche, Eero Saarinen, Charles Eames, Craig Ellwood and Gordon Bunschaft. That is a formidable group, with European counterparts like Egon Eiermann, Peter von Seidlein and

New National Gallery

Detlef Schreiber in Germany, Michael Scott in Ireland, Arne Jacobsen in Denmark, Bruno and Fritz Haller in Switzerland, Peter Smithson and Foster Associates in England.

The important edifices that reflect origins in Chicago are too numerous to mention here, but a number are worth citing as examples. The **IBM Central Utility Building** in Endicott, New York is one of **Harry Weese's** most felicitous designs. The steel structure, lucid, strict, enlivened by a horizontal pattern of delicately subdivided louvers and windows, reveals the glistening aluminum equipment within, lending it the look of abstract sculpture. Weese is also the designer of the widely-acclaimed **Washington, D.C. Subway,** in which, once again, a strong structural expression is evident in the handling of concrete.

Among several **SOM** projects in the San Francisco area, the **Oakland-Alameda Country Coliseum** is one of the most impressive. Designed chiefly by **Myron Goldsmith,** it is a cylindrical hall with a 420-foot diameter and a cable-suspended roof that rests on a ring of concrete cruciform columns. Goldsmith's initial design for this building was better proportioned than the version finally erected, but it remains an uncommonly refined structure, well sit-

IBM General Utilities Plant

Washington D.C. Subway

Oakland-Alameda County Coliseum

uated in relation to its neighboring open-air stadium.

Goldsmith and his Chicago SOM colleagues Bruce Graham and Fazlur Khan are among the leading international figures in the development of the tubular frame, a method which has opened up new economic possibilities in skyscraper design. Several of SOM's international projects have made various and pioneering uses of the tube: One Shell Plaza in Houston, a pair of office buildings in Rotterdam, the Tour Apogue in Paris, the Centre Sofil in Beirut (by John Turley and Khan), the First Wisconsin Center in Milwaukee and the BHP Headquarters Building in Melbourne.

One Shell Plaza, principally by **Graham and Khan** of **SOM,** is an example of the "tube-in-tube," in which an inner tubular form around the utility core supports the dead load, while an outer tube resists wind forces. The **Graham-Khan** team is also responsible for the BHP Headquarters and the **First Wisconsin Center** (with **James De Stefano**),

One Shell Plaza

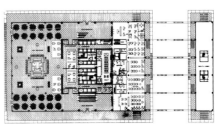

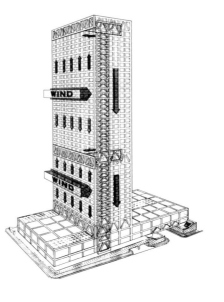

First Wisconsin Center

Oakland-Alameda County Coliseum

169

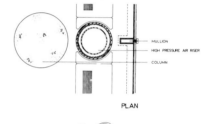

MULLION
HIGH PRESSURE AIR RISER
COLUMN

PLAN

INDUCTION UNIT
FLOOR SLAB
FIRE STOP

BLIND POCKET
DOUBLE GLAZING

SUSPENDED CEILING
MUNTIN

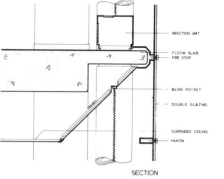

SECTION

First Wisconsin Plaza

both of which feature the belt truss, a device calculated to increase the stiffness of the structure by as much as 30 percent.

Graham and Goldsmith meanwhile have produced a number of distinguished smaller works as well, marked less by engineering audacity than by simple suavity of design. **Graham's**

First Wisconsin Plaza—designed in collaboration with **Thomas Rosengren** and **John Turley**—in Madison is one of the most compelling of these: a transparent mass of polygonal volumes encased in glass and supported by tubular steel columns. The building, well related to its street and a nearby park, encloses a richly landscaped interior space.

Goldsmith's plant for **"The Republic,"** a newspaper in Columbus, Indiana, is as severe a box as Graham's First Wisconsin Plaza is a complex exercise in reflecting prisms, but it has a kindredly discreet elegance about it. The window wall is divided into two lights of identical height, with the upper portion treated as an opaque plane concealing the columns at the end walls. The same designer's **Solar Telescope at Kitt Peak,** Arizona, is, on the other hand, a boldly sculptural work, consisting of a 100-foot-high tower connected to a massive 500-foot shaft which is inclined at 32 degrees to the ground.

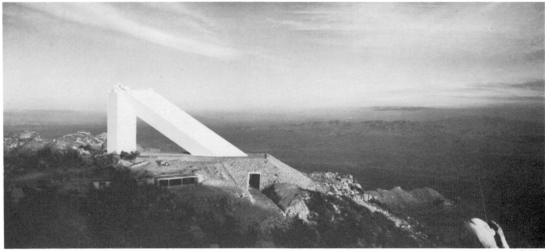

Solar Telescope, Kitt Peak, Arizona

Another large Chicago firm, **C. F. Murphy Associates,** is responsible for one of the most brilliantly conceived hall spaces recently built in America. It is the **R. Crosby Kemper, Sr., Memorial Arena** in Kansas City. Designed principally by **Helmut Jahn,** Kemper is a multi-purpose indoor stadium with a seating capacity of 17,500. An oval seating plan, with overlapping upper and lower seating tiers, brings spectators as close to the arena floor as possible. Externally, the arena's most spectacular feature is a powerful superstructure, 324 feet in span, which rides openly above and outside the mass of the building, thus allowing maximum depth of structure and minimum exterior skin.

To this group several more works deserve to be added, among them, from

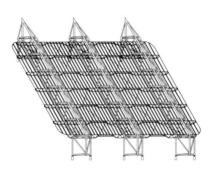

Kemper Stadium

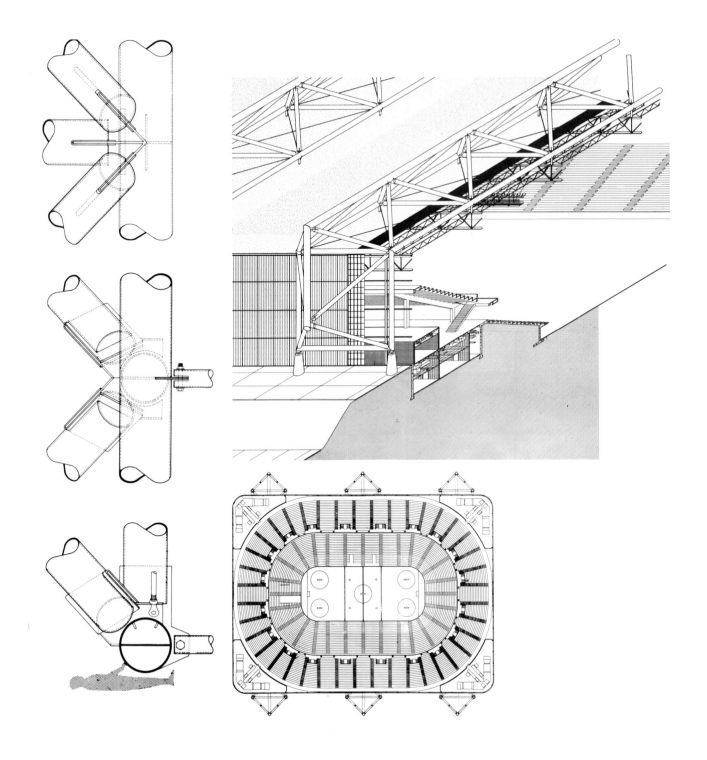

Toronto Dominion

Ripon Bank

Lincoln National Corporation Office Building

Mies's office, the plan and apartment buildings of Lafayette Park in Detroit, the Museum of Fine Arts in Houston, the Bacardi office buildings in Havana and Mexico City, **Toronto Dominion Center** in Toronto, Canada, Westmount Square in Montreal, Quebec and a new city square and office tower in London. The **Ripon Bank** in Ripon, Wisconsin, by **Hammond & Beeby,** and the **Lincoln National Corporation Office Building,** Fort Wayne, Indiana, by **Gerald Horn** of **Holabird & Root,** are yet two other handsome recent structures by Chicago firms.

Saint Mary's Athletic Facility

Michigan City Public Library

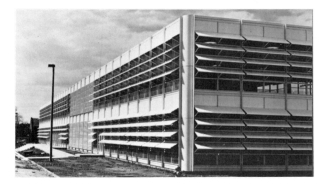

Auraria Library

88 Pine Street

Among the most recent buildings designed by **Helmut Jahn** of **C. F. Murphy Associates** are **Saint Mary's Athletic Facility,** Notre Dame, Indiana; the **Michigan City Public Library,** Michigan City, Indiana; and the **Auraria Library,** Denver, Colorado—co-designed with **David Hovey.** All three projects are unorthodox and innovative, yet continue the Chicago structural tradition.

Finally, there is occasion to mention the **88 Pine Street Building** in New York, which was designed by **James I. Freed,** a partner of **I. M. Pei Associates.** It has no articulated module except that of the structural bay, which is not covered with a curtain wall skin but with an infill clad system. Its lively white-painted aluminum skin stands out against the New York skyline.

If the work of Chicago designers now covers the globe, some final acknowledgment ought to be added of the role played by its architects at the academic level. Again Mies, who chaired the Illinois Institute of Technology School of Architecture and Planning for nearly two decades (1938–58), must lead any list of Chicago architect-teachers. His very able successors, George Danforth (1959–75) and James I. Freed (1975–), likewise merit mention, as do the former deans of the College of Architecture and Art: Leonard Currie (1962–72) and Bertram Berenson (1972–75), and the successive heads of the Department of Architecture at Circle Campus: Thomas Jaeger (1970–72) and Richard Whitaker (1972–). From 1938 to 1967, Ludwig Hilbers-

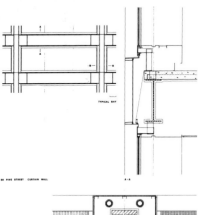

TYPICAL BAY

A-A

88 PINE STREET CURTAIN WALL

eimer, a colleague during their years in Germany, was chairman of the Planning Department at I.I.T. Five years ago, the brilliant Spanish-Mexican Felix Candela joined the faculty of the latter school. A remarkable number of the outstanding Chicago architects of the post-World War II period have been trained at Illinois Institute of Technology or University of Illinois—Circle or Urbana, a fact which underscores again the ongoing vitality of the city as a center of the contemporary building art.

Photos of Participants
Left to right, top row: Dorman D. Anderson, AIA; Charles B. Atwood; Thomas Beeby, AIA; Laurence Booth, AIA; Daniel Brenner, FAIA; Jacques C. Brownson, AIA; John Buenz, AIA; Daniel Burnham. *Second row:* Pao-Chi Chang; Bruno Conterato, FAIA; John Cordwell, AIA; George Danforth, FAIA; James DeStefano, AIA; Robert Diamant, AIA; James Ingo Freed, AIA; Joseph Fujikawa, AIA. *Third row:* R. Buckminster Fuller; Michael Gelick, AIA; Charles Genther, FAIA; Stanislav Gladych, AIA; Bertrand Goldberg, FAIA; Myron Goldsmith, FAIA; Ezra Gordon, FAIA; Bruce J. Graham, FAIA. *Bottom row:* David Haid, FAIA; James Hammond, FAIA; William Holabird; Jerry Horn, AIA; Helmut Jahn, AIA; William Le Baron Jenney; George Fred Keck; William Keck, FAIA.

Top row: Fazlur Khan; Phillip Kupritz, AIA; Jack Levin; Dirk Lohan, AIA; John Macsai, AIA; Ludwig Mies van der Rohe, FAIA; James Nagle, AIA; Walter Netsch, FAIA. *Second row:* John Novack, AIA; Michael Pado, AIA; I. M. Pei, FAIA; Lawrence B. Perkins, FAIA; Peter C. Pran, AIA; Henry Hobson Richardson; Louis Rocah, AIA; Martin Roche. *Third row:* Peter Roesch; John Wellborn Root; Eero Saarinen, FAIA; George Schipporeit; David C. Sharpe; A. James Speyer; Louis Sullivan; Gene Summers, FAIA. *Bottom row:* Alfred Swenson, AIA; Arthur Takeuchi, AIA; Stanley Tigerman, FAIA; Konrad Wachsmann; Harry Weese, FAIA; Benjamin Weese, FAIA; Frank Lloyd Wright; Y. C. Wong, AIA.

Bibliography

Architectural and Construction History

AMERICAN ARCHITECTURE COMES OF AGE
European Reaction to H. H. Richardson and Louis Sullivan
Leonard K. Eaton
The MIT Press, Cambridge, Massachusetts, 1972

AMERICAN BUILDING
Carl W. Condit
University of Chicago Press, 1968

AMERICAN BUILDING ART — THE NINETEENTH CENTURY
Carl W. Condit
Oxford University Press, New York, 1960

ANNUAL REPORT 1971
Public Building Commission of Chicago

ARCHITECTURE IN OLD CHICAGO
Thomas E. Tallmadge
University of Chicago Press, 1941

CHICAGO 1910-29
Building, Planning and Urban Technology
Carl W. Condit
University of Chicago Press, 1973

CHICAGO 1930-70
Building, Planning and Urban Technology
Carl W. Condit
University of Chicago Press, 1974

THE CHICAGO SCHOOL OF ARCHITECTURE
A History of Commercial and Public Building in the Chicago Area, 1875-1925
Carl W. Condit
University of Chicago Press, 1964
(revised and enlarged from the author's "The Rise of the Skyscraper," 1952)

GREAT BUILDINGS OF THE WORLD — MODERN BUILDINGS
John Winter
Paul Hamlyn Publishings Group Ltd., London, 1969

A GUIDE TO SIGNIFICANT CHICAGO ARCHITECTURE FROM 1872 to 1922
John D. Randall
Glencoe, Illinois, 1958

HISTORY OF THE DEVELOPMENT OF BUILDING CONSTRUCTION IN CHICAGO
Frank A. Randall
University of Illinois Press, Urbana, 1949

OFFICE BUILDINGS
An Architectural Record Book
The Editors of Architectural Record
F. W. Dodge Corp. McGraw Hill Co., New York, 1961

THE RISE OF AN AMERICAN ARCHITECTURE
Edited by Edgar Kaufmann, Jr.
Pall Mall Press, London, 1970

SPACE, TIME AND ARCHITECTURE
Sigfried Giedion
Harvard University Press, 3rd ed., 1954

STICKS AND STONES
A Study of American Architecture and Civilization
Lewis Mumford
Boni and Liveright, Inc., New York, 1924
(and subsequent editions)

UNITED STATES STEEL CORPORATION —
ARCHITECTURAL DESIGN DETAILS: EXPOSED STEEL
United States Steel Corp., 1965
(with periodic supplements)

Monographs

THE AUTOBIOGRAPHY OF AN IDEA
Louis H. Sullivan
American Institute of Architects, Inc., 1924
(subsequent edition with introduction and illustrations — Ralph Marlowe Line)
Dover Publications, Inc., New York, 1956

LOUIS SULLIVAN
Prophet of Modern Architecture
Hugh Morrison
W. W. Norton & Co., Inc., New York, 1935
(and several subsequent editions)

LOUIS SULLIVAN
(in Masters of World Architecture series)
Albert Bush-Brown
George Braziller, Inc., New York, 1960

THE IDEA OF LOUIS SULLIVAN
John Szarkowski
University of Minnesota Press, Minneapolis, 1956
Second Printing, 1960

LOUIS SULLIVAN — The Shaping of American Architecture
Willard Connely
Horizon Press, New York, 1960

GENIUS AND THE MOBOCRACY
Frank Lloyd Wright
(enlarged edition)
Horizon Press, New York, 1971

THE MEANINGS OF ARCHITECTURE
Buildings and Writings by John Wellborn Root
collected by Donald Hoffman
Horizon Press, New York, 1967

THE ARCHITECTURE OF JOHN WELLBORN ROOT
Donald Hoffman
Johns Hopkins University Press, Baltimore, 1973

BURNHAM OF CHICAGO — Architect and Planner
Thomas S. Hines
Oxford University Press, New York, 1974

THE BUILDINGS OF FRANK LLOYD WRIGHT
Henry-Russell Hitchcock
Plenum Pub., New York, 1942, 1969

FRANK LLOYD WRIGHT TO 1910
The First Golden Age
Grant Carpenter Manson
Reinhold Publishing Corporation, New York, 1958

THE MASTER BUILDERS
(sections on Frank Lloyd Wright and Mies van der Rohe)
Alfred A. Knopf Inc., New York, 1964

THE PRAIRIE SCHOOL
Frank Lloyd Wright and his Midwest Contempories
H. Allen Brooks
University of Toronto Press, 1972

TWO CHICAGO ARCHITECTS AND THEIR CLIENTS
Frank Lloyd Wright and Howard Van Doren Shaw
Leonard K. Eaton
The MIT Press, Cambridge, Massachusetts, 1969

TRIBUNE TOWER COMPETITION
The International Competition for a New Administration Building for the Chicago Tribune
MCMXXII
The Tribune Company, 1923

MIES VAN DER ROHE
Philip C. Johnson
The Museum of Modern Art, New York, 1947

MIES VAN DER ROHE
Ludwig Hilbersiemer
Paul Theobald and Co., Chicago, 1956

LUDWIG MIES VAN DER ROHE
(in Masters of World Architecture series)
Arthur Drexler
George Braziller, Inc., New York, 1960

MIES VAN DER ROHE
Die Kunst der Struktur
Werner Blaser
Verlag für Architektur, Artemis, Stuttgart, 1965
(in German)

MIES VAN DER ROHE
(catalogue of a retrospective exhibition at the Art Institute of Chicago in 1968)
A. James Speyer
catalogue entries by Frederick Koeper
The Art Institute of Chicago, 1968

MIES VAN DER ROHE
Library of Contemporary Architects
Martin Pawley and Yukio Futagawa
Simon and Schuster, New York, 1970

SOM — THE ARCHITECTURE OF SKIDMORE, OWINGS AND MERRILL 1950-1962

Sociology and Planning

Sociology and Planning

CHICAGO: GROWTH OF A METROPOLIS
H. M. Mayer and R. C. Wade
The University of Chicago Press, 1969

CHICAGO I WILL
Don Bronstein and Tony Weitzel
The World Publishing Co., Cleveland and New York, 1961

CHICAGO SOCIOLOGY 1920-32
Heritage of Sociology
Robert E. L. Faris
University of Chicago Press, 1971

CHICAGOLAND'S COMMUNITY GUIDE
Law Bulletin Publishing Co., Chicago, 1971/72

CULTURE AND DEMOCRACY
The Struggle for Form in Society and Architecture in Chicago and the Middle West during the Life and Times of Louis H. Sullivan
Hugh Dalziel Duncan
The Bedminster Press; Totowa, New Jersey, 1965

DESIGN OF CITIES — A Studio Book
Edmund H. Bacon
The Viking Press, New York, 1967

DIVISION STREET AMERICA
Studs Terkel
Pantheon Edition, New York, 1966

DIE ENTFALTUNG EINER PLANUNGSIDEE
Ludwig Hilberseimer
Verlag Ullstein GmbH., Berlin, 1963
(in German)

INVESTMENT IN TOMORROW
The IIT Campaign
The Illinois Institute of Technology, 1965

MID-WEST DEVELOPMENT AREA
Department of Development and Planning
City of Chicago, 1967

THE NATURE OF CITIES
Ludwig Hilberseimer
Paul Theobald and Co., Chicago, 1955

THE NEW CITY
Ludwig Hilberseimer
Paul Theobald and Co., Chicago, 1944

THE NEW REGIONAL PATTERN
Ludwig Hilberseimer
Paul Theobald and Co., Chicago, 1949

OLMSTED IN CHICAGO
Victoria Post Ranney
R. R. Donnelley & Sons, Chicago, 1972

PLAN OF CHICAGO
Daniel H. Burnham and Edward H. Bennett,
edited by Charles Moore
Chicago, 1909

PLANNING THE REGION OF CHICAGO
D. H. Burnham, Jr. and R. Kengerly
The Chicago Regional Planning Association, Chicago, 1956

PRAIRIE STATE
Paul M. Angle
University of Chicago Press, 1968

PULLMAN
An Experiment in Industrial Order and Community Planning, 1880-1930
Stanley Buder
Oxford University Press, New York, 1967

SETTLEMENT PATTERNS OF NORTHERN ILLINOIS
Sheldon Berest
Master's Thesis, Illinois Institute of Technology, 1972
(unpublished)

STADT UND KULTURRAUM ANGLOAMERIKA
Burkhard Hofmeister
Friedr. Vieweg & Sohn GmbH., Braunschweig, 1971
(in German)

Guidebooks

Guidebooks

CHICAGO—AN EXTRAORDINARY GUIDE
Jory Graham
Rand McNally Press, Chicago, 1968

CHICAGO ON FOOT
Second revised edition
Ira J. Bach
J. Philip O'Hara, Inc., Chicago, 1973

CHICAGO'S FAMOUS BUILDINGS
Second Edition
Edited by Arthur Siegel
The University of Chicago Press, 1969

ILLINOIS ARCHITECTURE
Frederick Koeper
University of Chicago Press, 1968

Periodicals

Periodicals

AIA JOURNAL
Washington, D.C.
January 1973

ARCHITECT AND BUILDER
South Africa
October 1966

ARCHITECTURAL AND ENGINEERING NEWS
Philadelphia
September 1966

ARCHITECTURAL DESIGN
London
April 1964; November 1966

THE ARCHITECTURAL FORUM
New York
(especially May 1962)

L'ARCHITECTURE D'AUJOUR'HUI
Paris, 1965
No. 122, Septembre-Novembre 1965
(in French)

ARTS AND ARCHITECTURE
Los Angeles
(especially November 1956; August 1958; July, August and October 1964)

BAUEN UND WOHNEN
Munich
(especially Oktober 1961; Mai 1964; Dezember 1966; Januar 1967; Juli 1970; März 1972; Februar 1973)
(in German)

BAUMEISTER
Munich
series Konstruktive Architektur in Amerika by Oswald W. Grube
Juni, August, September, Oktober and November 1970, and April 1971

BAUWELT
Berlin
Oktober 1962, (pp. 1173-1176); April 1963, (pp. 355-361)
(in German)

BAUWELT – STADT BAUWELT
Berlin
Vol. 38/39, 28 September 1970

CHICAGO MAGAZINE
Chicago
(especially September-October 1971)

CIVIL ENGINEERING
American Society of Civil Engineers
New York
July 1972

CONSTRUCTIONAL REVIEW
Australia
Vol. 43, No. 3, August 1970

DETAIL
Munich
März 1969

DU
Zurich
(special issue on Chicago)
Mai 1972

ENGINEERING NEWS-RECORD
McGraw-Hill, New York
3 June 1971

INLAND ARCHITECT
Chicago
(especially August 1970)

PROGRESSIVE ARCHITECTURE
Stamford
(especially December 1964; March 1965; – Ira J. Bach series – and October 1972)

QUARTERLY COLUMN
Japan
April 1963, (pp. 38-48)

STEEL CONSTRUCTION DIGEST
USA
Vol. 16, No. 3, 1954

WERK
Winterthur/Basel
Objektive Architektur – Mies van der Rohe
November 1964

Index of Buildings

The Authors

Oswald W. Grube is planning counselor with the government of Bavaria, West Germany, and a registered, practicing architect in that country. He is a member of the two professional architectural associations, BDA/DWB, in West Germany. He is the author of *Industrial Buildings and Factories* (Praeger, 1971). For a time he worked as an architect with Skidmore, Owings & Merrill in Chicago. He has subsequently returned to the city several times and studied the architecture of Chicago at great length.

Peter C. Pran is assistant professor of architecture at the University of Illinois at Chicago Circle, and senior architect with Skidmore, Owings & Merrill. He was formerly assistant professor of architecture at Washington State University. He is a registered architect in the United States and Scandinavia and an AIA and MNAL corporate member. For three years he worked with Mies van der Rohe. He received his bachelor of architecture from Oslo University, Norway, and his master of science in architecture from Illinois Institute of Technology. Over the years, he has written numerous articles for professional architectural magazines. He received—together with Warren Hendrickson—a Distinguished Building Design Award, 1977, from the AIA Chicago Chapter.

Franz Schulze, art critic of the *Chicago Daily News,* is also Hollender Professor of Art at Lake Forest College. He is a contributing editor of *Art News* and *Inland Architect* and a corresponding editor of *Art in America.* Following undergraduate training at the University of Chicago, he studied painting at the School of the Art Institute of Chicago and the Academy of Fine Arts in Munich. He is the author of *Fantastic Images: Chicago Art Since 1945* (Follett, 1972) and is at work on a biographical study of Ludwig Mies van der Rohe.